STYLES OF DISCOURSE

STYLES OF DISCOURSE

Edited by
NIKOLAS COUPLAND

CROOM HELM
London•New York•Sydney

Croom Helm Ltd, Provident House, Burrell Row,
Beckenham, Kent, BR3 1AT

Croom Helm Australia, 44-50 Waterloo Road,
North Ryde, 2113, New South Wales

Published in the USA by
Croom Helm
in association with Methuen, Inc.
29 West 35th Street
New York, NY 10001

British Library Cataloguing in Publication Data

Styles of discourse.
1. Discourse analysis
I. Coupland, Nikolas
415   P302

ISBN 0-7099-4852-2

Library of Congress Cataloging-in-Publication Data

ISBN 0-7099-4852-2

Typeset in 10pt Baskerville by Leaper & Gard Ltd, Bristol, England
Printed and bound in Great Britain by Mackays of Chatham Ltd, Kent

Contents

For Nen

Contributors

Paul Atkinson, Department of Sociology, University College, Cardiff.

Justine Coupland, Department of English, UWIST, Cardiff.

Nikolas Coupland, Department of English, UWIST, Cardiff.

Alan Davies, Department of Applied Linguistics, University of Edinburgh.

Howard Giles, Department of Psychology, University of Bristol.

Michael Hoey, Department of English Language and Literature, University of Birmingham.

Peter Hunt, Department of English, UWIST, Cardiff.

Martin Montgomery, Department of English Studies, University of Strathclyde.

Christopher Norris, Department of English, UWIST, Cardiff.

Andrew Pithouse, Department of Social Administration, University College, Cardiff.

Paul Tench, Department of English, UWIST, Cardiff.

Ian Whitehouse, Department of English, University College, Cardiff.

John Wiemann, Communication Studies Program, University of California, Santa Barbara.

Glyn Williams, Adran Gwyddor Cymdeithas A'i Sefydliadau, Coleg Prifysgol Gogledd Cymru, Bangor.

David Young, Department of English, UWIST, Cardiff.

Preface

There is great satisfaction in compiling a book that juxtaposes description and polemic, narrative analysis and D-J talk, philosophical history and conversation, and for that matter, children's books and nuclear deterrence. The possibility that, at each of these and several other poles, the book will have something to offer students not only of linguistics and communication, but also of criticism, sociology, social psychology and beyond is indicative of a *rapprochement* which is itself encouraging. Practitioners across this span can at times share a discourse. This is possible because of the growing recognition that textual and contextual analysis is a recognised common component of their ultimately unique purposes. Such coherence as discourse analysis now has is the result of multidisciplinary theorising, and it is fully appropriate that the insights it can derive are available across a broad field.

The book's theme is diversity and discourse, and its origins are in the diversity of backgrounds and interests of a group of teachers and researchers at the two university colleges in Cardiff, though invited contributions from other scholars have greatly added to the strength and coverage of the collection. Several contributions have grown out of the activities of the Cardiff Linguistics Circle (and more recently the UWIST Centre for Applied English Language Studies) which have provided a focus for language-related collaborative research, and to whose members a general debt of gratitude is owed. In some cases, analyses presented here are also distillations of workshop and seminar discussions to which undergraduate and postgraduate students in Cardiff have valiantly and valuably contributed. I hope that future students, in Cardiff and beyond, will find interest and insight in the lines of interpretation their predecessors developed, and will find means of adding to them.

The resources of UWIST Department of English have financed the major phases of the collection's word-processed preparation, and the project as a whole is heavily endebted to Julia Bullough and Jill Baily whose text-processing skills and (almost) inexhaustible patience saw the project through.

Nikolas Coupland
Cardiff

1

Introduction: Towards a Stylistics of Discourse

Nikolas Coupland

The need to account for discourse processes is pretty much universally recognised across the linguistic sciences, and is rapidly gaining recognition well beyond. On the other hand, there are widely differing views about what should be expected to derive from this endeavour, and therefore about what is involved both theoretically and methodologically. There are clearly different contemporary discourses of discourse analysis. The range of current and past conceptualisations and practices of discourse analysis cannot be comprehensively reviewed here, and this has in any case been recently done (by van Dijk 1985, particularly volumes 1 and 2). But a brief sketch of major current emphases will, I hope, establish a context for the diverse analyses assembled in this book, and allow me to present its collected chapters as showing a broadly agreed, distinctive orientation and enacting its own set of priorities for the analysis of discourse. These particular priorities, as we shall see, require a modification of several of the assumptions underlying more traditional work on discourse, towards a greater recognition of diversity, a more direct focus on contextual explanation at various levels, and more conscious integration with broader social scientific (beyond more narrowly linguistic) concerns. I shall present this realignment as the reimposition, in at least certain important respects, of the goals of stylistics (in explanation of the book's title) and work towards a definition of discourse analysis as the contextual interpretation of psycho-sociolinguistic diversity.

In British linguistics circles, discourse analysis tends to be associated with work inspired by Sinclair and Coulthard's analysis of classroom interaction (1975; cf. also Coulthard 1977; Coulthard and Montgomery 1982). The underlying rationale for the essentially structural account this paradigm offers is the need to capture aspects of the organisation of spoken interaction above the sentence level. A loosening of the confines of sentence or clause description is a pervasive theme of all approaches to discourse, both in the sense of operating with 'larger' or 'higher-order' units of expression, and in shifting the focus from formal, syntactic units to functional units, definable in relation to what is achieved in the contexts of their use, and in relation to one another. Analysis takes the form of exhaustively accounting for and labelling structured functional units in texts. The legacy of this model of discourse analysis is considerable. It feeds, for example, the discussion by Montgomery (in Chapter 4 of this volume) of how monologic, less obviously interactional discourse — such as D-J radio-talk — might be accounted for structurally. Again, the structural taxonomy of processes of self-disclosure (by J. Coupland *et al.*, Chapter 9) draws on what has come to be established terminology to identify hierarchical levels of functional organisation — 'moves' and 'acts'. Sinclair and Coulthard's schema has, with minimal modification, been applied to social settings beyond the classroom, for example in Coulthard and Ashby's analysis (mimeo) of doctor-patient interaction, and my own work on travel-agency talk (Coupland 1983). We might predict in fact that the principal functional 'levels' at which Sinclair and Coulthard have shown classroom talk to be organised — transactions, exchanges and moves — will be relevant in most 'transactional' (as opposed to 'personal', in Gumperz's senses of these terms) encounters and that similar patterings — e.g. of exchange structure — will tend to recur.

The important observation for our current interests, though, is that analyses of this sort are primarily motivated by concerns about descriptive linguistic adequacy rather than aspiration to social explanation. Though contextual/sociological insights *will* derive from analysis of this sort — leading to rather predictable conclusions, for example, about the distribution of power in the classroom through variable constraints on amounts and types of communicative contribution — the analysis is designed to display *linguistic* regularity. The classroom setting, as Sinclair and Coulthard acknowledge, is well suited to their analytic procedures (not vice versa) because of the rigid scripting that at least some school settings impose upon spoken interchange; their classroom discourse has 'structure and direction' (1975, p. 5). Though the units of analysis are not formal, the analysis is not essentially different from those of clause-level constituent-analysis, establishing criteria for segmentation and classification. Discourse itself is characterised as a further rank above the clausal rank at which structure is discoverable.

Another major strand of British linguistic studies — systemic linguistics — integrates 'discourse' focally into its theory and description. A moderately uncontroversial representation of the Hallidayan framework (though the precise distribution of categories and delimitation of descriptive planes and levels is a matter of considerable ongoing debate — cf. Halliday 1978, 1984; Halliday and Martin 1981; Greaves and James 1984) will view language as a tri-stratal system, comprising phonology, lexicogrammar and thirdly discourse. Discourse here broadly equates to core areas of the semantic/pragmatic components of alternative descriptive formulations, and is the stratum within which such sub-systems as reference, conjunction, cohesion and conversational structure may be specified. For example in Martin's (MS) account, discourse handles dependency relations between parts of a text. I shall return to Hallidayan accounts of the relationships between language and context and their discussions of register, genre and ideology a little later, where we shall find a discussion far more centrally relevant to the concerns of this book. For now the point is that systemic linguistics again adopts an orientation to discourse which seeks primarily to enrich the descriptive (and in this case also the predictive) adequacy of linguistic theorising. Halliday's theories are sociolinguistic theories to the extent that they work dimensions and categories of the social functioning of language into a systemic account of how language constructs meaning, the drift of argumentation therefore being from sociological to linguistic.

This is an observation that has been made in relation to quite different strands of sociolinguistic research (for example, about the seminal work of Labov 1972 and Trudgill 1974 in the area of dialect variation) — that established paradigms embody essentially *linguistic* priorities. But as in these cases (cf. Coupland 1987) so in relation to discourse, we can equally well adopt the converse perspective and embark on the analysis of language-in-context with an eye to the understanding of social processes and context itself. A stronger position, and one that many of the contributions to this volume will endorse, is that the language-to-social organisation schema for discourse analysis is theoretically *required* as a consequence of prior conclusions reached about the nature and constitution of social organisation itself. Arguing this position is in fact the epistemological corner-stone of sociological approaches to discourse analysis.

It is widely recognised that a major school of sociological theorising— ethnomethodology (cf. Garfinkel 1972, Psathas 1979) — has been influential in establishing a climate wherein discourse analysis (as a broad heading) is seen as an appropriate and even a necessary orientation to analysis and scholarly debate across many disciplines. Ethnomethodology as sociology distances itself from deterministic sociological analyses which it claims unjustifiably endorse the 'real' existence of demographic and institutional categories and 'facts'. Therefore, to take socio-economic stratification or indeed any social framing or coding as the point of departure for analysis is to misconstrue, it is argued, the nature of social organisation, which is an *imputed* organisation. However natural such categories are, and more particularly because of their conventionalised naturalness, we need to research whether and by what means they find their existence as natural categories for actors and analysts alike. These researches then become researchable in an inwardly spiralling analysis of methods of categorisation. A cognitive perspective at least begins to live up to our best understanding of the nature of social organisation, as established in and constituted by on-the-ground behaviours — and in particular through social interaction. By this account, it seems unlikely that social 'facts' will be available to linguistic theory-building, but it is to be hoped that delicate analyses of language in use will reveal acceptable truths — perhaps typically ungeneralisable, fleeting and partial — about aspects of social life.

The basic ethnomethodological perspective holds both a positive and a negative implication for discourse analysis: what might be obtainable, and what is not to be trusted. The sociological literature centring on conversation analysis (CA) has begun to show what might be obtained, but is arguably over-constrained by its definition of what is trustworthy. To the extent that CA is committed to an ethnomethodological re-working *ab initio* of social analysis, it needs to be relatively self-motivating and self-contained. The social structures it can recognise are essentially those demonstrated and created during interaction — structures of social action (cf. Atkinson and Heritage 1984)[1] — most obviously then structures *of* talk. CA derives its data meticulously though not unproblematically (cf. below) through transcription from recorded, naturally occurring interaction, which is clearly 'situated' and contextually relatable. On the other hand, concern about the bogus fixity of contextual categories seems to have led to *minimal* attention being afforded non-linguistic context in CA, subordinated to the primary status of the data as talk. The structuring and patterning of talk gives analyses their focus, under rubrics like closings, insertion-sequences, step-wise topic-transition, *oh*-prefaced responses, and so on. The focus on autonomous talk tends to drown out what individual protagonists bring to it — variables in their histories, relationships, motives and predispositions — and the effects of talk — satisfaction, dissatisfaction, attitude-change, relational change. Talk is presented as occurring in a rarified social context and sometimes in a world where all but talk is suspended (cf. the discussion in the Appendix to Chapter 9 in this volume).

CA has therefore arrived at a position where its primary input, and a vital one, to the analysis of language in context is in displaying the local mechanics of conversation. There is an irony: CA sociologists have shouldered the burden of pattern-building, which may be put to work doing social explanation (as in several contributions to this volume) in the works of analysts who are less obviously sociologists — linguists, sociolinguists, critics, ethnographers, philosophers, political theorists and social psychologists.

This diversity of disciplinary interest in discourse analysis (although in some of this book's chapters, the disciplines represented are encouragingly difficult to pin-point) is not entirely understandable as a spontaneous epistemological shift away from deterministic, overly empiricist social science, as I have sketched it in relation to ethnomethodology. At least, it is not entirely attributable to the negative implication — the mistrust of other approaches. A more humble explanation is that discourse analysis is, quite simply and within its limitations, a revealing way of doing social science. On the assumption that many or most social relationships, institutions, events and activities are mediated by communicative and specifically linguistic behaviours, it is reasonable to expect that detailed inspection of language-use, its relationship to and constitution of meanings in context, will give access to the dynamic workings of social processes. Discourse analysis does not therefore *have* to be sustained by a committed interpretivist, relativist epistemology, and be claimed to be the only theoretically enfranchised line of social scientific research. It can appropriately be a complementary practice to other modes of inquiry, over which it will have specific but not total advantages. A consensual view across this volume is that of discourse not as a delimitable technique or method or level of analysis, but as an orientation to social explanation — as an openness to the interpretation of situated communication events where some non-linguistic dynamic is a candidate for analysis. While this is a modest rationale for discourse analysis, it is a significantly different one from those offered, as we have seen, either by those linguists who see discourse as a further dimension to a linguistic theory or by those sociologists who are reticent to recognise social structures beyond those of talk.

A more ambitious formulation, however, would credit discourse analysis with the same explanatory power but against much higher odds, arguing that it is a nobler enterprise than an alternative focus on old questions. For some (cf. in particular Williams (Chapter 10), Norris and Whitehouse (Chapter 11) and Hunt (Chapter 7) in this collection), it is through the identification of broad cultural/sub-cultural discursive formations, and *only* through this, that the operation of societal power-codes can be read and conceivably broken. This tradition of discourse analysis (epitomised in the writings of Foucault, e.g. 1971, 1980 and overviewed by Kress 1985) argues a systematic relation between discourse, power and knowledge wherein self-justifying modes of discourse set the boundaries of and sustain ideologies — principally those of the dominant social groups and institutions. In consequence, critical analyses present the sole route to contextualising such discourses and possibly recovering rights over what may be said, what may be thought, what may be known. Thus, legal and nationalist discourse of 'ethnicity' and 'language' are argued (Williams) to dictate the progression of a tribunal hearing of a case alleging discrimination. Establishment discourses restrict definitions of 'literature' and 'children's books' (Hunt) in a way that preconditions the type of reading material offered to children, and critical response to it. In super-power heads-of-state pronouncements, the US employs a rhetorical mode premissed on quite different discursive principles (Norris and Whitehouse) from that of the USSR and sustains a position on nuclear deterrence which, these authors argue, cannot be rationally grounded.

In the chapters as a whole there is a pervasive theme of discourse analysis as a forensic detective activity, as a means of accessing covert but essential characteristics — of either individual communicative events (e.g. a poem), conversational modes (e.g. narrative/anecdote, self-disclosure), generic categories (e.g. various contexts of prayer, news-reading, D-J talk) or social institutions (e.g. social work). Working outwards from selective reading of texts — spoken or written — analyses are constructed to reveal processes salient to the constitution of these dimensions of social context. Certainly there are different levels of ambition here, and claims of varying strength are made by different contributors. The stronger the claim and the greater the explanatory leap from text to social implications, the more space remains (for critical readers) to give modified or alternative accounts. The analyses in fact mix textual description with interpretation in very different measures, and some contributors are at pains to mark the points at which their analyses cross from linguistic characterisation to more obviously subjective accounting. Hoey (Chapter 6), for example, notes where literary and theological observations are needed to carry through his linguistically-based analysis. Others are more ruthlessly interpretivist. There may even be an inverse correlation between chapters' readiness to move well beyond linguistic description and the level of linguistic technicality of the analyses themselves. (And perhaps the more descriptivist, the more likely to favour the term stylistics.) But the collection as a whole shows linguistics having outgrown the need to restrict its own compass, and equally as able to look outwards as inwards — towards psycho-social explanation as towards its own autonomy.

I do not want to overstate the unity of the book beyond claiming a broad communality of purpose. The chapters are noteworthy, most obviously so, for their diversity: of disciplinary inputs, of linguistic/communicative dimensions treated, and primarily of social contexts addressed. To this extent, the volume demonstrates analyses of discourse in the service of *stylistic* inquiry, exploring relationships of text and context. Stylistics and discourse analysis, however, cannot be easily conflated, given their distinct and complex histories and allegiances. Stylistics as conceived for example by Enkvist (1964, 1973) and Crystal and Davy (1976) has traditionally operated within the confines of sentence-based linguistics, sharing its propensity to autonomy and descriptivism. The waning of stylistics has arguably followed the erosion of confidence in precisely these two principles, and the growing recognition that characterising texts linguistically may in itself lead to *no* significant contextual insights (Hunt, Chapter 7 in this volume, quotes critics of over-ambitious literary stylistics on just this point). Stylistics of course pre-dates the 'socio' revolution in linguistic studies and the highly influential interaction between linguists and (other?) social scientists, only a small part of which I have referred to above. For this reason, we should consider how the greater 'depth' of discourse analysis (*pace* Hymes 1986, cf. below) might rejuvenate an ailing stylistics, but also how a revival of fundamental stylistic priorities might provide a structure for discourse analytic investigations of social context.

In a recent selective review of work on discourse, Hymes (1986) argues that there has a been a systematic underplaying of variability in discourse, which I shall take as corroboration of the need for greater stylistic awareness in discourse analysis. A critical survey of the well-known work of Bernstein, Austin, Grice, Goffman, Brown and Levinson, Garfinkel and others leads Hymes to conclude they have a certain common orientation:

> The worlds in which persons live and talk are secondary, not primary; in so far as these worlds have distinctive characteristics, these characteristics are departures, violations, limitations, not constitutive of order; discourse is to be analysed in terms of a speaker (and hearer) freely placed to relate words and world, and to each other, on the basis of a few universal principles. (p. 85)

An an ethnographer, Hymes is primarily concerned with the need to represent inter-cultural diversity, and the risk of ethnocentrism in discourse analysis, but his view that influential approaches lack a 'configuration' (p. 86) cuts even deeper than this. If discourse analysis is to recognise that 'the same behaviours, the same verbal conduct, may have different implications for different actors', and that 'the repertoires of individuals may differ in a given language and in a different range of discourse' (p. 87), it will need to represent social context in an altogether less idealised and much more explicitly variationist way than it has to date. The problem is how this might be achieved, and in a way that does not conflict with the epistemological requirements of discourse analysis. In the remainder of this Introduction, I shall suggest that social contexts may be represented in analyses either 'internally' or 'externally' and discuss the problems and possibilities associated with each; then I shall outline, in relation to the analyses offered in later chapters, a range of dimensions of social context that analyses might address, and that are in fact shown being addressed in the later chapters of this book.

Internal characterisation

Crystal and Davy (1976, p. 80 ff.) saw the primary goal of stylistics as the 'specification' of types, which in its simplest formulation implies characterisation of the linguistics of individual social contexts. This is clearly inadequate as a prospectus for the discoursal representation of context, but it might be useful to say why. Firstly, it suggests an 'inwardly' deterministic analysis (social-to-linguistic, as discussed earlier) which assumes that contexts consist of or condition linguistic selections. Secondly, there is no reason to believe that linguistic specifying will be informative or insightful (sociologically, psychologically, aesthetically, politically, etc.). Thirdly, there is an implication of dispassionate, unmotivated analysis here, which does not reflect the manner in which analysts (probably of *any* denomination) actually approach texts: there is always a hope of discovering, though more truthfully a wish to confirm and expound, an interpretation. On the other hand, Crystal and Davy's discussion is most helpful in the caveats it draws our attention to. There is an inherent selectivity and of course subjectivity within the notion of specifying — *what* to specify and *how* to specify.

There is a strong case for analytic eclecticism here and for the mixing of levels of analysis. And it is interesting that several of the chapters in this volume explicitly endorse such a standpoint. Hoey (Chapter 6), for example, demonstrates that he is able to reach his interpretive conclusions *only* by means of an analysis spanning lexical, phonological and clause-relational levels. Montgomery's account (Chapter 4) of the foregrounding of an interpersonal dimension in D-J monologue builds on simultaneous observations about modes of address, spatial deixis, the prevalence of certain utterance-functions and sequential aspects of the talk. J. Coupland *et al.* (Chapter 9) argue that an adequate taxonomy of the staging of self-disclosive sequences requires an admixture of formal, turn-based categorisation and a more functional means-ends account of their development and closing.

everal chapters are able to build coherent textual inter- s from wholly informal linguistic commentaries.

scourse analysis will only begin to offer an internal char- ation of context (or, as I shall suggest, more reasonably of r more dimension(s) of context) when it can show elements of the internal coherence or non-coherence of the contextualising process. The probably appropriate question is therefore not 'what are the linguistic determinates or correlates of this context?' but rather 'how are linguistic patterns constitutive of dimensions of social context?' This is not to rule out instances where 'contexts' have indeed established a permanence (as 'registers' or 'genres' — cf. below) in a way which exerts genuine constraints on the cognitions and behaviour of actors. In such cases, an analysis should reveal context as a potential site of struggle — as tensioned by the possible conflict between individual will and perceived normative behaviour. For instance, an elderly conversationalist may resist a stereotypically-based cluster of conversational roles imposed on her through the behaviour of a younger speaker; being a competent performer at a Quaker meeting for worship is influenced, but not dictated, by norms of ideal performances. Davies (Chapter 4 in this volume) remarks that contemporary Quakerism needs to be characterised by its on-the-ground practices, not its idealised formats — by its 'traditions' rather than by its 'charisma' — and the argument holds more generally.

If discourse analysis is to characterise social context, it will need to show a healthy mistrust for text, as a necessarily partial and idealised product of discourse process. All analyses in this collection focus on texts, wholly or partially transcribed, though they are *not* strictly analyses *of* texts. If, following Barthes, we conceive of text as a multiplicity of forms without context, then text becomes a potential obstacle as well as a potential aid to the analysis of discourse. Under these circumstances, transcription and its use in analysis assumes a considerable theoretical importance which it is not usually credited with. For example, the notion of a 'good' transcript is problematical: there are more and less useful transcripts but no 'correct' and ultimately verifiable transcripts. With conversation, the risk (as identified by Stubbs 1983, p. 227) is that the act of transcribing will re-fashion, re-encode 'the data' in more and less controllable and perceptible ways. Transcribing practices, probably rightly, earn credit for being 'meticulous', though their very meticulousness consolidates the illusion of perfection and objectivity, disguising processes of hearing, decoding and re-coding which are clearly subjective and bias-ridden. This argument contradicts established assumptions and priorities in, for example, conversation analysis where particularly strict, though I would suggest theoretically unjustified, criteria of 'accuracy' are met. Schenkein (1978, p. xi), for example, presents the transcription system used in his collection (based on that development by Jefferson) as aiming to produce written text 'that will look to the eye how it sounds to the ear'. The capabilities and limitations of the two modes — speech and transcript — surely make this pragmatically unachievable. What we find in conversation analysis is, rather, an elaborate set of conventions (often tacit) for representing speech which inevitably already impose an analysis on speech, packaged for a readership acculturated to its general form. For example, prosody and pronunciation are minimally represented in Jefferson's system (Atkinson and Heritage 1984, p. xii) though a few informal and atheoretical conventions are used. The system then deviates from orthography (Jefferson's *eether, git* (= get), *p'litical, liddle, ohgh, ju:ss,* etc.), offering unspecified and coded supplementary information to the textual reading process. We don't know precisely what *is* intended or conveyed; not phonetic realisations, since these deviations are the merest tip of a realisational iceberg, but perhaps there are coded inferences here as to affect, formality or even speaker-status.[2]

My purpose here is not to single out CA as exceptionally remiss in its orientation to text. It is only because CA has pursued natural data more relentlessly than most disciplines that it now has to face the implications of the procedures it has developed. Linguists are likely to take refuge from such criticism in the technicality of their own systems — their notational accuracy and internal coherence. Genuine benefits can follow (cf. Tench's demonstration, in Chapter 2 of this volume, of the role of intonational variation in register-identification, deriving from microphonetic analysis). Theoretically grounded transcription may increase the probability of reliably detecting patterns in the data but does not impinge on the general question of the status of text in contextual characterisation, and the inevitable need to transcend textual 'evidence' in analysing discourse.

There are apparent exceptions, notably in the case of literary analysis (Hoey, Hunt and Young in this volume), where it is often remarked that text — *the* text — has a singularly inalienable claim as the object of analysis. But it is important that, here too, analysis is likely to focus not on the text as isolate but on the text as composed and (in Hoey's case) as performed. A crucial component of Hoey's account of 'Vertue' is its phonological structure, an aspect of the social context of the text's enactment. Hunt too is ultimately concerned with the pre- and post-textual processes he presents as conflicting discourses — writers', children's, critics' and literary prize-givers' — of writing for children.

External characterisation

Stylistics has often discussed means by which contexts might be characterised externally, that is in relation to one another, and has wanted to ask 'what makes this style, this event, this context *not* others?' Style as deviation (e.g. Enkvist 1973, p. 15 ff.) is a well-known formulation, and in early accounts was conceived as a relation between two or more distributions, across contexts, of formal linguistic elements:

> the style of a text is a function of the aggregate of the ratios between the frequencies of its phonological, grammatical and lexical items and the frequencies of the corresponding items in a contextually-related norm. (Enkvist 1964, p. 28)

This thoroughly positivist announcement is hopelessly optimistic in view of the criteria for an adequate characterisation of context we have been discussing. But it encapsulates very clearly the contrastive focus that a stylistics of discourse must find ways of assimilating. Several contributions to this volume are explicit in their contrastive function, either directly setting analyses of quite distinct communicative contexts one against others (as in Chapter 2 by Tench), approaching a contextual delimitation through juxtaposing analyses of seemingly related discourses (Young), singling out contrasting participant-groups in a single interactional setting (J. Coupland *et al.*), or interest-groups in a single generic context and highlighting opposing rhetorical modes (Norris and Whitehouse) or ideological discourses (Williams). Even chapters which appear to offer *in*ternal characterisations of context make occasional reference to contrastable 'implied' norms — conversation versus Meetings for Worship (Davies), face-to-face dialogue versus radio monologue (Montgomery).

A grander design for the external characterisation of social context is suggested by the British tradition of stylistics and register-analysis, from J.R. Firth, through Gregory to Halliday and Martin. The emphasis here is on taxonomising contexts at various levels. A model is proposed where 'language' is seen as 'a denotative semiotic' (cf. Martin, MS) which acts as the expression-form of 'register', one of the three 'connotative semiotics' stacked above it in similar relationships. The four strata are (highest to lowest) 'ideology', 'genre', 'register' and 'language'. The four systems are semiotics in the sense that they make meanings rather than merely realise them. In this account, register is the level of abstraction at which options in the sub-systems of field, mode and tenor (cf., for example, Gregory and Carroll 1978), and genre is a culturally conditioned, staged, goal-oriented social process. Martin's work in particular is important as a coherent attempt to represent social context in a linguistic theory, to make categories of context, as he says in the paper cited, 'more predictive than they might otherwise be by orienting them to the specific systems in language whose meaning they may be seen to determine'. Again, then, the assumption is that contexts are primes, independently discoverable and having predictive, *determining* power over language, and Martin is highly critical of more sociolinguistic models (e.g. that of Hymes) which do not assume this. The whole approach is thus at odds with a discourse analysis of the sort this volume envisages. While Martin would downgrade non-predictive approaches to language and context (i.e. where context is not modelled to predict language selections) as 'mere' '*explication de texte*', his own approach continues to take for granted contextual taxonomising — intuitive and atheoretical — as a departure-point. Context itself cannot be unpackaged by these means.

Register, genre and ideology *are* useful concepts for contextual characterisation, though *not* for simple taxonomic purposes. There is a banality about early stylistic attempts to identify registers ('the language of journalism/advertising/law ...') stemming from an impoverished view of the role of social action in respect of context and too much faith in the stability and delimitation of categories. On the other hand, it is wrong to deny the relative stability of specific contextual structures or actors' potential awareness of them. Hymes seems to strike the right balance:

> To abandon the fixity of *a priori* general categories is not to be lost in a sea of exceptions. Persons, events, and groups have characteristic tendencies, dispositions and styles, recognizable to others and in principle describable by investigators. We do not experience conversational interaction as a chaos ordinarily. This is so for at least three kinds of reason:
> a. There are some recurrent types of sequence
> b. Persons, events, and groups have recognizable patterns, even though each sequence may not be predictable in advance
> c. Persons and groups bring to conversation expectations and resources which contribute to a sense of orderliness.
> Moreover, the very dimension of degree of predictability of fixity is an important dimension on which to compare and contrast persons, styles, activities, and events. (1986, p. 65)

Discourse analysis risks losing a significant interpretive resource if it denies the existence of culturally endorsed, cognitively represented blueprints or scripts for individual, group or institutional behaviour, modes of talk, categories of literary production or entire pattern-configurations of social interaction. Some of these (those more towards the end of this list) will more naturally attract the label of 'genre', but the recognition of potential fixity is more important than the coverage of any one category-label. 'Register', with its historical connotations of over-neat language/context correlation, may be a label to avoid, unless it is similarly taken to refer to the cognitive mapping of rather 'narrower' dimensions of communicative context — e.g. expected configurations of talk to addressee-groups ('baby-talk'/'old-speak'/'foreigner talk') or predicted by role or situation ('carer talk'/'teacher talk'/'interview talk'). Such labels cannot pretend to subsume totalities of communication behaviours in context. They are not categories of social context, which is not a carvable entity. They are either gross generalisations (unreliable correlational predictions that outside observers can make) or cognitive scripts (starting-points for participants' en- and de-coding options) of selective dimensions of social context.

Dimensions of social context

In this final section, it might be useful to summarise from the previous discussion the contextual dimensions whicl analyses address. The fundamental point that should that discourse analyses aiming to represent diversity context will necessarily approach the task selectively, si dimensions are of potential relevance to any and every municative manifestation. The following is not intended as another attempt to 'specify' social context exhaustively (cf. Firth 1957, Gregory 1967, Cazden 1970, Hymes 1972, and a recent review by Furnham 1986), but rather to preview the diversity to be found in subsequent chapters. None of the dimensions is self-sufficient or totally specifiable.

Interpersonal

As noted at the beginning of this Introduction, it tends to be assumed that discourse analyses will illuminate above all aspects of the interpersonal contexts of talk — the intermeshing of individual conversational contributions, but independently of actors' histories and circumstances either as individuals or as group members. It is perhaps significant that *none* of the following chapters dwells on inter-individual behaviours, *unless* it is to establish a contrast of some kind within another contextual dimension. Montgomery devotes a lot of space to interpersonal distance and relations, but specifically as a metaphorical re-casting of discourse between non-familiars (D-J and audience) across space. A discourse analysis motivated to explain diversity will presumably be drawn to more obviously *social* contextual dimensions and will relate interpersonal behaviours to them.

Socio-structural

In contrast, most chapters develop their analyses towards some characterisation of socio-structural context, in relation to social groups and/or institutions. For example, the analyses of self-disclosive behaviours (J. Coupland *et al.*) is directed at the different experiences, predispositions and satisfactions of 'painful' self-disclosure for older and younger conversationalists. Norris and Whitehouse's account of super-power discourse focuses on different philosophical and rhetorical traditions between East and West. Quaker discourse (Davies) and social work discourse (Pithouse and Atkinson) reify social groups and institutions simultaneously, and in each case the authors can claim that communicative conventions touch socio-structural essence — what Quakerism *is*, what social work *is*.

Modal

The focal contextual dimension of several of the analyses is less to do with actors or the social territory they inhabit and more to do with the packaging of texts and *their* environments. Tench's and Davies's analyses contribute to an account of what prayer is; Tench's and Young's to an account of narrative. Hoey's analysis of 'Vertue' is conducted in relation to what might be normative (in poetic and non-poetic discourse); Hunt's broader approach reviews multiple perspectives on the definition of children's literature. In some cases, such considerations of mode and genre are addressed in the establishment of *other* contextual dimensions (the patterning of self-disclosive talk opens up a means of differentiating social groups) and vice versa (foregrounding the interpersonal is a D-J strategy in response to apparent limitations on radio broadcasting).

Ideological

If ideology is taken to be a framework of social conceptualisations that resists modification and imposes an orientation upon reality, then no communicative manifestations will be totally devoid of ideological salience. As Kress (1985, p. 29) notes, 'ideologies ... find their clearest articulation in language', so any analysis from language to society is already ideological. The stronger formulation of Foucault (1971, 1980; and cf. again Kress) attends principally to the ideological output of social institutions and to the delimitation of power in situations of conflict (rather than to reality-orientation in general) whereby constraints are imposed upon what might be said. Several chapters pin-point discoursal contexts where overt conflict is in fact nullified under the weight of institutionally imposed authority, though this is not always negatively characterised. Davies sketches the 'novice' coming to terms with institutionalised Quaker discourse; Pithouse and Atkinson outline the pressures on social workers to show professional competence through their rhetorical skills. More divisively, Hunt presents the world of children's literature as constrained by establishment power-groups' definitions. There is the suggestion that elderly conversationalists are led into a self-disclosive role by the young's (and perhaps 'society's') stereotypes of how elderly talk and how talk between the generations should proceed. Williams traces the confused and conflicting discourses of written reports and counsels' arguments at a discrimination tribunal-hearing back to legal and even national presuppositions about the definition of language as an ethnic identity.

Pragmatic

A discourse analysis directed at contextual accounting has no obvious outer limit, and analysts will set the boundaries of their interpretations quite differently. If we conceived of contextual explanation as occupying a series of concentric circles, moving outwards from text, what would be the outer ring? With discussions of ideology, we are already concerned with social conflict and processes of social maintenance and change that influence the ways lives are lived. Theories of language as social action have produced a discourse analysis which can talk elegantly about the nature of language and language-context relations, but has as yet made little contribution to the causal and consequential aspects of particular language-uses in particular context. But ultimately, discourse analysis will itself be evaluated for what it does rather than what it is. The pragmatic dimension of contextual analysis will come naturally to the fore as discourse analysis takes more interest in diversity. Returning to some of the issues raised in the chapters to come, patterns of talk between the generations are more than fodder for structural analysis and require interpretations in terms of the preconceptions of an ageist society, the diverse functioning of talk — recreational, emotional, therapeutic, instrumental — across the generations (cf. Wiemann, N. Coupland, Giles *et al.*, MS), perceptions of degrees of satisfaction in contexts of talk, and the consequences of miscommunication (cf. N. Coupland, Giles and Wiemann, forthcoming) — for life-satisfaction and even health. Conflicting discourses about Welshness and the Welsh language are of central relevance to patterns of employment in Wales and questions of linguistic and cultural change. There can be no clearer pragmatic context for language than the nuclear threat, which is directly contingent upon reading and second-guessing super-power discourses of aggression and deterrence. The agenda for a variationist discourse analysis is open-ended, and that in itself will force practitioners to select social contexts where their analyses will impact most strongly. Under these circumstances, discourse analysis will be increasingly recognised as an explanatory resource open to the social sciences as a means of accessing dynamic processes in the diverse episodes of our social lives.

Notes

1. An illustrative anecdote: at a recent CA conference (University of California, Santa Barbara, April 1986), a distinguished keynote speaker consciously re-directed the theme of the conference — 'Language and Social Structure' — towards the preferred CA territory of 'Language and structures of social action'.

2. Another illustrative anecdote: it even seems permissible for CA practitioners whose data is not in English to subscribe to Jeffersonian *English* conventions of this sort when reporting their data in translation!

References

Atkinson, J.M. and Heritage, J. (1984) *Structures of social action: studies in conversation analysis.* Cambridge: Cambridge University Press

Cazden, C. (1970) 'The situation: a neglected source of social class differences in language use.' *Journal of Social Issues,* 26, pp. 35-60

Coulthard, M. (1977) *An introduction to discourse analysis.* London: Longman

Coulthard, M. and Ashby, M. (mimeo) 'A linguistic description of doctor-patient interviews'. University of Birmingham

Coulthard, M. and Montgomery, M. (1982) *Studies in discourse analysis.* London: Routledge & Kegan Paul

Coupland, N. (1983) 'Patterns of encounter management: further arguments for discourse variables'. *Language in Society,* 12, pp. 459-76

—— (1987) *Dialect in use: sociolinguistic variation in Cardiff English.* Cardiff: University of Wales Press

Coupland, N., Giles, H. and Wiemann, J. (eds) (forthcoming) *The handbook of miscommunication and problematic talk.* Clevedon: Multilingual Matters

Cystal, D. and Davy, D. (1976) *Investigating English style.* London: Longman

Enkvist, N. E. (1964) 'On defining style: an essay in applied linguistics'. In N. E. Enkvist, J. Spencer and M. J. Gregory, *Linguistics and style.* Oxford: Oxford University Press

—— (1973) *Linguistic stylistics.* The Hague: Mouton

Firth, J. R. (1957) *Papers in linguistics, 1934-1951.* London: Oxford University Press

Foucault, M. (1971) 'Orders of discourse'. *Social Science Information,* 10, 2, pp. 7-30

—— (1980) 'Prison talk'. In C. Gordon (ed.) *Power/Knowledge.* New York: Pantheon, pp. 37-54

Furnham, A. (1986) 'Situational determinants of intergroup communication'. In W. B. Gudykunst (ed.) *Intergroup communication.* London: Edward Arnold, pp. 96-113.

Garfinkel, H. (1972) 'Remarks on ethnomethodology'. In J. J. Gumperz and D. Hymes (eds) *Directions in sociolinguistics.* New York: Holt, Rinehart & Winston, pp. 301-24

Greaves, W. S. and James, D. (1984) *Systemic perspectives on discourse: selected theoretical papers from the Ninth International Systemic Workshop.* Norwood, NJ: Ablex

Gregory, M. (1967) 'Aspects of varieties differentiation'. *Journal of Linguistics,* 3, pp. 177-98

Gregory, M. and Carroll, S. (1978) *Language and situation: language varieties and their social contexts.* London: Routledge & Kegan Paul

Halliday, M. A. K. (1978) *Language as social semiotic: the social interpretation of language and meaning.* London: Edward Arnold

—— (1984) *A short introduction to functional grammar.* London: Edward Arnold

Halliday, M. A. K. and Martin, J. R. (eds) (1981) *Readings in systemic linguistics.* London: Batsford

Hymes, D. (1986) 'Discourse: scope without depth'. *International Journal of the Sociology of Language,* 57, pp. 49-90

Kress, G. (1985) 'Ideological structures in discourse'. In T. A. van Dijk (ed.) *Handbook of discourse analysis,* 4 vols. London: Academic Press, vol. 4, pp. 27-42

Labov, W. (1972) *Sociolinguistic patterns.* Philadelphia: University of Pennsylvania Press

Martin, J. R. (MS) 'Lexical cohesion, field and genre: parcelling experience and discourse goals'

Psathas, G. (ed.) (1979) *Everyday language: studies in ethnomethodology.* New York: Irvington

Schenkein, J. (1978) 'Explanation of transcript notation'. In J. Schenkein (ed.) *Studies in the organisation of conversational interaction.* New York: Academic Press, pp. xi-xvi

Sinclair, J.McH. and Coulthard, M. (1975) *Towards an analysis of discourse: the English used by teachers and pupils.* Oxford: Oxford University Press

Stubbs, M. (1983) *Discourse analysis.* Oxford: Blackwell

Trudgill, P. (1974) *The social differentiation of English in Norwich.* London: Edward Arnold

van Dijk, T. A. (1985) *Handbook of discourse analysis.* 4 vols. London: Academic Press

Wiemann, J., Coupland, N., Giles, H. *et al.* (MS) 'Beliefs about talk: intergenerational perspectives'

2

Projection and Deixis in Narrative Discourse

David Young

The purpose of this paper is to study some features of the language used for reporting on the use of language. It will look at the ways in which the grammatical resources employed may vary from one kind of discourse to another. Reporting on the use of language includes not only telling what people said, but also what they thought. I have chosen three kinds of narrative for the purpose, though the term 'narrative' is used loosely here in a non-technical sense to mean any recounting of events from the past, real or imagined. The kinds of narrative chosen are (A) reports of parliamentary proceedings in the press, (B) conversational anecdote and (C) prose fiction.

The texts

The analysis will be based on a series of examples from these narrative contexts. An analysis of the discourse structure will be given when we come to examine the texts in detail. For the moment I am simply presenting the texts with some description of their contexts. Texts A1 and A2 are photo-reproduced below. The marginal numbers relate to my analysis of the texts, referred to below. Both are taken from the reports of parliamentary proceedings in the *Guardian* of 6 December, 1985. A1 is part of a report about 800 words in length of a debate in the House of Lords about a Conservative Government bill to compel the routing of a new trunk road through the Dartmoor National Park. The Government's bill was going against the decision of a joint select committee. The bill was opposed by a Conservative peer, who was moving a 'wrecking' amendment. The opposition

Text A1

2.1 Moving the bill for the Gov-
2.2.1 ernment, |the **Earl of Caithness**
said it was convinced that the
southern route, which passed
through the edge of the
National Park, was the right
.2 route. | The Government stood
by the policy of the not routing of major roads through
national parks, but argued that
this was an exceptional circumstance in that there was no
reasonable alternative route
which could be built within an
acceptable time scale.

.3 "We do not believe that any
northern route would be a
reasonable alternative means
of bypassing Okehampton."

.4 The Earl said the Government did not apologise for
bringing forward the bill and
believed it was right that the
issue should be decided on the
floor of the House rather than
upstairs in committee.

.5 He said he could give cate-
gorical assurances that the decision on Okehampton would
not form a precedent for any
other roads to be routed
.6 through national parks. He argued that the southern route
could be completed within five
years whilst the alternative
northern route, advocated by
environmentalists, would take
a minimum of nine years and
that would only be possible if
there was no public
consultation.

Text A2

Pressure from MPs on Sunday trading

SHOPS BILL

By Alan Travis

1 THE Government's commitment to the concept of a moral and Christian country was questioned by MPs yesterday as ministers insisted they will push ahead with legislation to allow Sunday trading and a relaxation of the licensing laws.

2.1 Mr Douglas Hurd, the Home Secretary, said during Home Office questions that he had an open mind on relaxing the licensing laws. He is waiting for a report from the Office of Population Census and Statistics due to be published in February on the effect of the licensing laws experiment in Scotland before taking a decision.

2.2 Mr Hurd said he needed reassurance that the proposal would have substantial support in the country before going ahead. He had been told by Mr Andrew MacKay (C, Berkshire E) that it was high time that licensing laws were relaxed, bearing in mind the experience in Scotland.

3.1 Home Office ministers still face strong pressure from MPs of all parties over the bill to deregulate Sunday
3.2 trading. | Nine Conservative MPs yesterday tabled a motion protesting that the imposition of a party whip when the bill is voted on in the Commons will be unjustified.

3.3 Twenty-four Labour MPs also tabled a separate Commons motion which strongly protested that Sunday trading would considerably worsen the conditions of shop workers.

3.4 MPs claim that they have received more letters opposed to Sunday trading than on any other issue of
3.5 the moment. | But Mr David Waddington, the Home Office minister, insists that the bill will go ahead despite his receiving 6,688 letters against Sunday trading. He said that was only to be expected: "We seem to very rarely get letters from people saying they like what the Government is doing."

4 These potential liberalisation measures prompted Mr Dennis Skinner (Lab. Bolsover) to ask, "What's all this here? Is the Home Secretary really telling the house that, notwithstanding what the chairman of the Tory Party had to say about the permissive society of the sixties, that not only is he going to have Sunday trading but is also going to relax the licensing laws? I don't know what the Tory Party is coming to."

to the Government, however, was weakened by the fact that the opposition parties did not want to oppose a measure which had previously passed with a large majority in the Commons. The whole report has the following structure, in which section 2 forms our text Al:

1. Summary of what the Government was attempting and of the main lines of opposition.

2. Report of what the Government mover said.

3. Report of what the supporter of the amendment said.

4. Report of an opposition spokesman's disapproval of the Government's measure, while, however, declining to vote for the wrecking amendment.

Text A2 is a whole article and speaks for itself.

Text B, reproduced on pp. 38–40, consists of two extracts from the conversational anecdote cited by Paul Tench on pp. 62–7 of this volume.[1] The extracts in question are lines 33-54 and 76 to the end. The conversation took place in November 1985 between a male academic (a Senior Lecturer in Electronics) and his wife and daughter when he had just arrived home from work at about five o'clock. The passage cited is itself only a short extract (about one-fifth of the whole) from an anecdote which lasted about seven minutes. The anecdote relates how on the previous day the narrator set out from Cardiff and met up with a colleague to go to a meeting in Birmingham, but never reached their destination because they got on the wrong train.

Text C is reproduced below.[2] It is taken from Charlotte Brontë's *Villette* (1853) and consists of four paragraphs from Chapter 38, 'Cloud' (p. 426 in the Collins edition of 1953). The novel is a first-person narrative of an autobiographical kind. The narrator, Lucy Snow, is a woman of the English Protestant middle class without private means of any sort and with no close relatives. She is telling the story of her childhood and young womanhood and is very much concerned with the development of her personality and the search for her own identity. She lays stress on the way she now perceives and the way she did then perceive what other people did and said and her relationship with them. She is quiet, often superficially timid, but inwardly determined by means of an intense self-discipline. She presents herself as one whose lot in life it is to be lonely, and to suffer hardship. Her loneliness is heightened by her living in the capital city (Villette) of a foreign Catholic country, where she finds employment as an English teacher in a girls' school.

The head and proprietress of the school is a cool efficient woman, Madame Beck, who is unscrupulous in her control of the school, keeping the teachers, pupils and servants under strict, often surreptitious, surveillance. Nevertheless, relations between her and Lucy are outwardly smooth. They respect each other and each keeps her distance from the other lest any open breach should occur. Lucy gradually forms an attachment to M. Paul Emanuel, a senior teacher of the school and a cousin of Mme Beck's. She at first sees him as 'a dark little man ... pungent and austere' (p. 133). Under his astringent and unpromising exterior there is a passion, an intellect and a self-denying generosity that win her admiration and love. The feeling is returned, despite his initial criticism of her Protestant upbringing.

At the point in the novel from which our extract is taken, Mme Beck has announced to the school that M. Emmanuel is intending to leave. The news is a shock to all, including Lucy. She suspects that Mme Beck knows and is opposed to her attachment to M. Paul and that a certain Jesuit priest is also bent on preventing any association between them. She feels sinister forces silently working to frustrate her, while all daily routines and relationships appear calm and normal.

The 'they' of the first sentence of the extract refers to the staff, pupils and servants of the school. Zélie St Pierre is one of the teachers.

Text C

They talked so much, so long, so often, that, out of the very multitude of their words and rumours grew at last some intelligence. About the third day I heard it said that he was to sail in a week; then, that he was bound for the West Indies. I looked at Madame Beck's face, and into her eyes, for disproof or confirmation of this report; I perused her all over for information, but no part of her disclosed more than was unperturbed and commonplace.

> 'This secession was an immense loss to her,' she alleged. 'She did not know how she should fill up the vacancy. She was so used to her kinsman, he had become her right hand. What should she do without him? She had opposed the step, but M. Paul had convinced her it was his duty.'
> She said all this is public, in *classe*, at the dinner table, speaking audibly to Zélie St. Pierre.
> 'Why was it his duty?' I could have asked her that. I had impulses to take hold of her suddenly, as she calmly passed me in *classe*, to stretch out my hand and grasp her fast, and say, 'Stop. Let us hear the conclusion of the whole matter. Why is it his duty to go into banishment?' But madame always addressed some other teacher, and never looked at me, never seemed conscious that I could have a care in the question.

The grammar

The areas of English grammar that are relevant to our study of these texts can be called 'projection' and 'deixis'.

Projection

Projection can be loosely defined as language representing the use of language. In the sentence *He asked her where the Titanic was, and she said it had gone down*, the clauses *where the Titanic was* and *it had gone down* represent utterances from a former occasion. That is, on that former occasion the people talking, he and she, encoded meanings in verbal messages, and these messages are now projected into the current utterance. By way of contrast, in sentences such as *He got up* or *He spoke to her*, no projection takes place; what is encoded is immediate, that is, given at first hand. An 'utterance' may be either a spoken or a written utterance. It is to be understood that henceforth when I use the words *utter*, *utterance*, *speech* and *speaker* I am not distinguishing between the spoken and written media unless I explicitly state otherwise. Thus *speaker* will mean 'speaker or writer', etc. This may be thought an awkward use of terminology, but there is no alternative, since there are no everyday words that are neutral to the distinction.

When projection occurs, it normally occurs as a separate clause, so that we have a projecting clause and a projected one. *He asked her* ... projects, i.e. it announces that a projection is about to take place, while ... *where the Titanic was* is projected. We must not understand from this that all combinations of two clauses have this relationship of projection between them. In the sentence *When she approached, he got up*, each clause is of a non-projecting type; no prior encoding of meaning is being introduced into a current utterance. One of the marks of projection is the use of a 'projecting verb' in the projecting clause: e.g. *say, ask, tell, wonder, believe, think, know, argue, be convinced, be sure, insist, shout, work out, forget, allege.* What is projected need not be an utterance — a verbal event. It may be simply a meaning entertained by someone — 'held in the mind' as it were, whether or not in some verbally encoded form. Thus in *He wondered where the Titanic was,* it is not necessary to think of the idea of where the Titanic was as having been put into words by him, though it may have been, at least 'to himself'.

The projections illustrated above are all of the kind traditionally known as 'indirect speech', though as we have seen, they do not always represent utterances. They are 'indirect' because, if they do represent utterances, they do not guarantee that the words actually used were the same ones. *He asked her where the Titanic was* does not guarantee that he uttered the words *Where is the Titanic?*; he may have said *Will you please tell me what has happened to your ship?* The report of this utterance as *He asked her where the Titanic was* would be perfectly normal.

Another kind of projection is that in which the projected clause is, or claims to be, the very words used, as in *He asked her, 'Where is the Titanic?'* The traditional name for this construction is 'direct speech'. It is 'direct' because it claims to be an exact reproduction of the original utterance. (Again, it need not be literally uttered, it may be an inward idea: e.g. *He asked himself, 'Where is the Titanic?'*) Naturally, what is reproduced from the original utterance includes the 'mood' features, i.e. whether it was interrogative, declarative, imperative, etc. The difference between direct and indirect can be seen in the following examples:

interrogative:	He asked	'Where is it?'
		where it was.
		'Is it there?'
		whether it was there.

declarative:	He said	'It is there.
		(that) it was
imperative:	He told us	'Go there.'
		to go there.

The first example in each pair is direct and the second is indirect. (To use other terms that are current, the first is a 'quote' and the second is a 'report'.) In direct projections the projected clause could stand as an independent communication with an addressee (e.g. *Where is it?*). In indirect projections the projected clause is dependent and the dependency is usually marked by a difference of word order (e.g. ... *where it was*) or the use of a subordinator (e.g. ... *whether it was there*; ... *that it was there*). The only exception to this is that in indirect 'declaratives' the subordinator *that* is often omitted. This results in a potential ambiguity: if the sentence *He says the ship has gone down* is spoken aloud, it may not be clear which kind of projection is intended. In writing, inverted commas would normally indicate direct projection.

So far we have established four kinds of projection. It may be (A) direct or (B) indirect, and it may at the same time be a projection of either (1) an utterance or (2) an idea — the substance of something that could be uttered. These alternatives are illustrated below.

A1 He asked her, 'Where is the Titanic?'
'Where is the Titanic?', he asked her.
'Where is the Titanic', asked Tom.
She said, 'The Titanic has gone down.'
'The Titanic has gone down', she said.
'The Titanic has gone down', said Susan.

A2 He wondered, 'Where is the Titanic?'
'Where is the Titanic?', he wondered.
'Where is the Titanic?' wondered Tom.
She thought, 'The Titanic has gone down.'
'The Titanic has gone down', she thought.
'The Titanic has gone down', thought Susan.

B1 He asked her where the Titanic was.
She said it had gone down.

B2 He wondered where the Titanic was.
She thought the Titanic had gone down.

In type A, either the projecting clause or the projected one may come first. If the projecting one comes second, there is the option also of putting the subject after the verb (e.g. ... *asked Tom*). Type B also has some possibilities of varying the sequence of the clauses, but only under restricted circumstances which I shall not describe here (see Young 1980, p. 251). There is perhaps something anomalous about type A2, since, if the idea was merely an idea and not encoded in words, there is no occasion to claim an actual wording. Thus A2 strongly suggests silent verbalisation — 'talking to oneself'. This kind of sentence is used quite commonly in certain circumstances as we shall see.

A further kind of projection is illustrated in the following. This type is named by Halliday (1985, p. 238) 'free indirect'.[3]

C1 Where was the Titanic, he asked her.
The Titanic has gone down, she said.
C2 Where was the Titanic, he wondered.
The Titanic had gone down, she believed.

This type combines features of A and B in a way that will be elucidated below, pp. 30–1. Although there are some restrictions on the grammar of the free indirect construction, it is a type that, within its limitations, is much used in certain kinds of discourse as we shall see. The neutral sequence of the clauses in this type has the projected clause first, and reversal of this favoured sequence seems to be very restricted. However, it is possible to split the projected clause and have, for instance: *Where, he asked her, was the Titanic?*

Much more could be said about the grammar of projection, and in fact some further points will be made later in this chapter, but the above must suffice for present purposes. One major area not dealt with in this chapter is the embedding of projections in nominal groups, e.g. ... *the statement that the public would not tolerate it*; ... *the train which they told me was late.*[4]

Deixis

When people speak they need to refer to things in their environment. They can identify things by pointing and saying *this* ('near me') and *that* ('not near me'). Obviously the words *this* and *that* cannot be defined other than by saying that they identify by pointing — that is, by deixis. They identify what they are pointed at, and what this is will vary from one occasion to another. Similarly, the words *I*, *you*, *he*, *she*, *it*, etc. vary in what they identify: it depends on who is speaking, and to whom, and what third parties there are in the environment. So we have place-deixis (*this*, *that*, *here*, *there*) and person-deixis (*I*, *you*, *he*, *it*, etc.). We also have time-deixis (*yesterday*, *today*, *tomorrow*, *this morning*, *last year*, etc.). More subtly, there is tense-deixis, which has much in common with time-deixis. Here the tense of a finite verb is varied. It may be either present or past. *I am hungry* may be true if uttered by Mr X before lunch, but after lunch he would have to say *I was hungry* to refer to the same instance of hunger. The different tenses are realised in the first word of the verbal group whether the verbal group is simple (e.g. *is*, *was*; *sinks*, *sank*) or complex (e.g. *has gone*, *had gone*; *is being told*, *was being told*).

To summarise, deixis is the phenomenon in which the speaker orients certain references to the situation of utterance. Of course, not all references are deictic. In *The Titanic has gone down*, the Titanic is referred to by name; it does not matter when or where it is said, or who says it. This is therefore, not deictic. In contrast, in *It has gone down*, the *it* refers to the Titanic only if the context points to the Titanic as being the nearest thing of which 'going down' might be predicated.

Now, if you report what someone has said or thought, there are two 'situations of utterance'. There is the immediate, current or primary situation in which you are addressing some listener or reader. Let us call this S1. And there is the original, remote or secondary situation which you are telling about. We will call this S2. When you report on S2 the deictic features you use may be those appropriate to S2 as it originally was. This is what happens in direct projection:

She said, 'You are sitting in my chair.'

deixis → S2
you, *my* and the present tense refer to features of the remote situation

On the other hand in indirect projection, one does not necessarily report the very words used but only the import of what was said. The deixis is oriented to features of the primary or current situation:[5]

She said, I was sitting in her chair.

> deixis → S1
> *I*, *her* and the past tense refer to features of the current situation

The use of inverted commas in writing is a device for alerting the reader to the presence of direct projection. Spoken language has its own devices (rhythm and intonation) to distinguish direct from indirect projection. These partly compensate for the lack of inverted commas. However, it is not by any means always the case that there would be an inconvenient ambiguity if the punctuational and intonational devices were not used.

The free indirect type of construction, as was stated above, shares features of the other types in a kind of blend. The projected clause has the mood features of the secondary situation but it has the deictic features of the primary situation:

I was sitting in her chair, she said.

> deixis → S1
> *I*, *her* and the past tense refer to features of the primary situation

The fact that this is free indirect rather than an anomalous form of indirect is shown by the possibility of having a free interrogative mood in the projected clause:

Was I sitting in her chair, she asked.

The writer of such a sentence might well hesitate whether to use inverted commas or not. Texts A1 and A2 do not use them. Text C does. Similarly, there is a problem with the use of a question mark. The projected clause is definitely interrogative, and the projecting clause definitely is not. But putting a question mark in the middle of a sentence goes against conventional practice. Whether the projected clause is a quote or a report is an interesting question. It has been modified by the shifting of the deictic orientation, but are we to understand that everything else is untouched? In other words are we to understand that she certainly said *Are you sitting in my chair?*, or might she have said *I believe that's my place, isn't it?* It seems to me that the same wording is implied (but see Halliday 1985, p. 240).

Analysis

Texts A1 and A2: press reports

The first of the press reports (A1) has the following structure. (The place it has in relation to its context has already been described above.) The section numbers below refer to the marginal numbers in the photo-reproduced text:

2.1 Orientation: statement of who was speaking and in what phase of the debate

2.2 Account of pronouncement: the Earl's statement of the Government's case:

- 2.2.1 statement of the Government's decision
- 2.2.2 justification for going against usual policy
- 2.2.3 rejection of alternative solution
- 2.2.4 justification for circumventing the decision of the committee
- 2.2.5 assurances against establishing a precedent
- 2.2.6 justification of the decision

There is, of course, no guarantee that the grouping and emphasis of the points in the newspaper report correspond to the grouping and emphasis made by the Earl of Caithness in his actual speech. The whole of phase 2.2 is devoted to an account of what was said and contains nothing else. Several of the sub-phases, namely 1, 4, 5 and 6, consist of a short projecting phase (A) and a longer phase representing what was said (B), e.g.

A — PROJECTING	B — PROJECTED
The Earl of C said	it was convinced . . . right route.
He argued	that the southern route . . . consultation.

The projecting phase identifies the speaker (*the Earl of C, the Earl, he, he*) and indicates the rhetorical force of his utterance (*said, said, said, argued*). The Earl was, of course, acting as spokesman for the Government, and hence there are in places two 'layers' of projection, as suggested in the following analysis of 1, where *it* refers to the Government:

A — PROJECTING	B — PROJECTED	
	B1 — PROJECTING	B2 — PROJECTED
Earl of C said	it was convinced	that . . . route.

I shall call the first layer a first-order projection and lower layers second-order projections.

The standard grammatical form for the projected phases in this text is that of indirect projection, as illustrated in the examples analysed above. However, it is a very marked stylistic characteristic of this kind of discourse that the projecting phase is often omitted. Once the idea of projection has been introduced it may be taken as understood. The following analysis shows this:

A — PROJECTING	B — PROJECTED	
	The Government stood by . . . parks	
	PROJECTING	PROJECTED
	but argued	that . . . time scale

Of course, even though there is no projecting phase A, the clauses in B are still projected — we have to interpret them as such, otherwise the rhetorical force of what is said would be radically altered. What the Earl actually said was presumably *The Government stands by . . . but argues . . .* The fact that it is put in the past tense serves as a clue that this is a projection of what the Earl said. If we failed to get this point, we would have to read the sentence as first-hand comment by the reporter. The grammatical type of projection in the clauses where there is no projecting phase A is free indirect. The mood is derived from S2 and the deixis from

S1. If the Earl had been asking a question rather than making a statement, it might have been reported: *When would the critics of the Government begin to realise that* . . ., which has interrogative mood (. . . *when would they* . . .? rather than . . . *when they would* . . .) and past tense (*would* not *will*).

In phase 2.2.3 of Text A1 we have a rather different case. Here the projection is direct. There has been a sudden switch to present tense (*do* instead of *did*).

PROJECTING	PROJECTED
	'We do not believe that . . . Okehampton.'

There is no danger of misinterpreting the clause as non-projected (the journalist's comment with an editorial 'we'!) both because of the inverted commas, and also because of the unlikelihood that the journalist is interpolating a remark at this point. Moreover, there is no difficulty in taking 'we' as the Earl's reference to the Government of which he is a member.

It is not at all clear why the journalist chose to switch to direct projection at this point, other than to introduce some variation of style into a long and wordy report. He does the same in a similarly arbitrary way at one other point in the whole article from which Text Al is taken, which runs for 870 words. However, if we look at Text A2 (3.5 and 4) we can see better motivated instances of the switch to direct projection of utterances. I shall here briefly anticipate our look at A2 to draw attention to this point. In A2, 3.5, the journalist wishes to draw attention to an unintended ambiguity in what Mr Waddington said, so it is necessary to cite the actual words used. Again the words of Mr Skinner, quoted in A2, 4, are heavily ironical. The irony would be weakened if indirect projection was used (e.g. *He asked whether the Home Secretary was really telling the House that* . . .). (See my comments below, p. 45, on the irony inherent in the use of direct projection of utterances.)

When direct projection is used in this type of discourse, especially when a projection of utterances by the same speaker (either direct or indirect) is already in progress, it is often sufficient to indicate it with inverted commas and the use of the present tense without recourse to a projecting clause (e.g. in A2, Mr Waddington's words, and Mr Skinner's second and subsequent clauses). The difference between direct/utterance with and without a projecting clause is not recorded in Table 2.1 but as a

Table 2.1

	Text A1 (whole article) (c.870 words)	Text A2 (c.340 words)	Text B (whole anecdote) (c.1,500 words)
Independent clauses	29	14	190
1st-order projections			
indirect/utterance	8	5	2
indirect/idea	0	0	11
direct/utterance	3	4	38
direct/idea	0	0	7
free ind./utterance	10	1	0
free ind./idea	0	0	2
	21	10	60
Proportion 1st-order projections to ind. clauses (per cent)	72	71	32
2nd-order projections			
indirect/utterance	1	4	0
indirect/idea	8	2	0
others	0	0	0
	9	6	0

matter of fact, of the seven instances in A1 and A2, only two have a projecting clause.

The amount of first-order projection in a text can be measured as follows. Every independent clause (including those conjoined to independent clauses) is counted as a potential locus for a first-order projection to be introduced, unless it is itself a direct projection with an independent clause projecting it (e.g. *He said, 'You are late'*; this counts as only one independent clause). The number of first-order projections can be seen as a proportion of the number of independent clauses. In the whole article from which Text A1 is taken there are 29 independent clauses. Table 2.1 shows the number of first-order and second-order projections in this and the other texts, and the numbers of the various types of projection. Many of the independent clauses have other clauses dependent upon them, producing clause complexes of considerable length. This is why the number of independent clauses is quite low for a text of this length measured in words. Sometimes, a projecting clause is dependent without introducing a second-order projection (e.g. the first sentence of Text A2: ... *as ministers insisted* ...); I have not included these among first-order projections. A point of interest in connection with the analysis of the whole A1 article is that it opens with eight non-projecting independent clauses. Thereafter, starting from the last independent clause in episode 1, every independent clause is projecting or projected, i.e. there is 100 per cent projection from that point on.

Text A2 is not a report on a single debate but a combination of a report on parliamentary questions with miscellaneous comments attributed to various individuals and the reporter's own account of the progress made by the Government in seeing though certain legislation. Let us first look at the structure of the piece:

1. Summary introduction: account of events; yesterday's events in the progress of legislation on matters A and B

2. Progress in matter A: account of pronouncement; Home Secretary's pronouncement in question time

   2.1 the Government's open mind
   2.2 awaiting assurance of popular support

3. Progress in matter B: account of present state of affairs including yesterday's events and a pronouncement; sources of pressure on Home Office against the proposed measure and Home Office reaction to this

   3.1 pressure is from all parties
   3.2 motion tabled by Conservative MPs
   3.3 motion tabled by Labour MPs
   3.4 evidence of popular disapproval
   3.5 Home Office's determination to proceed

4. Coda: account of spoken comment; ironical question of opposition MP

(The headline does not give an accurate indication of the content of the article, since it mentions only Matter B.)

An analysis of the proportion of projection in Text A2 and of the various types can be found in Table 2.1 alongside that for Text A1. Text A2 has a far more complex discourse structure than Text A1, since here projections of what other people said are interspersed with first-hand comment and accounts of events. This more complex structure is partly reflected in the repeated switching of tense between past and present. In Text A1 present tenses were used only in direct projection of utterances. Everything else followed the 'standard' mode of past tense indirect projection backed up by free indirect projection, also using the past tense. In Text A2 we also find these modes of reporting, but here the alternation of present and past tenses sometimes has other functions.

Since, as we have seen, it is possible for a clause to represent a projection when there is no explicit mark of projection in the sentence, it may be simply, or principally, a switch of tenses from past to present that signals whether or not projection is continuing. Thus in phase 2.2 we have: *Mr Hurd said he needed* ... *He had been told* ... (meaning 'Mr Hurd said he had been told'). This is followed immediately by *Home Office ministers still face* ... The present tense is a principal signal that the account of what Mr Hurd said has come to an end (another is the new paragraph, though projections can probably sometimes survive a paragraph break; absense of inverted commas is but a negative signal). The reader may judge how difficult it would have been to maintain a fluent reading of the passage if by some accident the word *face* had been misprinted as *faced.* This would have been taken as a positive signal that projection was continuing.[6] An interesting case of a switch of tenses comes in phase 2.1. *He is waiting for a report* ... Because of the present tense (*is*) the first reaction of the reader could be to interpret this as a first-order statement made by the journalist, not a projection of what Mr Hurd said — as though the journalist were offering an explanation of Mr Hurd's open-mindedness. If he had written *He was waiting* ... we would have been more likely to take this as a free indirect projection. It is only with hindsight that we might review our interpretation and query which the journalist really meant; but the point is that it is the tense of the verb which makes the difference.

There are two further points to make about the use of present tense in this text, which were not applicable to Text A1. The first is the use of the present tense in projecting clauses. So far we have concentrated on projections in which the projecting clause is in the past tense: *Mr Hurd said* ... ; *ministers insisted* ... ; ... *prompted Mr Skinner to ask* ... However, phases 3.4 and 3.5 contain projections where the projecting clause is in the present tense. Projection is not only used to report people's past words and ideas; the intention might be to declare one's own or other people's current opinions or states of mind:

I always say 'Where's the harm in that?'
I believe the election is next Thursday.

People are wondering what all the fuss is about.
The Chairman thinks the matter is unimportant.

Or it might be to report a rule imposed by authority:

Mother says you mustn't do that.

Moreover, when people's words and ideas are being reported, this is not always done in the past tense. The present tense is regularly used in recounting the plot of a play or novel, etc.: *Then he shouts 'My kingdom for a horse!'* or to give a sense of immediacy to an anecdote (though not in the one from which Text B is taken): . . . *and she says 'Well, I know you're only saying that'*, or to a report of an interview with a well-known personality, say a recording artist:

'It's necessary to play solo from time to time', says Annette, 'but chamber music is what we enjoy most.'

Returning now to the present tense projections in Text A2, phases 3.4 and 3.5, the present tenses (*MPs claim* . . . and *Mr Waddington insists* . . .) seem to indicate that the reporter is here not giving an account of yesterday's events, but stating these people's present attitudes, which somehow he knows about. (The fact that this appears to conflict with the past tense projection in *He said* . . . leads to a difficulty in interpreting this text which I have not space to comment on.)

The second point concerns the 'sequence of tenses' between projecting and projected clauses. All the examples given earlier showed a concord of tenses in the indirect projections: e.g. *He asked where the Titanic was*, rather than *He asked where the Titanic is.* Of course the Titanic is still in the same place as it was when he spoke, but it is customary to employ a concord of tenses to emphasise that a past occasion is being spoken of. The whereabouts of the Titanic was the absorbing question on that past occasion, rather than at the present time. But the use of a concord of tenses is not grammatically obligatory, and if the proposition mooted in the past is still of current relevance, one might well choose a present tense for the projected clause. The difference of meaning between *Keats said that beauty was truth* and *Keats said that beauty is truth* has nothing to do with what Keats said, but with how we are regarding his assertion from our present-day standpoint.

In Text A2 phase 1 is a past-tense account of events. However, it contains a projection: ... *as ministers insisted they will push ahead* ... The projected clause has *they will push ahead,* where it would have been possible to write *they would push ahead.* It would have been difficult to predict whether the journalist would have favoured a past or a present tense in this case. We may note that in phase 2.1 we get *Mr Hurd ... said ... that he had an open mind ...* not *Mr Hurd ... said that he has an open mind ...*

To summarise our findings on the use of projection in these texts, we note that

1. when the reporter is recounting what people said the standard form is indirect projection and the projecting clause is in the past tense;
2. a past tense clause immediately following an indirect projection is likely to be taken as free indirect projection;
3. a switch to present tense indicates a cessation of the projection;
4. direct projection, incorporating present tense, is occasionally interpolated; if it immediately follows a projection, it may occur without a projecting clause; inverted commas mark the directly projected words;
5. past tense projections are normally projections of utterances (ideas may be projected as second-order projections, e.g. *The Earl said he was convinced that* ...); hence a past tense projection of an idea is likely to be interpreted as free indirect projection of an utterance (e.g. if the text had read: *The Earl was convinced that* ... this would be likely to mean *The Earl said "I am convinced that* ... "There are no clear examples in the texts cited above.)

Text B: conversational anecdote

The two pieces taken from the extract of conversational anecdote on pp. 62–7 of this volume are given below with discourse structure divisions indicated by numbers. Functional labels are added: Or = orientation; Ac = action; Ev = evaluation. These labels are explained below, pp. 42–3. Tonic syllables are underlined.

Extract I

Or 1.1 Em, anyhow
I got to the station now,

Ac	1.2	and they said
		the half past train will be twenty minutes late
Ev	1.3	I could hear this
		I was listening very carefully
		going on
Ac	2.1	so another train came in
Ac	2.2	and they said
		this train em coming in now
		approaching the other platform
		a little train
		is going to - Weston super Mare via Newport
Ev	2.3	oh I'll get on that one then
Ac	3.1	so I got in there
		and it was there for about three minutes
Ev	3.2	and I thought
		they're going to stick . keep this train here
		and let the other one go through I'll bet
Ev	3.3	this is because I'm the son of an engine driver (laughter)

Extract II

Or	1.1	I got my bit sorted out
Ac	1.2	Newport station
		sure enough he was right by the door
		in he comes
		sit down
Ev	1.3	Great. Everything is going well, like
Ac/Ev	2.1	I said
		oh you know exactly where we're going don't you then David?
Ac/Ev	2.2	and he said
		yes we've got it all arranged he said
		we're catching we're changing at at Parkway
		and catching the Plymouth train he said
		There'll be a buffet on there
Ac/Ev	2.3	I said
		well I'm not sure about this buffet
		I'm going to have my breakfast now
Ac	2.4	So I had a cheese and toasty sandwich and a cup of coffee
		and he had er bacon sandwiches I think

Ev 2.5 fortunately, as the story goes
em we was convinced
we didn't need to bother at that stage
Or 3.1 We had this
Ac 3.2 Got out at Parkway
He looked at his watch
Ev 3.3 and he said
Oh good he said
the train will be here in another minute
Because we're late we don't have to wait at Parkway
Ac 4.1 and he looked up and the train was coming in
Ev 4.2 Great!
Diddliddle here it comes
Or 5.1 and the announcer was saying something
Ac 5.2 and I switched off
Ev 5.3 because I said
you're looking after me Dave
I won't even listen to anything
you know I'm just talking to him
I thought
I'm going to enjoy myself
Or 6.1 I've had a tremendously hard day the day before
I was working for twenty three hours round the clock more or less, wasn't I
It was very x longest day I've ever had actually, that one
Ev 6.2 and I thought
well this is it
Or 6.3 because I'd got up at four o'clock in the morning
and was working till three the next day with one thing and another
or at least I was awake
Ev 6.4 em, so I thought
I'd better have a day off
You know what I mean
I'm going to go with him and enjoy it
Or 7.1 anyway,
Ac 7.2 we went we did
Ev 7.3 in the wrong damned direction! (laughter)

The ranking of the units suggested by the numbering and line divisions of the above transcription represents an attempt at a principled analysis of the text, though I have to admit that it is tentative. One can perceive the speaker moving from stage to stage in his discourse, but it does not always seem easy to group the shorter moves together to form higher-ranking units. Some of the reasons for this will be discussed below. In the discussion that follows, I refer to the higher-rank units as episodes and the lower-rank units as phases.

It is not the events recounted that give structure to an anecdote, of course, but the 'packaging'. No doubt the narrator sees a structure in his experience, but he has selected and perhaps rearranged his material, and above all made decisions on how to make an impression on his audience. The structure of the anecdote is interactional. The immediate intention is to entertain the auditors with an account of personal experience. There are obviously deeper purposes, too. The presentation of one's personal view of experience serves to create or recreate for the speaker and his auditors the world in which they see themselves. One of the main points made by this speaker (and, later on, by his auditors) is that his getting on the wrong train was uncharacteristic behaviour; in fact he presents himself as someone whose strong point is careful planning and meticulous execution of plans. His adventure is seen as essentially comic and he tells the story 'against' himself. Explanations are offered — the narrator was tired after an exceptionally long day the day before; he was in the hands of a companion who alone had responsibility for seeing that they got to their destination; they were engrossed in technical discussion. Another feature of his telling of the experience is the way he represents his reaction to the event once the mistake had been discovered — not alarm or resentment, but embarrassed facetiousness and self-deprecation.

Labov (1972, p. 369), in a chapter entitled 'The transformation of experience in narrative syntax' says:

> A complete narrative begins with an orientation, proceeds to the complicating action, is suspended at the focus of evaluation before the resolution, concludes with the resolution and returns the listener to the present time with the coda. The evaluation of the narrative forms a secondary stucture which is concentrated in the evaluation section but may be found in various forms throughout the narrative.

(For Labov the 'orientation' sets the scene; it gives background information to make the story intelligible. I modify this definition somewhat below.) The narratives that Labov is mainly concerned with are fairly short and self-contained. Unlike these the narrative from which Text B is extracted is long, and though it has a very definite beginning (*Did I tell you what happened yesterday, Vi?*) it has no very clear ending. The final episodes are a discussion between all three people present of the narrator's characteristic carefulness, and the reasons for his appearing careless on this occasion.

Labov acknowledges that there may be complications of his simple schema; in particular, 'evaluative devices' may be 'distributed throughout the narrative'. Sometimes orientational phases are placed in mid-course too; for instance, later in our anecdote the narrator explains:

> So — we were engrossed talking away
> now we were in one of these carriages now
> you know the sort of thing
> where you sit there
> and there's — there's like six of you in the carriage

Thus, whereas the beginning and end of an anecdote are likely to consist of clearly demarcated episodes with definite structural functions, and, if the anecdote is short, the middle is likely to consist of one or two discrete episodes, in a longer anecdote the middle is likely to be a sort of fricassee of action and evaluation with little pattern in it. This is why I am hesitant about claiming any authority for the episodic structures in my divisions of the text. However, the principle I have followed is to take orientations as opening new episodes and evaluations as terminating episodes — though there may be a series of evaluations in one termination.

The functional categories marked in the left-hand column of the transcriptions above are as follows (my category of 'orientation' is more inclusive than Labov's):

Orientation. The addressee is prepared for a new episode of the narrative. The orientation may take the form of (a) a formal device for marking a new episode of the discourse just beginning (e.g. Extract I, section 1.1), or (b) it may summarise the events narrated immediately before as a kind of announcement that that episode is behind us and we are to move on (e.g. I, 1.1; II, 1.1; II, 3.1), or (c) it may provide background knowledge, as in Labov's definition (e.g. II, 6.1 and 6.3); or there may be a combination of these devices.

Action. A phase in which the events of the story are advanced (e.g. I, 2.1; II, 2.4, 3.2). Labov points out that an action phase may contain evaluative detail (e.g. in II, 1.2 the words *sure enough* emphasise the fact that everything is going according to plan, an evaluation which is given more explicitly in the exclusively evaluating phase 1.3). It might happen that the evaluation, if any, is mere detail in a predominantly action phase; but it can happen that action and evaluation are blended so equally that it is not possible to decide between them. Hence, some phases in my transcription are marked Ac/Ev.

Evaluation. The events recounted are evaluated to ensure that the auditors get the point of the story as the narrator wishes them to see it. For example:

> II, 1.3. The story of catching the wrong train is organised so as to stress the travellers' sense of success and security up to the point where they discover their mistake.
>
> II, 2.5. The narrator's characteristic caution in taking breakfast while they had the chance is justified.
>
> II, 3.2. The companion's expression of satisfaction at their progress serves the same purpose as 1.3 (similarly 4.2).
>
> II, 5.3. The narrator's sense of relaxation and reliance on his companion emphasises the smooth course of events (similarly 6.2 and 6.4).
>
> II, 7.3. All the sense of smooth running of the expedition is shown to have been unjustified. (Note that the brevity of episode 7 contrasts with the long-drawn-out build up.)

We turn now to the functions performed by projections in the structure of this discourse. The whole anecdote contains approximately 190 independent clauses uttered by the narrator. (The number is approximate because moodless expressions sometimes have the status of a clause, and it may be a delicate matter to judge whether they have or not.) There are in all 60 projected clauses (I have not included certain formulaic devices such as *You know what I mean, you know, you see* as projections.) Table 2.1 shows the various types of projection alongside the analysis of

Texts A1 and A2. We see that the types of projection used contrast strongly with those in the press-report texts. There the basic pattern was a preponderance of indirect and free indirect utterance. There was a small proportion of direct utterance — about 0.2 of the total. There was also a considerable amount of second-order projection. Here, on the other hand, there are few indirect utterances, and no free indirect utterances, and almost everything projected is either a direct utterance, a direct idea or an indirect idea. Moreover, there is no second-order (or otherwise dependent) projection.

The direct ideas are usually, as it turns out, the thoughts of the narrator during the course of his experience (e.g. I, 3.2 *and I thought they're going to stick — keep this train here*, etc.; II, 6.2 *and I thought well this is it*). I interpret I, 2.3 as a direct idea, though there is no audible projecting clause. The indirect ideas are such as that which occurs in II, 2.5 — *we was convinced we didn't need to bother at that stage.* (Others that occur later in the anecdote are *I'd decided I wasn't going to make a fuss or anything*, and *I'd worked out that this train was going to be waiting in Cardiff when the main train came through.*) They usually have the purpose of explaining the state of mind of the narrator and his companion. One of them occurs as an aside and is strictly not part of the anecdote. This is where the narrator forgets the name of Didcot station (*I've forgotten what it's called now*).

By far the most numerous type is the direct utterance. Almost all utterances that were actually made are represented as direct projections. (The two indirect utterances come right at the beginning of the anecdote — *Did I tell you what happened yesterday, Vi?* and *Did Mum tell you?* Apart from these there are none.) It is interesting to note the style of the utterances represented 'directly'. In I, 1.2 and I, 2.2 it is evident that the wording of the station announcer is in fact not reproduced exactly. The late train would not have been called the *half past train*, but something like *the 8.30 to Paddington.* Again, the arrival platform would not have been referred to as *the other platform*, and the description *a little train* is obviously an interpolation. On the other hand the word *approaching* suggests the style of the original utterance. Similarly in II, 2.2 it is clear from the hesitations and backtracking that the narrator is making up his companion's speech as he goes along. He is remembering the gist, recomposing the wording and presenting it as direct. This seems to be a quite legitimate technique in telling an anecdote, though it would not do in press reporting of parliamentary debates (which does not mean to say that it never happens).

If exact reproduction of wording is not the object of direct projection of utterances, why is direct projection so commonly used? The answer seems to be that direct projections of utterances are a useful means of combining evaluation with action. The direct representation of the speech of the participants emphasises the separation between the original situation of utterance and the immediate one (the separation between S2 and S1). There is an effect of dramatic irony. A particularly clear example is to be found in II, 2.1, 2.2, 2.3. The words uttered express the confidence of the companion (*know exactly*, *got it all arranged*) and the caution of the narrator (*not sure*), but while this very conversation is going on, and the victims of circumstance are as yet unaware of their plight, we know what is destined to happen to them. The expressions of confidence and caution, suggesting praise of the way the expedition is being managed, together with the irony introduced by direct projection, are what give these phases a strong evaluative function.

Text C: prose fiction

The last of our texts, the short extract from *Villette*, falls into four paragraphs, with the following plan:

1. Account of unconfirmed rumours
2. Account of Mme Beck's utterances
3. Circumstances of Mme Beck's speech particularised
4. Account of narrator's reaction to the situation

There is no point in making an analysis in this short text of the distribution of the types of projection, as was done for the other texts above. The point I want to make is that there is much variety of different projection techniques within a short space, and that the shifting of technique has a symbolic value in the narrative. The narrator represents herself as desperately anxious and in need of information which she cannot openly seek. The inward turmoil and the outward calm are represented by the syntactic devices for projecting speech and thought.

The first paragraph has only two projections in it and these are indirect utterances (*I heard it said that he was to sail in a week;* . . .

then, that he was bound for the West Indies). Indirect projection is 'low key', contributing no sense of drama, no disturbance of the first-order description of events. The second paragraph represents Mme Beck's words. This character is the principal holder of the information which the narrator is desperate to obtain. Her speech therefore has a key importance. Her words are projected as free indirect utterance. (Unlike the writers of Texts A1 and A2, Charlotte Brontë uses inverted commas for this purpose.) Had it been direct utterance we would have had:

> 'This secession is an immense loss to me,' she alleged. 'I do not know how I shall fill up the vacancy ...'

Only the first sentence is explicitly marked as a projection by the use of a projecting clause (*she alleged*), but the force of cohesion with the context makes it clear that all the following sentences are to be interpreted as free indirect speech too. The effect of using this form instead of direct speech is of great interest. The reader might consider what difference it would have made if Mme Beck's words had been projected directly, as illustrated above, throughout the paragraph. We noted in Text B how the use of direct utterance projection contributed to the irony of the narration. Here also there is an ironical effect; there is a discrepancy between what Mme Beck knows and what she divulges, so that if we are given her actual words and thus an illusion of her very tone of voice, her insincerity is dramatised. The irony is even more marked by the use of free indirect projection than it would have been by direct projection.

The short third paragraph has no projection in it. But in the fourth the narrator's thoughts in reaction to the situation are projected. The first instance is again in the free indirect mode, without a projecting clause. But we are not told *I asked her that*, but *I could have asked her that.* In other words, this is a projection of an utterance that was not uttered. At the next stage the author actually switches to direct projection to represent words that were not spoken: *Stop. Let us hear ... Why ...?* She is anxiously making demands but not uttering a word. The 'high key' direct projection is used here to contrast the acuteness of the narrator's anxiety with the irony in which Mme Beck's words are presented.

Conclusion

The text studies conducted above demonstrate that the grammatical resources available to the English speaker for reporting people's words are richly varied and that the selections actually made in particular cases are sensitive to the use of language as described in terms of discourse structure. In particular there is a subtle interplay of selections from the systems of mood (including dependent mood) and tense. This finding serves to underline the point that it is not, or not mainly, in the subject-matter that one should seek the structure of discourse, but in the devices employed for interacting with addressees and for managing the linguistic event.

The analyses of texts provided above are exploratory. They demonstrate how the superficially simple task of reporting people's use of language may be carried out in a variety of ways. It is scarcely possible to draw wide-ranging conclusions from the small amount of evidence that these analyses afford. What is of interest is that the varying techniques for projecting the former use of language into existing discourse seems to be in some measure, perhaps in large measure, predictable by reference to situational factors. The texts selected for examination in this paper were chosen as making an initial impression of being reasonably normal (not stylistically eccentric) for the kind of situation to which they belonged, and indeed I have here and there appealed to what I assume the reader will agree with me is a recognisable stylistic trait. But though we might have guessed that the reporting mode in the written medium would make more use of free indirect projection than the anecdotal mode in the spoken medium, and that, conversely, anecdotal texts would contain more instances of direct projection, the extent to which these assumptions are justified could only be determined by close examination of what are assumed to be typical texts. Nor perhaps was it initially obvious that one of the things that gives the Brontë passage its quality of verbal magic was the rich assortment of so many kinds of projection in such a short space, combined with its ironic use of direct projection for what was not uttered and free indirect projection for what was.

Moreover, the relationship of the various kinds of projection to the rhetorical structure of the discourse could certainly not have been predicted in any detail. For instance, there is not a total absence of indirect projection in the anecdotal text. The analysis reveals that for the most part it has, however, a particularly specialised function in being used for the narrator's own thoughts supposed to have been thought at the time of the incident, and that these 'thoughts' are now reported as an evaluation of the events in the story.

Further research is obviously needed to verify the tentative findings of these analyses, and also to extend the enquiry to other kinds of text (e.g. journalistic reports of interviews, news broadcasting, narrative writing for children, etc.).

One might wonder why attention has been given to the grammatical topic of projection, rather than to the whole set of features that constitute particular kinds of discourse. The answer to this is that it satisfies a certain field of curiosity. There is an interplay between the structure of discourse and the linguistic system which is employed to encode the speaker's meanings. The distribution of certain grammatical categories in discourse is of interest both to the discourse analyst and to the grammarian, who might, for instance, find it necessary to give a more prominent place to free indirect projection in his description of the language than he had hitherto done.

Notes

1. Paul Tench and I are indebted to Jeanette Meredith for the recording from which this anecdote was transcribed.
2. I have used this passage from *Villette* in another publication (see Young 1980, p. 282), but in a context where I had not so much space to examine it alongside other texts; so I do not apologise for using it again.
3. In Young 1980, pp. 272-82, it is less felicitously called *pseudo-report.*
4. A fairly detailed account of the theory of projection can be read in Halliday 1985, pp. 192-251; see also Young 1980, Chapters 20-2.
5. It is not the case that the features of the situations S1 and S2 are always different. For example suppose Mary says to John in the library on 1 May, 'I have seen you here twice today.' Then if George reports this utterance to Susan in the park on 2 May, all of the features, speaker, addressee, place and day, have been changed, and George might say 'She told him she had seen him there twice yesterday.' But if the report is made in the same library on the same day, it will be 'She told him she had seen him here twice today', thus using the words 'here' and 'today' as in the original utterance. Again, if Mary reports her utterance immediately afterwards to the same addressee, all of the features except the tense will be the same: 'I said I had seen you here twice today.' This detail is important but often overlooked in explanations of the difference between direct and indirect speech.

6. The fact that the switch of topic to *Home Office ministers* inaugurates a new phase of the press report is a fact that only comes to light as we read on. A change of topic at this point is no bar to a continuation of the projection since, if the projection is in the free indirect mode, a change of topic is not surprising; the selection of topic belongs to the original discourse.

References

Halliday, M.A.K. (1985) *An introduction to functional grammar.* London: Edward Arnold

Labov, W. (1972) *Language in the inner city.* Oxford: Basil Blackwell

Young, D. J. (1980) *The structure of English clauses.* London: Hutchinson

3

The Stylistic Potential of Intonation

Paul Tench

We have often had the experience of being able to hear the sound of a television or radio in an adjoining room, muffled and somewhat at a distance, and of being able to tell what kind of event is happening even though we can not hear the actual content of the words. We can immediately identify events like the commentary of a horse race, the reading of the news, a quiz or drama, without being able to identify a single word. That is because these events all sound different. There is a general shape or pattern of sound that we, in our society and culture, associate with these different kinds of events. It is not the sound of consonants and vowels and word-stress; *they* are used primarily for the identification and recognition of words operating in phrases, clauses, sentences and in text as a whole. The sound that helps us to identify events is a different kind of sound, often referred to as *prosodic* and *paralinguistic.*

Prosodic features include pitch, stress and tempo, which are different in nature from consonants and vowels in at least two ways. Firstly, consonants and vowels act as segments of a syllable, i.e. its structural components; whereas the three prosodic features are characteristics of a syllable itself and of units far larger than syllables as well (hence an alternative term for them: *suprasegmental*). Secondly, although consonants and vowels are absolutely essential for the identification and recognition of words, not all of them need necessarily appear in an utterance. The sequence *hold your horses* does not contain any nasals, for instance. But you can not utter that clause without some degree of pitch (even if it was spoken on a monotone), or some degree of loudness (even if it was spoken pianissimo) or some degree of tempo (allegrissimo or lentissimo). These prosodic features are ever-present and accompany every use of (spoken) language.

Pitch, stress and tempo have two functions: a basic, linguistic function, and a secondary, paralinguistic function. Linguistically, they are the basic components of rhythm and intonation of any language; paralinguistically, they are part of the means by which 'tone of voice' is expressed by any speaker. Pausing is also often considered as part of the prosody of a language. Pauses, which are usually silent — although hesitation pauses are often voiced — are basically absences of articulation. However, they too have both linguistic and paralinguistic functions. Consider the difference in the meaning of these two (part-) utterances:

my brother who lives in Nairobi ...
my sister — who lives in Weston ...

The surface grammar looks identical: NP with a rank-shifted relative clause; but the first identifies which brother is being referred to (i.e. not the one who lives somewhere else), but the second does not identify at all; it just adds an extra piece of information. The pause (—) here performs a linguistic (syntactic) function, by distinguishing a non-defining relative clause. On the other hand, pauses can be used to produce paralinguistic effect — emphasis, a dramatic effect, etc. (cf. Abercrombie 1971). Thus, pauses operate in rhythm and intonation, and in paralanguage.

The three prosodic features and pausing have both linguistic and paralinguistic functions, but in addition to these, there are specific (non-prosodic) *paralinguistic* features. Paralinguistic features are not integral to speech (as prosodic features are), but are additional, marginal features of speech which do not rely on pitch, stress and tempo for their effect. The most common of these features are whisper, breathiness, huskiness, creak, falsetto, resonance ('booming' voice) and 'tension' (which includes 'tense' voice — a harsh, metallic effect — and 'lax', and also precise and slurred articulation — all variations of muscular tension). Vocalisations (or 'extra-linguistic effects') are also included in many paralinguistic studies, like grunts (*hm*), clicks (*tut-tut*) and emissions (*phew*). Thus you can utter *hold your horses* with all the necessary segmental phonemes, and with any combination of prosodic features, but with or without any kind of paralinguistic effect.

Of all this phonetic material, what do we use to identify (and produce) different speech events, or genres? Mainly, the prosodic features, but paralinguistic features also, to a certain extent; for instance if we heard the use of whisper, or resonance, or tension, or even any of the 'vocalisations', we might assume an event which is typically informal, or it may be drama. However, what distinguishes a racing commentary, news reading and a quiz programme are mainly prosodic features: for a racing commentary, speech that is allegrissimo (tempo) and a high, often almost monotone, pitch; for news reading, a slower tempo, a predominance of falling and low rising intonation patterns (for 'major' and 'minor' information respectively), and clearly identifiable phonological paragraphs (corresponding to sections and sub-sections of the news content); and for a quiz programme, a wide variety of tempo, stress and pitch (which is typical of lively, informal conversation), considerable pauses at times (and, obviously, a variety of voices).

By speech events, we obviously do not confine ourselves to what may be broadcast by television and radio, but we do at least mean 'talk', as opposed to singing, chanting, and so on. Any human event which at least includes talk, is potentially a speech event. *Genres* are categories of speech events that a given society recognises as distinctive in its culture. British people recognise a racing commentary as distinctly different from other speech events, even from other types of sports commentary. There is something about the style of speech associated with it which we recognise, whoever the commentator may be or wherever and whenever the racing takes place; in other words, there is a conventional aspect to genre, which is separate from a person's individual speech characteristics and certainly separate from incidental details such as a race meeting at Chepstow or Heydock Park. Furthermore, an individual will enter into a considerable range of genres in the course of a single day. Peter O'Sulliven, a well-known racing commentator, does not speak allegrissimo with a high pitched voice and a narrow range all day. Even when on the air, he is not always commentating: he announces the names of the runners, gives results, conducts interviews, and each of these events 'sound' different from a commentary.

It must be pointed out that each genre is characterised not only by its prosodic features but by other linguistic features too — grammatical, lexical, textual and graphological; and it may be argued that some of these other features may be more important. Maybe; it depends on the genre. But sometimes, the prosodic features may be crucial. In many church services, it is considered bad manners for late-comers to enter during prayer or Bible reading. Late-comers have to listen at the door and decide from the evidence of the 'talk', whether prayer or Bible reading is being conducted or not. The grammatical, lexical and textual features of prayer, Bible reading and preaching are extremely similar in their very nature; the late-comers depend, therefore, very heavily on the prosodic features, to make their particular judgement: that evidence determines their decision to enter or not.[1]

The most thorough descriptions of prosodic and paralinguistic features in English are to be found in Crystal and Quirk (1964) and Crystal (1969). The first significant attempt at incorporating such features in the identification and description of different styles of English is presented in Crystal and Davy (1969). The precise prosodic features involved in intonation are pitch height (high, mid, low), pitch movement (falling, rising, falling–rising, rising–falling, or level, i.e. *no* pitch movement) and pitch range (narrow/wide, high/low, ascending/descending), together with degrees of stress. These features operate in such a way that they realise three separate systems within English intonation: (i) *tonality*, i.e. the division of spoken text into discrete units of intonation; (ii) *tonicity*, i.e. the location of the most prominent syllable within each intonation unit, commonly referred to as the *tonic* (or *nuclear*) *syllable*; and (iii) *tone*, i.e. the contrastive pitch movement accompanying the tonic syllable. In general terms, tonality indicates the division of spoken text into units of information, tonicity indicates the focus of information in each unit, and tone the status of information (either major/minor, or final/incomplete) and the type of communicative interaction (e.g. statement, question, command, request, etc.). (For full descriptions of English intonation, see Pike 1945; O'Connor and Arnold 1973; Crystal 1969; Halliday 1970; and Brazil *et al.* 1980.) Other aspects of non-intonational prosody that appear in speech include degrees of loudness (forte, fortissimo, piano, pianissimo, crescendo and diminuendo) and of tempo (allegro, allegrissimo, lento, lentissimo, accelerando and rallentando); also types of rhythmicality (rhythmic, arhythmic, spikey ˊorˋ, glissando ˊorˋ, staccato and legato). Paralinguistic features are listed above.

Not many studies have followed the pioneering work in the prosodic description of style in English, although Crystal and Davy themselves ventured further in the description of conversational English (Crystal and Davy 1975). Johns-Lewis (1986a) notes a few studies on pausing characteristics in spontaneous and non-spontaneous speech, and on French discourse modes. Her own research (1986a, b) and Graddol (1986) represent the closest parallels to Crystal and Davy. The general conclusions of both pieces of research are that two forms of non-spontaneous speech (acting and reading aloud) are characterised by (a) higher mean pitch and (b) greater degree of variety of pitch, than conversation; that this is the case for both men and women; but that there are 'powerful social conditioning forces [that] constrain men to exploit a narrower pitch band than women do' (Johns-Lewis 1986a, p. 217). Amongst her general comments she concedes:

> In order to identify a particular prosodic parameter (in this case, pitch) as signalling a particular social dimension, comparison between *acting* and *other* public modes (e.g. political speeches, sermons) would be required. In other words, before claims can be made that high variation about a mean is characteristic of public address for a multiple audience, and small variation about a mean is characteristic of private communication for a unique, single audience, measurement of Fo in several discourse modes involving public address for a multiple audience, and several discourse modes involving private communication for a unique audience, would be necessary. (Johns-Lewis 1986a, p. 213)

Against this background,[2] the present study is an attempt to provide further evidence of the stylistic potential of intonation in the description and categorisation of genres of spoken English. We shall start from Crystal and Davy's own analysis (and definition) of conversation as represented in Crystal and Davy (1975). These authors' original material will be used as one data-source here not only in recognition of the value of their pioneering work, but also because it is publicly available in taped form and it should be therefore possible for the reader to refer to it and assess any comments directly.

Prosodic characteristics of informal conversation

Conversation is of course a very varied kind of activity. It can vary in length, in number of participants, in degrees of seriousness and formality and in types of settings (e.g. face-to-face, telephone, public, as on the radio and television). It varies from intimate tête-à-têtes to formal, public discussion. Variations in the activity are matched by variations in the kind of language used; and the varieties of conversation 'sound' different, i.e. prosodic and paralinguistic features are involved, besides the grammatical, lexical and other semantic features. An attempt at a definition of 'conversation' has been provided by Crystal and Davy (1975, p. 86):

> A *conversation* is any stretch of continuous speech between two or more people within audible range of each other who have the mutual intention to communicate, and bounded by the separation of all participants for an extended period.

The reference to a separation by participants 'for an extended period' is meant to exclude incidental interruptions. Generally speaking, in our culture, we feel that we know when a conversation comes to an end; admittedly, there is no hard and fast rule, since we sometimes feel that we are 'picking up where we left off last time'. The question of the extent of the conversation affects the structure of it, not its characteristics, and we will not consider this problem further here.

The kind of conversation which will be treated in this section is the kind that we all engage in most of our talking lives, 'natural, everyday, informal conversation' as Crystal and Davy call it. They have described it in detail in two places: Crystal and Davy (1969, Chapter 4), and (1975), the latter providing 15 samples as well as commentaries and a general discussion. They have drawn attention to at least twelve characteristics of informal conversation (Crystal and Davy 1975, pp. 4 ff.):

1. a wide variety of linkage between sentences

2. intonation

3. ellipsis

4. hesitations

5. gestures and facial expressions that affect the interpretation of intonation

6. interruptions and cues

7. indications of giving attention

8. variations in rhythm
9. variations in tone of voice (paralinguistic features)
10. variations in speed
11. segmental simplifications (i.e. assimilation, elision)
12. 'extra-linguistic effects' (p. 16) e.g. laughter.

The prosodic features previously outlined directly contribute to 2 (intonation), 8 (rhythm), and 10 (speed); but indirectly they also accompany, in a significant way, 4 (hesitations), 6 and 7 (the management of conversation participation); they are necessarily involved in 5 (the 'evidence' of gesture and facial expression) and 11 (simplifications, due mainly to speed), and are incidentally involved in 1 (linkage) and 3 (ellipsis) in types of tone and length of intonation units. Paralinguistic features are mentioned in 9 and 12.

Three other major features of informal conversation were presented in Crystal and Davy (1969, pp. 102-5): namely (i) *inexplicitness,* due to the extra-linguistic context, which accounted for the frequency of incomplete utterances and phonologically obscure items as well as the obvious semantic assumptions between participants who have possibly known each other well and for a long time; (ii) the *randomness* of subject-matter, the inevitable and excusable result of a general lack of planning in *informal* conversation; and (iii) *normal non-fluency* — hesitations, backtracking, restructuring, slips of the tongue, overlapping and simultaneous speech, and the like, which result from the creative process of thinking and planning and are expected and tolerated by all those engaged.

Conversation is distinguished from other genres (except drama and oral storytelling, for obvious reasons) by allowing the full range of paralinguistic effect, i.e. the paralinguistic use of the prosodic features and the paralinguistic features themselves. However, this full range does not necessarily *dominate* conversation; it is not as if one paralinguistic effect (e.g. allegrissimo) must of necessity follow another (e.g. resonant voice) in a continuous succession of effects. Rather, they are simply available, ready for use as the occasion demands. In fact, most of the time, the intonation and rhythm are quite unexceptional, and even predictable — not everybody, on every occasion throughout every conversation, produces 'dramatic' effects. Most conversation is plain ordinary 'natural, everyday, informal conversation'. Crystal and Davy's 15 samples offer a corpus of ordinary conversation, totalling 40 minutes of informal speech. A study of these reveals both stated characteristics: the unexceptional, even predictable, rhythm and intonation on the one hand, and the availability of practically the whole range of prosodic and paralinguistic features on the other. Speech is interrupted, for instance, by laughter and giggles, but understandably, other 'extra-linguistic effects' (or 'voice qualifications') like tremulousness, sobbing and crying are not exemplified in such publicly available materials. Interjections like *coo, cor, ooh* abound, as do clicks, grunts (*hm*) and other vocalisations. Hesitations occur frequently, both silent and voiced, and so do indications of attention, e.g. *mm, yes, oh.* Of voice qualities, breathiness featured in seven of the 15 extracts, creak in three, tension also in three, huskiness in two, and there were just two instances of resonant voice (one to quote children, and the other a mock expression of incredulity); whisper and falsetto happened not to be present in these extracts. Onomatopeia occurred occasionally too, e.g. *c-r-unch.*

Variations in tempo, loudness, pitch level, pitch range and rhythm occurred very commonly. Turns of speed to allegro were noted in five extracts, accelerando in five and to lento (and drawl) in eight, but rallentando in only one. Forte was noted a couple of times, but piano much more often. Monotone was noted once, and occasionally a generally high pitch level; but a narrow pitch range was very common indeed, especially in monosyllabic responses and markers of attention, while a wide pitch range occurred less often — it was obviously kept in reserve for the right occasion, but often accompanied interjections. Distinct changes in rhythm occurred in eight of the extracts, by far the most common being a switch to glissando with falling or rising pitch; spikiness, staccato and legato were not noted at all, but nevertheless are known to occur in ordinary informal conversation. Interruptions were frequent and this often had the effect, of course, of leaving an intonation unit incomplete. Cues — handing over the role of speaker to another participant — are less common than one might think; demanding the role of speaker hardly featured at all, as it would in a lively argument (Crystal and Davy's samples were all *friendly*, 'natural, everyday, informal' conversations!). Cues were often with a falling tone — specifically giving the role of speaker to someone else; occasionally they were accompanied with a rising tone, which is more in the nature of an offer of the role of speaker to another.

Within the parameters specific to intonation, we can look at the length of intonation units (tonality), the placement of the tonic syllable (tonicity) and the proportion of falls and rises, etc. (tone) and the types of pretonics. First of all the tonality. In the extracts studied, no units of intonation contained more than seven accented syllables; those that contained seven *could* be analysed differently — into two separate units:

I 'think he 'said there was 'only 'one 'modern 'ground in England

well 'some of the 'gates 'might be a'bout as 'wide as 'that room

And similarly some of the intonation units with six accented syllables could be interpreted in the same way:

I 'thought they 'always had these 'wooden 'benches and 'stands and 'that

and 'every 'time a dis'aster 'like this 'happens

but if 'you ve got 'so many 'thousand 'quid s worth of 'stand 'there

The intonation units with five, six or seven accented syllables always contained a full clause. Of those with four accents 63.6 per cent contained a full clause, 27.3 per cent contained just the complement of a clause, and 9.1 per cent were relative (defining) clauses. Of intonation units with three accounts 50 per cent were full clauses; 14.3 per cent contained SPC but not the totality of the clause; 14.3 per cent contained the complement and 21.4 per cent an adjunct. Of the intonation units with two accented syllables, only 20.1 per cent contained full clauses, 8.3 per cent contained SPC but not the totality of the clause and 8.3 per cent just SP; 29.2 per cent contained adjuncts, 8.3 per cent the complement and the remainder contained just a subject, just a predicator, a linker and a subject, a relative (defining) clause, an exclamation or post-modification in a noun phrase. Of intonation units with a single accented syllable 33.3 per cent contained a full clause, but they were in the vast majority of cases clauses like *you know, you see,* or simple equative clauses like *he's a director*, or verbless bound clauses like *if anything.* To these could perhaps be added the 12.5 per cent that contained a simple response structure like *Yes, true, mm,* or an exclamation like *coo!, cor!*; they are in effect full clauses, after all. 16.6 per cent contained adjuncts; 16.6 per cent contained complements, and the remainder contained a fairly even spread of tags, subjects, post-modifications, predicates and SPC structures that were not the totality of the clause.

The average length of intonation units in these samples of informal conversation was 2.2 accented syllables. The usual upper limit seems to be five accented syllables, for most units that contain more than five are susceptible to alternative interpretation, namely into two units (or what Halliday would call a 'compound tone group'). Even these so-called 'compound' units rarely contain more than seven accented syllables. The tentative upper limit would correspond to (a) the syntactic structure S P C1 C2 A: *The 'lady s al'ready 'paid the 'club her 'dues*; or (b) if one element of structure was realised phonologically by an unaccented syllable, then some kind of expansion to one of the other elements of structure, e.g. SX P C1 C2 a: *the 'old 'lady s just 'paid the 'club her 'dues* (where *X* = accented expansion of a given element, and *a* (as opposed to *A*) = a phonologically unaccented realisation of a given element — similarly, s, p, cl, c2); or (c), if two or more elements of structure were realised by unaccented syllables, then some kinds of expansion to one or more other elements of structure, to make up five accented syllables, e.g. s PX CX c A: *she 'tried 'yesterday to 'pay them her 'annual 'dues*; or (d), if one or more element of structure was not selected, then some kinds of expansion to the elements that were, to make up five accented syllables, e.g. (i) PX-X C A *Try to 'plan 'paying your 'dues 'annually*; e.g. (ii) s p CXXX-X; *She's a 'new 'paid up 'member in the 'pensioners 'club.* A full listing of possibilities is beyond the scope of this discussion; equally, a full listing of possibilities of syntactic structures within intonation units comprising four, three or two units, or a single unit.

Clauses frequently contain complex, expanded elements of structure, which in total are realised by more than five accented syllables. How does a speaker cope intonationally with such clauses? Usually, by splitting the clause into two or more intonation units, the 'splits' reflecting, as noted previously, a degree of informational structuring, and occurring at appropriate syntactic boundaries. I say a 'degree of informational structuring', because the intonational splitting may well result in an intonation unit not corresponding exactly to an information unit. Take a familiar announcement:

> the ˈtrain arˈriving at ˈplatform ˈ<u>two</u> // is the ˈten o ˈfive from ˈSwansea to <u>Pad</u>dington

The whole announcement is a single clause with eight accented syllables, too many for a normal unit of intonation. The speaker 'splits' the clause into two intonation units that happen to correspond syntactically to subject and predicate. However, the first intonation unit hardly corresponds to a separate unit of 'information'; nothing in it is new — the train, its arrival, and platform two are all given, because they are all present in the situation to both speaker and hearers, and we may assume that no other train is arriving elsewhere and that no other train is present at (or departing from!) platform two. The motivation for the distribution of intonation units is simply the fact that there is too much to say in a single unit. The motivation for the location of the splitting is a degree of informational structuring, namely 'theme' in one unit, and 'rheme' in the other — which corresponds exactly in syntactic terms to subject and predicate in this example.

We must note, however, that on average a unit of intonation in informal conversation has only two or three accented syllables; thus, even a clause with five accented syllables could easily be split into two intonation units:

> he ˈused to <u>spend</u> // a ˈbout a ˈthousand a <u>year</u>

This is a simple clause with five accented syllables, right up to the tentatively established maximum. The speaker decides to split that clause into two separate intonation units, splitting the complex complement (three accented syllables) from the SP. This may reflect the speaker's perception of the information as two separate pieces; on the other hand, the first intonation unit might, again, contain simply the 'theme' ('spending'), and the second the 'rheme'.

Although length of utterance is *not* equivalent to length of intonation units, it is nevertheless worth noting a characteristic of informal conversation that Crystal and Davy (1969, p. 109) discovered, because it *does* have a bearing on the length of intonation units. Utterance length varies according to the stage of development of the conversation. Utterances are short at the beginning, longer as topics are introduced, and longer still if an anecdote is related or argumentation is established, and then utterances are reduced in length again as an end approaches.

Secondly, the tonicity. The distinction between neutral and marked tonicity has been regarded as standard since Halliday (1967) proposed it, and subsequent evidence confirms it too. For example, Crystal (1975, p. 23) reports, 'from the statistical point of view, 80 per cent of all multi-word tone-units in the corpus' displayed the neutral tonicity pattern, i.e. that the tonic syllable occurs within the final lexical item of the intonation unit. A brief study of some of Crystal and Davy's extracts confirms that kind of proportion: 87.5 per cent of intonation units exhibited neutral tonicity, while only 12.5 per cent exhibited marked tonicity (of which cases, two-thirds had the tonic on a non-final lexical item, and one-third on a grammatical item). It must be pointed out, though, that 40 per cent of the total cases of neutral tonicity were information units with a single accent only, of which 53 per cent were responses, markers of attention, interjections, connectives like *you see.* If the latter (i.e. single accent responses, etc.) were removed entirely from the calculations, then neutral tonicity still accounted for 84.5 per cent of the intonation units.

Thirdly, the tones. Calculations from a number of the extracts showed that 64.8 per cent of all tones were falls. Of all falls 39.9 per cent involved a step up in pitch (↑\`); these were never used, of course, in single accent responses, markers of attention, etc. These latter accounted for 32.6 per cent of the other falls. 19.5 per cent of all tones were low rises, i.e. not the high rising pitch usually associated with 'yes/no questions', of which there were extremely few. Of all tones 5.5 per cent were level; their distribution was very similar to that of low rises — principally, incomplete utterances and markers of attention — and thus level tones may be combined with low rises to account for a full 25 per cent of the total. The remaining 10.2 per cent was accounted for by the high rises (0.5), fall–rises (9.1) and rise–falls (0.6). (What are called compound tones were re-interpreted either as sequences of simple tones or instances of complex tones, i.e. fall–rises and rise–falls.)

And finally, the types of pretonic. Crystal (1969, pp. 225-33) has provided the fullest description of the different pitch patterns that occur in the head of the pretonic segment. He and Davy (1975, p. 106) come to the conclusion that in informal conversation the sequence of gradually descending syllables within the head is the most frequent type, that gradually rising syllables are almost completely absent and that equally absent are heads involving wide pitch jumps between the syllables, 'which are common in most other spoken varieties'. In the extracts investigated, gradually descending heads accounted for 79.1 per cent of the intonation units with heads; an occasional rise or couple of rises in the head accounted for the remaining 21.9 per cent. These rises do not amount to a gradually ascending head, as if they were all stepping up to a peak at the tonic syllable, for the pitch of the syllables in between usually drops lower. These rises indicate relative semantic prominence in the intonation unit.

Extract 1 is another specimen of informal conversation, but it takes more the form of an anecdote. The father (speaker A) has had a long and unusual day and, after a good meal, he explained he was feeling very relaxed. His daughter (speaker B) and his wife (speaker C) have received snippets of information about the unusual event of the day but now while he is relaxed, they insist on a full and detailed account. His account comes in a light-hearted and casual manner, and there is a good deal of laughter. Besides the laughter, notice the variety of other paralinguistic features, the variations in speed, rhythm and pitch range and level, the hesitations and overlaps and the indications of attention. In this extract, there happen to be no interruptions or cues.

Extract 1: Anecdote

A well I 'went to 'Cardiff 'station in the ˏmorning (high)
to 'catch a 'train at 'half past ↑ˋeight
'all 'rather a ˏpleasant 'time
B 'on your ˋlonesome
A 'on my ˏlonesome (low)
ˏyes (low)
--- whats ˋthat mean (A, B: laughter) (piano)
C 'that s ˋLancashire
for on my ↑ˋ tod (C: laughter)
A ˋoh (forte, wide)
I underˎstand now
and I . I ar'ranged . that I was 'going (B: incogˋnito) with
a ˋguy
called 'David ˇJones (?: m)
-- wi'thout ˏlocker (?: m)

- who was 'getting on at ↑` Newport (allegro)
((x)) and had `organised it all (allegro)
- I 'didnt really 'want 'quite 'have` time to 'go
,really (B: 'I ˎsee) (C: laughter) (allegro)
but . he d . 'sort of - (C: laughter) he* ` talked (*allegro)
me into it*
`finally (allegro)
because its `actually 'very im'portant (allegro)
'what we were' going to ↑`see
(xxx) *'one of the 'things Id 'write my* (*allegro,
↑` report on ascend)
(?: ` yeah)
for a'bout 'hundred 'thousand ↑` pounds (?: ' I ˎsee)
- was as' sociated with this ↑` visit . you see
so I 'thought well I ll ˎ go then (lento, low)
- but I al ᵛready had a - 'good idea ' what it was all (high)
a'bout . you know
- but 'not the'nitty'gritty . 'technical ↑` details
- - - I 'knew the 'sort of ` funding problems (diminuendo
descend)
and the - and the specifiˎcations (dim. desc.)
and techniˎcalities (?:m) (dim. desc.)
- and ˎ so on (pianiss, low)
-um . `anyhow
I 'got to the , station now (piano, low)
and they 'said - the* 'half 'past -train (*crescendo,
rhythmic)
will be 'twenty ′minutes ↑` late*
(?: laughter)
I could ˎ hear this (low)
I was 'listening 'very, carefully going on (low alleg)
so - a` nother 'train 'came in (high)
- and they 'said 'this train um 'coming in -now . .
approaching the`other 'platform (allegro)
a ᵛ little 'train
is 'going to - 'Weston super, Mare
via ` Newport (wide)
'oh (?: -m) I ll 'get on` that one
then
? ` yes (piano)
A - so I 'got in , there

- and it was 'there for about 'three ↑` minutes (wide)
- and I -thought (narrow)
- they re going to 'stick . keep this 'train ˏ here
and 'let the 'other one 'go -through (allegro, narrow)
'I ll bet (wide)
- 'this is be'cause I m the 'son of an `engine driver
(low, piano, gliss`)
(laughter)
so I 'jumped 'back ˏ out a'gain (high, forte, wide)
and I 'waited on the 'other 'plat ˏ platform a'bout 'five
or (x)
- and 'sure e ˏ nough (high)
the 'other 'train 'came ˏ in* (*held consonant)
- I *'got into the 'train* 'right by the (*allegro)(*lento)
er -* ˏ coffee place*
you ˏ know
? `oh yes (piano)
(` yes)
A (by the) - re ˏ freshments
the - ˏ ((x)) 'sort of thing
- I got (a'nother) 'seat. 'right by the ˏ side (crescendo)
of me
(?: oh ˎyes)
ˏbooked
because it got 'full it 'gets very ` full (diminuendo)
these ˏ trains you see (?:` yes) (piano, low
it was 'one of these 'one 'two ` five things (allegro)
- and I 'got my ˏ coat
and I got it *'all*ˏ ready for when (*drawl)
and when he 'comes -in
'two ˏ seats
ˎ smashing (you know) (*drawl)
? (-m)
A I 'got 'my bit ˏ sorted 'out (piano)
? - ˏ yea (piano)
A - - 'Newport ˏ station
'sure e ˏ nough (high, allegro)
he was 'right by the ˏ door (high, stacc)
'in he ˏ comes (descend)
'sit -down
ˏgreat (low, piano, clipped,
breathy)

- 'everything is going ˏ well 'like (low, allegro)
- I 'said oh you 'know e`xactly (high)
'where we re ˏ going
'dont you then ˏDavid (allegro, piano)
and he said *-yes* (*drawl)
we ve got it 'all arˏranged he said (wide, allegro)
we re catching we re 'changing at (lento, gliss')
- atˏParkway
? -m
A and 'catching the ˏ Plymouth train (lento, gliss')
he 'said there ll be a ˇ buffet on' 'there
I said' well 'I m not`sure (allegro)
about this ˏ buffet
'I m going to 'have my 'breakfast `now
. so - I had a 'cheese and - (?:`yes) 'toasty ˏ sandwich
and a 'cup of coffee
and 'he had er 'bacon ˏsandwiches I 'think
. *ˏ for*tunately (*clipped)
. as the 'story ˏ goes (ascend, piano)
-- em we was con'vinced we 'didn t need to -bother (high, allegro)
at ˏ that 'stage
? -m
A ((x'xxx)) we -had this (narrow)
- got 'out at ˏ Parkway (wide)
he 'looked at his ˏ watch (allegro)
and he 'said - * 'oh `good* he said (*lento, breathy)
. the 'train will be'here in a'nother `minute (allegro, spiky)
be'cause 'we re ˏ late
we 'dont have to 'wait at ˎ Parkway
- and he 'looked ˏ up
. and the 'train was 'coming ↑` in (ascend)
? -yes (piano)
A `great
'diddle 'iddle 'here it -comes (high, drawl)
and the an'nouncer was - 'saying ˏsomething (high, narrow, allegro)
and . I 'switched `off
- because I -said
-- ˇ you re 'looking 'after me 'Dave (high, wide, allegro)
I won t 'even 'listen to ˎ anything (narrow, allegro)

you know I m just *\talk*ing to him (allegro, *drawl)
I 'thought I m going to en *\joy* myself (*drawl)
I ve had - tre*\ mendously 'hard day* (*wide)
the 'day be,fore
I was 'working for 'twenty three\hours
'round the\clock
'more or,less
? \yes (piano)
A - \wasnt I (piano)
- it was 'very x 'longest' day I ve 'ever \had (narrow, allegro, piano)
,actually that one
- and I 'thought 'well . 'this is ,it (narrow, piano)
because I d got 'up at 'four o'clock in the ,morning
and was working till 'three the \next' day (allegro, stacc)
. with 'one 'thing and a,nother (low, allegro, stacc)
- or at 'least I was a,wake (low, narrow, allegro, husky)
- em - so I 'thought I d 'better have a 'day\off* (ascend, wide, *drawl)
'you ,know what I mean
I m 'going to *ˇgo* with him (*forte, drawl)
and en,joy it (narrow, piano)
- anyway we 'went we did in the *'wrong* 'damned di\rection (ascend, *giggle)
(laughter)

The average length of the intonation units in this specimen of informal conversation was 2.5 accented syllables, slightly longer than for ordinary informal conversation. There was the same kind of variety of lengths with many units (24.1 per cent) with only a single accent; this specimen — no doubt because of its anecdotal nature — had, in fact, more two-accented intonation units, 30.3 per cent; 19.7 per cent had three accents, 16.9 per cent four, and three intonation units (2.1 per cent) had five (lines 28, 40, and 135), while there were two instances of units (1.4 per cent) with more but they both contained instances of faltering (lines 17 and 56).

Neutral tonicity accounted for 80.3 per cent of intonation units. The proportions of cases of marked tonicity were again:

approximately two-thirds (67.9 per cent) had tonics on non-final lexical items and one-third (32.1 per cent) on grammatical items.

The proportion of falling tones was considerably lower than in Crystal and Davy's samples — no doubt, once again, the consequence of the anecdotal character of this specimen. Falls comprised 48.2 per cent, 36.8 per cent were low rises, 7.1 per cent were level, and 6.4 per cent were fall-rises. There was one instance (0.7 per cent) of a high rise (line 77). The fall-rises were not usually indicative of incomplete information, but marked contrast, emphasis and the expression of personal opinion. The vast majority of pretonics had descending heads, although four (2.8 per cent) were ascending (lines 23, 101, 113 and 142).

All in all, the statistics and characteristics of this specimen accord well with those of Crystal and Davy. Differences can be attributed directly to the anecdotal nature of this specimen. These differences are shown in sharper focus in another speech event of reporting — news reading.

News reading

News reading is a stretch of continuous speech, a monologue spoken by one person, or by a set of people speaking strictly in turn, reading from a script, to an audience that is remote from the immediate setting, with the communicative intention of simply reporting on events. It is distinct from other news programmes such as current affairs, documentaries, etc. by taking the form of monologue, retaining a formal style and seeking to eschew the expression of opinion, emotion or suasion. In contrast to informal conversation, it is characterised by (i) its independence from extra-linguistic context, e.g. no reference is made to items in the immediate setting (of a recording studio); (ii) its deliberate and carefully planned structure of subject-matter; (iii) its deliberate and conspicuous division of topics; and (iv) its normal fluency and its almost complete absence of hesitation and slips of the tongue, due to a prepared script and rehearsal.

There are no extralinguistic effects or vocalisations, although occasionally a deep drawing of breath is audible. There are no paralinguistic features such as breathiness or creak, and no significant variations in tempo or stress. There is no glissando, spiky, staccato or legato featuring of rhythm. There are just occasionally cases of hesitation, as in line 52 below, but otherwise rhythm is normal — not 'rhythmic', however, as in the reading of poetry or prose aloud.

The most noticeable kind of variation is in pitch. A wide pitch range is not encountered, nor, on the other hand, is monotone; narrow pitch range is fairly common. The distinctive kinds of variation are high and low pitch ranges, typically found in a sequence of intonation units gradually stepping down, one after another, until a new pitch level is reached (usually preceded by a pause). Although this is noted by Crystal and Davy (1969, p. 33), it is Brazil, Coulthard and Johns (1980, pp. 61-7) and Coulthard and Brazil (1979) who have described these 'pitch sequences', as they call them, in greater detail. (These are also called 'intonation groups' by Tench (1976, p. 13).) So, in addition to the pitch variation within an intonation unit, there is a discernible pitch range variation between successive units. This latter kind of pitch range variation is discernible to a certain extent in informal conversation, too, but in news reading it is regular and expected. 'Pitch sequences' or 'intonation groups' correlate with the presenting of information in 'chunks', and because the semantic content of news reading is thought out and carefully planned in advance, the 'intonation groups' correspond to it in a systematic way. In fact, the 'intonation groups' correspond almost directly with what would be considered full and complete sentences in the written mode: Units 1-4, 5-9, 10-14, 15-19, 20-6, 27-9, 30-6, 37-9, 40-1, 42-7, 48-54, 55-61, 62-5, 66-9, 70-3, 74-6. There are 16 'intonation groups' with an average of 4.7 intonation units each.

Above the intonation groups, Tench (1976, pp. 13-15) has proposed the term 'phonological paragraphs' for even greater structural units. It is obvious that in fluent, rehearsed speech, pauses of the magnitude displayed between units 19 and 20, between 29 and 30, between 47 and 48, and between 65 and 66 have a particular significance. The pitch level after such a lengthy pause is very high. The combination of lengthy pause and high pitch correlate usually with a distinct change of subject-matter, and just as intonation groups correspond to sentences in the written mode, these larger units correspond to paragraphs; hence the term 'phonological paragraphs'. No doubt, such phonological paragraphs could be discerned in informal conversation, too, but the careful semantic planning of news reading makes them easily identifiable. In fact, the slightly shorter pauses between 29 and 30 and between 47 and 48 suggest that the three contiguous paragraphs (from 20 to 65) belong more closely together than they do with either paragraph preceding or following.

To return to matters of tonality, tonicity and tone, a number of differences are noteworthy from the characteristics of informal conversation. Intonation units are longer in news reading; the average in the specimen below is 2.9 accented syllables. Very few units have only a single accent, and the longest unit has eight accents. The tendency, thus, is to use longer units in news reading. Neutral tonicity is found in 88 per cent of the intonation units in the specimen below; thus, no difference is apparent in this respect from informal conversation. Even in the proportions of kinds of marked tonicity, no difference can be found: two-thirds, approximately, of cases of marked tonicity involved non-final lexical items, one-third involved grammatical items (e.g. *this, all, her*). Falls accounted for only 51.3 per cent of the tones in the specimen below; the low rises, most of the fall-rises and all the level tones principally functioned as indications of incomplete information. This more or less balanced, one-to-one, proportion of falls, which indicate completed information, and other tones indicating incomplete information, suggests careful and planned information structuring. The proportion is distinctly different from that of informal conversation, and, of course, in news reading there are no instances of responses, indications of attention and so on, which would have affected the ratio of tones. The pretonics displayed a much greater variety than in informal conversation. Of the 60 intonation units with heads in the following specimen, 25 (41.7 per cent) were reckoned to be descending and 20 (33.3 per cent) level. Level heads are strongly associated with narrow pitch range; i.e. the pitch varied little, not just through the pre-tonic segment, but through the tonic segment as well. Ascending heads accounted for 10 per cent; and the complex heads, chiefly associated with long heads, accounted for the remainder: descend–ascend 6.7 per cent, ascend–descend 5 per cent, and descend–ascend–descend 3.5 per cent. One final point: the news is normally introduced and terminated by an appropriate announcement:

ˈBBC news	(high, narrow range, level tone)
. at eleven o clock	(falling tone)
BBC	(narrow, level tone)
. radio news	(low, descending head, falling tone)

The point throughout the above description is that a person familiar with British culture will recognise the news reading genre without any reference to these announcements. If the introductory announcement is missed, they will identify the genre without any difficulty through the kind of prosodic features described above.

Extract 2: News reading

the ˈfinal ˈgroup of ˇbritons (high)
eˈvacuated . from the ˈheavy ˏfighting (ascend)
in ˈSouth ˏYemen (ascend)
has arˈrived in ˎLondon
- ˈthirty six ˏbritons (high level, narrow)
inˈcluding the ˈbritish am ˏbassador in ˈAden (level)
mister ˈArthur ˏMarshall (low, level, narrow)
ˈlanded at ˈHeathrow ˎAirport
this ˎmorning (low, narrow)
- ˈmister Marshall ˈsaid it was inˋcredible (high)
that ˈno ˈbritons were ˋkilled (level, narrow)
or ˋinjured in the ˈfighting (narrow)
although ˋseveral ˈpeople (narrow)
ˈtold of aˈmazing esˋcapes
- he ˈsaid - ˈhe and his ˈwife ˏCheryl
ˈsheltered under a ˋtable (narrow)
in their-house
for ˈfifteen ˋhours (level)
. while ˈshots were ˈfired aˈround the ˎpremises (low)
- - - theˋpound (high)
ˏfell (high)
aˈgainst ˈmajor ˏcurrencies (high, level, narrow)
in ˈearly ˈtrading . on the ˈforeign (descend–ascend)
exˈchanges in ˏLondon
- and then reˈcovered ˏslightly (ascend)
to ˈstand at ˈone ˈdollar . thirty (ascend–descend)
eight ˎcents
- ˈdown ˈone and a ˈquarter ˈcents (low, ascend–descend,
on ˈFridays ˎclose narrow)
- the ˈpounds ˈfall in ˈvalue was ˈsaid to be ˈdue (high)
to the continuing ˈnervousness about ˇoil prices
- and . in adˈvance of this (high, level)

'afternoons 'Commons de`bate
on the 'latest developments in the (descend–ascend–
'Westland 'Helicopters af ̖fair descend)
- the 'board of 'Westland ˏHelicopters (high, narrow)
has an'nounced re'vised pro ˏposals
de'signed to se'cure the `future (level)
of the 'troubled ˏcompany (level)
- as be ˏfore
the 'board . sup'ports a 'link up (high,
with Si-korsky descend–ascend)
and `Fiat
- 'however 'this 'time
- it will be 'seeking 'just a 'simple (level, narrow)
ma`jority
of 'shareholders ̖ votes (low)
- the 'company has 'called a `new (high)
'shareholders 'meeting
on 'February the ̖ twelfth (low, narrow)
- 'Westlands ˏ Chairman
. sir 'John-Cuckney
.' says the 'company re'mains in a (ascend–descend)
pre'carious fi`nancial 'state
and its `future (low)
. must be `settled (low)
`soon (wide)
- -the prime 'minister is preparing to 'face the (high,
'Commons in this 'afternoons descend–ascend)
emergency de-bate
on the 'Westland 'Helicopters af ˏ fair (high, level)
- she s 'meeting 'senior (ascend, narrow)
ˏ colleagues this 'morning
to dis'cuss her 'Commons ˏ speech
'which . she ˏworked . on (low, level, narrow)
'over the week ˏend (level)
at 'number 'ten ̖ Downing Street
- she s 'promised to give `all the 'facts (high, level)
about ˇher 'role
in the `row
'over the 'leaked ˏletter (ascend)
from the so'licitor ˏgeneral (ascend)
. to the 'former de'fence`secretary (low)

. mister 'Michael `Heseltine (low)
- this 'afternoon s de ˏbate (low, level)
. will be 'broadcast -live (high, level, narrow)
. on 'radio 'four 'vh'ff ˏ m (narrow)
from a'bout 'half past ˎthree (low)
--- the 'dutch au'thorities are
re'ported to have 'dropped - charges (high, descend–ascend–descend)
against 'William 'James `Kelly
. who was ar`rested . 'earlier this 'month (narrow)
in ˎAmsterdam (low, descend)
- he was ar'rested with 'Brendan
Mc'Farlane and 'Gerard ˇKelly (high)
. who es'caped from the 'Maze prison
near -Belfast (narrow)
in 'nineteen 'eighty ˎthree (low)
- he was 'charged under 'dutch
'fire arms ˏlaws (high, descend–ascend)
- po'lice are still `checking (low, level, narrow)
his 'Irish ˎpassport (low)

Prayer

Prayer takes many forms; it can be either private or public, written or spoken, prepared or impromptu, recited individually or in unison. Its content varies according to circumstances and emotional conditions, and according to the variety of religions and traditions. Crystal has drawn attention to the prosodic features of spoken prayers that are recited from written texts, by individual clergymen and in unison, in the Anglican and Roman Catholic traditions (Crystal and Davy 1969, Chapter 6; Crystal 1975, Chapter 6). Here are the main characteristics that he noted for prayers recited in unison from a written text.

> Each punctuation group is a prosodic unit, but it is a prosodic unit of a rather different kind from the tone-unit (or primary contour) found in all other varieties of spoken English, as it requires only two obligatory prosodic features — a most emphatic syllable, and stress conforming to the

> distribution of lexical words within the unit. The introduction of variation in nuclear tone-type (e.g. rising, falling-rising tones) or in pitch-range (e.g. high falling or low falling) is optional, and usually not introduced. Any participant in a congregation may, if he wishes, articulate his words with as much feeling as possible, introducing a wide range of pitch patterns; but as far as the total, cumulative auditory effect is concerned, such effort is unnecessary, and few speakers bother. A congregation — or any speakers in unison — has very much one voice. When a group speak an utterance together, differences in the phonology of their articulation become blurred, and the outside listener is left with a 'single voice' impression, consisting solely of variations in emphasis. The pitch level on the whole is low and monotone, though towards the end of a longer stretch of utterance than normal there may be a noticeable descending movement. This is absolutely predictable at the very end of a prayer, where the 'Amen' (and often the words immediately preceding it) is given a marked drop in pitch. But otherwise pitch contrasts are regularly reduced to zero, leaving monotone and rhythmicality as the defining characteristics of unison liturgical prayer. (Crystal and Davy 1969, pp. 158-9; and Crystal 1975, p. 102)

The specimens of prayer in this chapter are taken from a nonconformist evangelical service held in Cardiff and broadcast on BBC Radio Wales. The recitation in unison of the Lord's prayer follows very closely Crystal's description above. The intonation units follow punctuation groups (cf. the Authorised Version text of Matthew 6) very closely; but not exactly: see lines 5 and 6, and 7 and 8, the latter case being considered too long for a single intonation unit; the division into two keeps the rhythm steady — two, or at most three accents, per intonation unit. The average length is 2.3 accents per unit. What is also particularly noticeable is the regular pause between each unit; the pauses maintain the rhythm of the speech. The pauses are briefer between lines 5 and 6, 7 and 8, 10 and 11 because of syntactic 'cohesion'. Neutral tonicity is very high too (88.2 per cent) since there are only two cases of tonicity falling on a (final) grammatical item, and there are no cases at all of marked tonicity on a non-final lexical item.

Perhaps the most remarkable feature of prayer in unison is the lack of tone variation. All the tones are level in the specimen below, with the exception of the low fall on the final intonation unit. The pretonics are level too, but there is a clear step down to the tonic. There are two degrees of downstep: a *half downstep* in lines 5, 7, 10 and 14, indicating incomplete information — as it happens, it coincides with incomplete clause structure in these cases (e.g. line 5: S P, line 6: Loc); and a *full downstep*, indicating a complete unit of information.

Extract 3: Prayer in unison

ˈour * -father* (*trem)
- which ˈart in -heaven
- ˈhallowed ˈbe thy *-name* (*trem)
- ˈthy ˈkingdom -come
- ˈthy ˈwill be -done
. in ˈearth . ˈas it is in -heaven
- ˈgive us this -day
. our ˈdaily -bread
- and forˈgive us our -trespasses
- ˈas we forˈgive -them
. that ˈtrespass aˈgainst -us
- and lead us ˈnot into temp-tation
- but *deˈliver us* ˈfrom -evil (*trem)
- for ˈthine is the -kingdom
. the ˈpower and the -glory
- for ˈever and -ever
- aˋmen

The lack of tone variation is quite remarkable. Right throughout the above specimen of prayer in unison, there is no single instance of pitch movement on the tonic; level tones thus account for a staggering 94.1 per cent (i.e. 16 out of 17!). In Crystal's transcription of a similar specimen (Crystal 1975, p. 100), ten of the thirteen tonics are level (76.9 per cent), and of the three that are falls, the two in the middle of the text are often, from my observation, given simply a lower level tone, marking a semantic boundary — rather like the intonation groups noted in news reading. The final intonation unit contains a significant drop in pitch, with a fall to very low, thus signalling the end of the prayer.

The regular rhythm is also noteworthy; there are generally two prominent beats per intonation unit — the onset syllable and the tonic; other accents in between are less prominent. The onset and the tonic syllables seem to act as the end points of the rhythmic 'swing'. Prayer in unison involves rhythmic speech (Crystal and Davy 1969, p. 36) *in extenso.*

The only notable differences between Crystal's description of prayer in unison and the present one is that the specimen transcribed above is not spoken in monotone (there is a clear step down in pitch on each tonic), and that one paralinguistic feature in particular is common, namely tremulousness. This tremulousness is heard in the lead voice and seems to express a serious and sincere fervency and reverence. Tremulousness would be lost in the 'cumulative auditory effect' of the congregation. Crystal seems to suggest the above features are unique to prayer in unison. But they are not quite. The features also characterise public praying on behalf of a congregation by a minister in non-conformist worship. Here are two more examples: Extract 4 is the introductory prayer and Extract 5 is from the main prayer part way through the service.

Extract 4: Public prayer

alˈmighty -God
. and our most ˈmerciful -father
- we ˈthank Thee that we can ˈcome to -Thee
- in ˈthat ˈname which is above
  ˈevery ˈother *-name* (*trem)
- the *ˈname* of our ˈLord and
  ˈSaviour ˈJesus -Christ (descend)(*trem)
- and ˈas we esˈpecially reˈmember to-day
- the resurˈrection . of ˈJesus -Christ
- we ˈask Thee in Thy -mercy
- that Thy ˈpresence ˈ. will be -with us
- and with ˈall who will ˈshare . this -service (descend)
. with us as -well
- for ˈthis we -ask (ascend)

- in the ˈnameˈ. of ˈJesus ˈChrist ˈ. our -Saviour (descend)
- a\men

This prayer is not scripted, but it is very typical of introductory prayers. The features that it has in common with prayer in unison are its regular rhythm, the pattern of pauses between intonation units (with occasional brief pauses on account of incomplete clause structure), the total lack of tone variation apart from the final intonation unit, the high degree of neutral tonicity, and the level pretonics with a clear step down to the level tonic (apart from those cases, in lines 1 and 11, where there is less of a step down because of incomplete clause structure). Three pretonics, however, have a descending movement; they are relatively long pretonics and come close to semantic boundaries. One pretonic (line 12) has an ascending movement: it is semantically unimportant as it is a mere repetition of line 8, which carries the main performative verb.

The general pitch is high, compared to prayer in unison, news reading and most of informal conversation. This prayer is also forte, for obvious reasons. It is also slower in general tempo than news reading and most of informal conversation. Tremulousness is featured again, and occasional slight hesitations occur as well (lines 7, 9 and 10) which reinforce the impression of creative thinking in impromptu speech. The pausing in line 13 is not hesitation but what Abercrombie (1971, p. 151) calls the 'terminal function' of silent stress; it is not a feature of conversation, but it is of public speaking: 'what it does is to signal an immediately impending transition'. If it is felt that the above introductory prayer is a stereotype and thus akin to a scripted or at least rehearsed prayer, then Extract 5 should belie that view. It is taken from the middle of a two-minute impromptu prayer.

Extract 5: Public prayer

and we *ˈthank Thee our -father* (*trem)
- that the ˈChristian ˈchurch has a (descend)
ˈmessage to man -kind

- so that wherˈever we -are
- in ˈthis ˈmornings -service
either * -here* (*trem)
- in ˈthis ˈchapel -building (descend)
- - ˈor in ˈscattered -homes
- that ˈwe might be ˈgiven -grace
- to ˈhearken to the *ˈWord* of -God (descend)(*rall)
- and that our ˈhearts might be (descend)
ˈstrangely -warmed (*trem)
- that in * ˈthese ˈtroubled ˈtimes (*trem)
that we -live in*
and we ˈare con -cerned
- and ˈpray for the ˈsorrows of this -world (descend)
- -yet
- in the ˈGospel of ˈJesus -Christ
-ˈ is the *ˈhope* of man -kind (*husky, cresc)
- for it is *-there* (*rall)
we have ˈpeace with -God

Again, the same features emerge as for prayer in unison: regular rhythm, the almost automatic pausing between intonation units (except where close syntactic 'cohesion' requires at most only a brief pause), the lack of tone variation, the high degree of neutral tonicity, the level pretonics with a step down to the level tonic (except where close syntactic 'cohesion' requires only a narrow step down). What distinguishes individual impromptu prayer from prayer in unison are, again: the descending movement in the pretonic at semantic boundaries, the general high pitch, the forte degree of loudness, the occasional hesitation and tremulousness, and the silent stresses with the 'terminal' functions. Occasionally, other paralinguistic features appear, as in the above specimen. The features of rhythm and intonation decribed here must be kept clearly distinct from chanting, which involves a singing voice.

There are also intonational differences between public prayer and public Bible reading. As was noted above, there is evident and understandable overlap between prayer and Bible reading in lexis, grammar and semantics, but there are prosodic differences. Here is a specimen of Bible reading from the same nonconformist evangelical service as the extracts of prayer; it is the same speaker in all cases.

Extract 6: Bible reading

in the 'end of the . / sabbath (high)
- 'as it began to / dawn (high)
to'ward the 'first 'day of the ↓-week (descend)
- 'came . 'Mary . -Magdalene
- 'and the 'other -Mary
to 'see the \ sepulchre (low)
- - 'and be/ hold (high)
- there 'was a 'great \earthquake (ascend)
- for the 'angel of the 'Lord des
'cended from 'heaven (narrow)
- 'and / came (high)
and rolled 'back the -stone
. 'from the \door
- and 'sat up \ on it (low)
- - his / countenance
- was like ↑\ lightning (extra high tonic)
- and his / raiment
'white as \ snow (low)
- 'and 'for 'fear of / him (high)
- the 'keepers 'did \shake
- and be'came 'as 'dead \ men (descend)
- - and the 'angel -answered (high)
and 'said . 'unto the \ women
- 'fear 'not ↓\ *ye* (*creak)
- for I / know (high)
that ye 'seek \Jesus
- 'which was *\crucified* (*trem)
- 'for he is *'not \here* (*trem)
- for he is \risen
- 'as 'he has \ said
- / come (high)
- 'see the -place
- 'where the 'Lord \ lay
- - 'and 'go \quickly (high)
- and 'tell His dis\ciples

- that *ˈhe . is ˈrisenˈ. from the ˎdead* (glissˈ)
- - ˈand be, hold (high)
- he ˈgoeth be, fore you
- intoˋGalilee
- and ˈthere shall ye -see him
- -lo
ˈI have ˎ told you (low)
- - ˈand . they de↑ˈparted ˋquickly (low–high)
ˈfrom the ˋsepulchre
- with *ˈfear ˈand ˈgreat ˋjoy* (*trem)
- and did ˈrun . to ˈbring his diˈsciples . ˎ word (descend)

Some features will be identified immediately from the above transcription which distinguish it from public prayer: variations in tone (55 per cent are falls) and a wider variation in pretonics. There is also a much more discernible phonological paragraphing. These three distinctive features are shared by news reading. The intonation units follow punctuation very closely as they do in other forms of speech which are scripted. Silent stresses signal a 'terminal function' as in other forms of public speech. However, there are, specifically, features that public Bible reading share with public prayer: regular rhythm, with a kind of balancing of onset and tonic syllables, while other accented syllables are less prominent in between; the average length of intonation units is 2.4 accents, but it is noticeable that many grammatical items are accented that would not normally be in informal speech — this helps to maintain the regular rhythm; and lento speech. It was noted above that the general tempo of public prayer was slower than that of news reading; this is also true of public Bible reading. In the news, an average of 107 accented syllables occurred per minute; in public prayer, only 80 accented syllables occurred per minute; in public Bible reading, 84 accented syllables. The impression of lento speech is enhanced by the regular pausing, and, in the case of Bible reading, by the considerable use of accents on grammatical items without semantic significance.

Public Bible reading shares with public individual prayer three other features, namely a generally high pitch, a generally forte degree of loudness — the result of speaking up to be heard at a distance — and paralinguistic features for expressiveness.

We have been considering the claim that people can regularly identify different genres in spoken English by means of prosodic and paralinguistic clues, and we have been adducing descriptive evidence in an attempt to justify that claim. We have considered particularly the evidence from intonation in a number of recognisably different genres, viz.:

(a) informal conversations and
(b) an informal, conversational anecdote, both of which are private and unscripted;
(c) a news bulletin, which is public, and scripted;
(d) unison prayer, which is also public, and scripted, but is uttered by a body of people simultaneously;
(e) individual public prayer, which is unscripted, but uttered by one person on behalf of a body of people; and
(f) public Bible reading, which, like a news bulletin, is public and scripted.

We have noted also whether paralinguistic effect is involved in these six genres. The prosodic and paralinguistic evidence is summarised in Table 3.1.

A number of interesting points emerge from the tabulation. Firstly, the length of intonation units does seem to correlate with the degree to which the semantic content is already prepared. The semantic content of informal conversation is the least prepared and the average length of intonation unit is short, only about 2.2 accents per unit. In news reading, the semantic content is fully prepared, and the length of intonation units is longer, about 2.9 accents per unit. The anecdote occupies an intermediate position, 2.5 accents per unit, and this seems to reflect neatly an intermediate degree of semantic planning; with an anecdote, a speaker knows the whole semantic content beforehand, but has nevertheless the task of organising it during the telling of the anecdote, whereas with news reading the speaker does not have to. In informal conversation, the speakers do not plan the whole of the semantic content; the planning is short-term and depends largely on the input from other participants; the result is that less information is processed in each unit of intonation.

However, it must be noted that in both kinds of prayer and in public Bible reading, the intonation units are also short. The planning of the semantic content is already established in

Table 3.1

	Informal conversations	*Anecdote*	*News reading*	*Bible reading*	*Individual prayer*	*Prayer in unison*
Paragraphing		yes	yes	yes		
Punctuation groups	n/a	n/a	yes	yes	n/a	yes
Short units	yes			yes	yes	yes
Neutral tonicity	yes	yes	yes	yes	yes	yes
Tone variation	yes	yes	yes	yes		
High proportion of falls	yes					
High proportion of pretonic variation			yes	yes		
General high pitch				yes	yes	
Forte				yes	yes	
Lento				yes	yes	yes
Rhythmic				yes	yes	yes
Paralinguistic features	yes	yes		yes	yes	
Hesitation	yes	yes	rare	rare	yes	

scripted prayer and Bible reading, as it is in news reading. Why, then, short units? Firstly, there is a much slower pace of delivery; secondly, there is a much more rhythmic type of delivery, with each intonation unit consisting mainly of just two accents. The degree of semantic planning in unscripted prayer would be equivalent to that of anecdotes — the whole content is in view and interruptions are not expected. On the other hand, this kind of prayer is public, called out over a distance and is uttered more slowly. The extra energy involved in public speaking demands, in general, a slower pace of delivery. News reading is public in a different way since the distance between the speaker and the immediate receiver (i.e. the microphone) is small.

The degree of preparedness and semantic planning also correlates with the proportion of falling and rising tones. Rising tones in the anecdote and the news bulletin relate to incomplete or minor information; the sequences incomplete/completed information and major/minor information suggest a degree of planning, since the two items of the sequence must have been planned together. There is a very high proportion of rising tones in both the anecdote and the news bulletin, and a much lower proportion in the relatively unplanned, informal conversation.

The lack of paralinguistic effect in news reading and prayer in unison distinguish them both from the other genres; the attitudinal function of intonation is tightly constrained. That is not the case in conversation, anecdotes, public prayer and Bible reading. In the former two, there is the freest use of paralinguistic features, and in the latter two, the dominant features express fervency and deep feeling. Again, the lack of tone variation in the two forms of prayer is an interesting phenomenon. It is as if the informational function (major/minor information; incomplete/completed information) and the communicative function (statement, question, command, request, etc.) of intonation are both abrogated. Linguistic communication with God does not anticipate a linguistic response.

Thus the stylistic potential of intonation in these genres relates particularly to the degree of preparedness in semantic content (scripted/rehearsed v. unscripted/unrehearsed), to the audience (private v. public, or in the case of news reading, private for a public purpose), to the degree of formality (paralinguistic effect v. none) and to the peculiarly different linguistic situation in prayer.

Notes

1. Try an experiment: Welsh and English society and culture share a very wide range of genres — indeed, the very same events are often covered by both English-medium and Welsh-medium broadcasting. Listen to Radio Cymru and S4C (without vision) and try to identify different genres in their programmes. (If you can't tune in to those, or if you understand Welsh, try it on the radio with other European stations; Europe (Western, at least) shares a similar wide range of genres.)

2. The analysis of data reported here was completed before John-Lewis's research appeared in print, and was conceived as an extension of Crystal and Davy's work, rather than hers.

Transcription conventions

1. Each unit of intonation occupies a separate line of transcription. In those cases where a unit is too long for a single line, the continuation is indented.

2. The tonic/nuclear syllable is underlined.
3. The tone is marked by a system of accents ˎ, ˋ, ˏ, ˊ, ˇ, ˆ, -.
4. A noticeable step up or down in pitch is marked by ↑, ↓
5. Accented syllables are marked ˈ.
6. Pausing is marked: . (brief), -, –, — (relative degrees of length)
7. Simultaneous speech is either marked by brackets: (B: ...) within the speech of another, or by two sets of brackets, one below the other: (   )
(   )
8. Unidentifiable speech is marked by x; the number of x's indicate the number of syllables.
9. Additional prosodic and paralinguistic information is given in brackets to the right. Continuing features are indicated by a series of brackets down each line; *...* indicates the limit of a feature identified by * in the right-hand brackets.

References

Abercrombie, D. (1971) 'Some functions of silent stress'. In A.J. Aitken, A. McIntosh and H. Palsson (eds) *Edinburgh studies in English and Scots.* Harlow: Longman, pp. 147-56

Brazil, D., Coulthard, M., and Johns, C. (1980) *Discourse intonation and language teaching.* Harlow: Longman

Coulthard, R.M. and Brazil, D.C. (1979) *Exchange structure.* Discourse Analysis Monographs, 5, University of Birmingham

Crystal, D. (1969) *Prosodic systems and intonation in English.* Cambridge: Cambridge University Press

——— (1975) *The English tone of voice.* London: Edward Arnold

Crystal, D. and Davy, D. (1969) *Investigating English style.* Harlow: Longman

——— (1975) *Advanced conversational English.* London: Longman

Crystal, D. and Quirk, R. (1964) *Systems of prosodic and paralinguistic features in English.* The Hague: Mouton

Graddol, D. (1986) 'Discourse specific pitch behaviour'. In C. Johns-Lewis (ed.) *Intonation in discourse.* London: Croom Helm, pp. 221-37

Halliday, M.A.K. (1967) *Intonation and grammar in British English.* The Hague: Mouton

——— (1970) *A course in spoken English: intonation.* Oxford: Oxford University Press

Johns-Lewis, C. (1986a) 'Prosodic differentiation of discourse modes'. In C. Johns-Lewis, (ed.) *Intonation in discourse.* London: Croom Helm, pp. 199-219

——— (1986b) 'Conversation as listening material: the prosodic bases of difficulty'. In P. Meara (ed.) *Spoken language.* London: CILT, pp. 85-94

O'Connor J.D. and Arnold, G.F. (1973) *Intonation of colloquial English.* 2nd edn Harlow: Longman.

Pike, K.L. (1945) *The intonation of American English.* Ann Arbor: University of Michigan Press

Tench, P. (1976) 'Double ranks in a phonological hierarchy'. *Journal of Linguistics*, 12, pp. 1-20

4
D-J Talk

Martin Montgomery

> Radio . for me . is the opportunity . to really exploit . the listener's mind as much as possible to encourage them as much as possible . to join you . to make your job easier
> (Noel Edmonds)

This chapter[1,2] attempts to characterise some features of the discourse produced by D-Js between playing records on BBC Radio One. Because of legal restrictions on the amount of broadcast time that can be devoted purely to playing music, various strategies have evolved for 'filling the spaces' between records — including quizzes, phone-ins, interviews, jingles, and so on. None of these, of course, remains pure and simply a 'space-filler'; each performs a determinate range of functions such as including the audience or dramatising the station's broadcast identity, each having its own special interest. This paper, however, focuses on a particular sub-variety of talk between records on Radio One — that spoken by the D-J as extempore (and sometimes less than extempore) monologue. Monologues, where speech is produced and controlled exclusively by a single speaker — in this case the D-J, comprise a substantial component of talk on this channel, and yet they raise particular challenges both for the study of broadcast talk and for the study of talk in general.

Issues in the analysis of monologue

Monologue raises particular kinds of problems for both discourse analysis (DA) and for conversation analysis (CA) — two of the main traditions devoted to the study of talk. In each case the boundary between one turn and another provides a crucial point of entry to the analysis. In conversation analysis, for example, the orderliness of talk is actually displayed in the relation between one turn and another. As Sacks and Schegloff put it in an early but characteristic formulation:

> Our analysis has sought to explicate the ways in which the [conversational] materials are produced by members in orderly ways that exhibit their orderliness, have their orderliness appreciated and used, and have that appreciation *displayed and treated as the basis for subsequent action.* (Schegloff and Sacks 1973, p. 290; my italics)

Displays of orderliness are thus most transparent and evident precisely in the relationship between turns by successive speakers, of which adajcency pair formats and their attendant preference organisations provide the prime examples. There have, of course, within CA been some studies of the organisation of extended turns, but these have depended heavily upon the presence and placement of some kind of receipt token produced by co-participants — e.g. laughter in Sacks' account of a joke (Sacks 1974 and 1978), and applause in studies of speech making (see Atkinson and Heritage 1984, and Atkinson 1984). The situation within (interactional) discourse analysis is broadly similar (see, for example, Sinclair and Coulthard 1975, and Coulthard and Montgomery 1981), since there the identification of the boundaries of discourse units depends heavily on speaker change; and description of their function depends heavily on relations of mutual implication between a move by one speaker and the succeeding move by another.

It is in just these respects that the monologue character of D-J talk constitutes something of a challenge. Put quite baldly, since turn-taking is suspended for much of this talk, there is no possibility of using notions of turn transition to determine boundaries of units. Nor is it possible to use exchange of speaking turns as a guide to what aspects of an utterance might be doing: there is no second turn or answering move to help define how a first has been deployed. It is in these respects, therefore, that D-J monologue poses problems to general accounts of the operation of talk.

Issues in the study of language and the media

There is also, however, another tradition of work to which D-J talk poses something of a challenge; and this is work — especially from a basis within media studies — that treats language as crucially implicated in the production and circulation of ideologies (see, e.g., Trew 1978, Hartley 1982). Here, language is seen very much as a resource for making statements about the world, or shaping our experience of it, in ways which may be more or less true, more or less misleading. The process of representation is seen as heavily dependent on linguistic practice and at the same time never neutral or disinterested. Consequently, work within this tradition is most at ease when handling representations from the social, political or economic spheres — such as strikes, demonstrations, and forms of civil disorder, especially where these occur in the form of 'reportings' — TV news bulletins, newspaper headlines, and so on.

I have no wish to take issue with this kind of project; it provides an important critical instrument for unravelling one dimension of the textual practices of the media. But it does not provide an exhaustive and comprehensive account of those practices. D-J talk, for instance, sits uneasily within this kind of approach, precisely because so little of what it does is actually bound up with reportings. (Announcing future events is, if anything, more central.) Where events are reported, they are more likely to concern either station personnel or media personalities than the world of social, political and economic affairs. And even here such accounts tend towards parody:

Ex. 1 I can now exclusively reveal that this morning the keyboard player in Matt Bianco got up and was mugged by his rabbit.

In general, it may loosely be characterised as a discourse of the present and future tense rather than the past, projecting forwards rather than backwards in time. Where it is concerned with events, these tend to be drawn from the small change of the everyday lives of media personalities (including the station's own staff) or of the audience itself. Indeed it may be more accurate to characterise it as a discourse obssessively concerned with its own conditions of production and consumption. It tends to foreground the relationship of the D-J to the talk, and the relationship of the talk to the audience, rather than the relationship of the talk to 'the world at large'. Unlike news programmes, for example (where the role of the newscaster in particular and the broadcasting institution in general is often elided from the discourse so that its preferred mode is third person, past tense, with little direct reference to the audience), D-J talk operates much more frequently along the axis between first and second person, between *I* and *you*. In schematic terms, it tends to occupy the shaded rather than the unshaded areas of Figure 4.1.

Figure 4.1

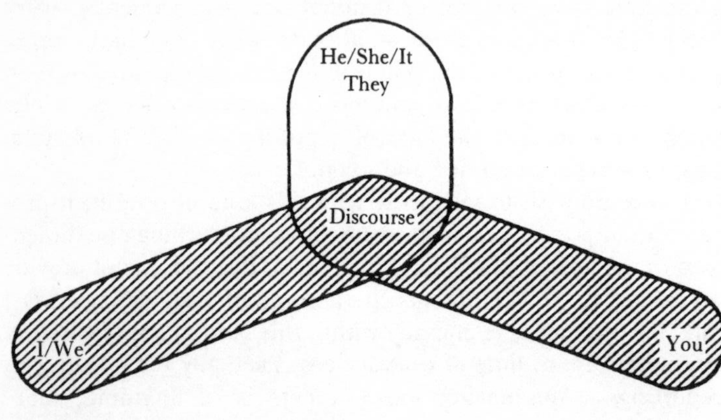

Work in language and ideology, in fact, tends to be more concerned with the unshaded areas of the diagram, rather than the shaded. Its primary emphasis is on representation — on the relationship of words to world; and, in keeping with this emphasis, it tends to focus on the ideational components of discourse, particularly those, such as transitivity, most concerned with the *representational* or *observer* function of language 'as the expression of the processes and other phenomena of the external world, including the world of the speaker's own consciousness' (Halliday 1978, p. 48). There is something of a consequent neglect of interpersonal dimensions of the discourse, precisely that dimension most foregrounded in D-J talk. D-J talk, therefore, can be seen as a kind of limitating case, both for work on language and ideology within media studies, and for the analysis of talk in general. It is in just these respects, however, that its interest lies. If we are to have a comprehensive account of the role of media discourse in the reproduction of social life, then it must be one that includes the interpersonal dimension of talk as well as its ideational aspects — the social-relational as well as the ideological (see Montgomery 1986, pp. 62-3, and Hartley and Montgomery 1985, pp. 233-5);

and yet, paradoxically, it must also be able to handle the monologic utterance as well as the dialogic. To this end I shall try to outline some further characteristics of D-J talk in fairly rudimentary terms but in more detail, and then return to these points in conclusion.

Foregrounding the interpersonal

Foregrounding the social-relational dimension of talk is done in a variety of ways. For one thing, the quality of the relationship between the D-J and the audience can become the explicit focus for comment, as in the following, where the exact degree of formality adopted by a correspondent is used as a topical resource:

Ex. 2 I(t)s now fourteen minutes to two: — on Gary's-Bit-in-the-Middle and hi to Bob Sproat in erm Charford Bromsgrove — in Worcestershire (0.5)
(Who) said HEY: — Howya doing
I love these informal ways that you're writing to me now forget the dears you know dears are a thing of the past I mean it's just so formal — just put HEY: howya doing or summin like that you know (0.3) especially when you're writing to your bank go: —
HEY: howya doing boss you know gonna give me the dosh or what (0.3) simple (0.3)
er anyway Bob says just thought I'd write

Modes of address: social deixis

More significantly, perhaps, it is a discourse that frequently addresses its audience in direct terms. This is done most commonly and basically by the use of the second person pronoun '*you*'. While this not uncommonly refers to the audience as a whole, its field of reference is frequently narrowed down by the use of an accompanying 'identifier'. Thus, *you* may be identified by name:

Ex. 3 *Alison and Liz* you are now official listeners for Ward Eighteen

Ex. 4 *Ian Schlesser* hello happy birthday to you

Ex. 5 you are now (*Marjorie*) the official Radio One listener for Princess Street

Ex. 6 Yeh okay then *Bob Sproat* in er Worcestershire er … T-shirt on the way to you

by region:

Ex. 7 coming up
some information for *anyone listening in Edinburgh*
because I need your legs your hands your arms
and the rest of you tomorrow morning in Princes Street
9.30
tell you about it after this

Ex. 8 and er I don't know about where you are probably
if you're nnn sort of in Scotland at the moment
you got some quite nice weather but in London
it's really dark and doomy

by occupation:

Ex. 9 and *anyone who's a typist in a hospital*
and has to read that writing by doctors
congratulations

by event:

Ex. 10 *if its your birthday today* then you share it
with all those people

Ex. 11 *if its your birthday* here's where the birthday file starts with
your Horriblescope coming up in just a second

by age, or other characteristics:

Ex. 12 now *if you're healthy and you're over ten years old*
(I emphasise that 'cos that one thing I don't wanna er anybody to do is to get sick as a result of doing it)

on Friday November fifteenth might be a nice idea
if you just didn't eat

and by star sign:

Ex. 13 *Hello Scorpio*
although it takes a considerable amount to realise a cycle
or a chapter in your life has already come to a close
you must now face up to situations as they really are

And, of course, these occur not only singly but also in combination. They range in specificity from the fairly general (by region) to the highly restrictive (by name). The field of reference of *you* is thereby constantly shifting. The item, indeed, lends itself to this kind of variation, but it is instructive to note that the audience, though directly addressed, is not identified in stable terms but in shifting ones.

Direct address may be made all the more so by combining it with greetings tokens, as in the following:

... *hi* to Bob Sproat ...
... Ian Schlesser *hello* happy birthday ...
... official listeners *hi* ...
... *hello* Scorpio ...

The most obvious everyday use of a greetings token is to open an encounter of a reciprocal kind under conditions where participants are mutually present to each other in some way. Given the monologic character of D-J talk and the absence of actual reciprocal co-presence between the D-J and audience, it is something of a curiosity that the talk should quite commonly be interspersed with such items. In effect, absent recipients are here treated *as if* co-present in a continual reopening of the discourse. By combining them with identifiers, then, new addressees are being continually greeted into the discourse, as if they were capable of responding. Even so, while the use of identifiers has the effect of singling out sometimes quite specific addressees, it is none the less important to note that they never exhaust the full range of the talk's intended recipients. The talk is always available for others than those directly named as addressees. There can at the very least be a kind of bifurcation between those whom the talk directly addresses and those for whom it is intended, as in the following:

Ex. 14 okay Fleet Street
(they're all awake now)
I have news of a rock star

The ostensible addressees of this overall fragment are print journalists (metonymically identified as *Fleet Street*). Interpolated within it, however, is a comment (*they're all awake now*) which refers to these same journalists in the third person, and thus redirects the utterance at that moment to alternative segments of the audience.

Another instance of bifurcation of addressee can be detected in the following example:

Ex. 15 Libra
(oi! Libra stop that it's dirty)
Libra let partners . . .

Initially in the fragment, *Libra* is used to identify a segment of the audience 'out there', viz. Librans — anyone with a birthdate between 23 September and 24 October. It is then used to address one, individual, uninhibited Libra fictionally constituted as co-present to the speaker — as somehow within the speaker's visual field (*stop that it's dirty*). Then the fragment switches back to address Librans in general. The discourse shifts its alignment with the audience by continually addressing different segments within it. Members of the audience are thereby cast and recast into different positions: any listener may vary from being addressed directly in particular terms, to being addressed directly in general terms, to being some kind of non-addressed recipient of the talk. Indeed, since any use of a specific identifier (e.g. *anyone listening in Edinburgh*) singles out a determinate sub-segment of the audience, it thereby has the simultaneous effect of excluding others, so that it is quite common for the audience to be in the position of overhearing recipient of a discourse that is being directly addressed to someone else.

Despite relegating substantial sections of the audience to the status of overhearers, it does not seem that the use of identifiers — even of the more specific kind — actually reduces the capacity of the discourse to engage the audience in general. On the contrary, the combination of identifiers with greetings and with direct address would seem to be part of the way in which a relatively dynamic relationship is achieved between the discourse and its broadcast audience.

Simulating co-presence: spatial deixis

Whereas deixis of a social or personal type is heavily implicated in the activity of direct address, deixis of a spatial kind is prominent in what might be considered an extension of direct address — namely, making reference to conditions of co-presence. The absence of co-presence may be made the explicit focus of attention, as in:

Ex. 16 I wish you could see this place
it's full of disk-jockeys getting themselves all made up
and looking nice

Or co-presence may expressly be simulated, as in:

Ex. 17 er got my pumpkin in the studio here
i(t)s really good (i) got a real pumpkin honestly
I mean you probably think that I'm ninety
but here hang on
let me just hold this up in front of the microphone
so you can see my pumpkin
can you see that
a real Halloween pumpkin

There are references here to the immediate environment of the speaker (*this* place, pumpkin *here*) as if the details were visible to the audience (can you see *that*). In one respect this may be seen as playing with properties of the medium — treating an exclusively aural medium as if it had a visual dimension. In other respects, however, it can be understood as a device for erasing a sense of distance between speaker and audience — assuming a common visual field thereby implies a form of co-presence.

'Response-demanding' utterances

D-J discourse is rarely if ever in some kind of seamless declarative mode. It is quite common for it to contain interrogatives and imperatives such as the following:

... how's Virgo doing? ...
... what's the gossip today? ...
... have you noticed the penny for the guy things are starting
to appear? ...
... can you see that? ...
... stop that it's dirty ...
... listen ...
... but here hang on ...

Since the normal operation of these as response-demanding utterances (either question or command) would involve (as in the case of greetings) some kind of reciprocal co-presence, these can be seen yet again as a further way of implicating the audience into the discourse. To treat the audience as if they were in visual contact with the speaker, available for greeting and capable of responding to the discourse, is to construct a sense of reciprocity even in its absence.

Expressives

In addition to direct address, spatial deixis, questions and commands, the interpersonal possibilities of discourse are further foregrounded by the common use of speech acts of the type described by Searle (1976) as expressives. Expressives are speech acts primarily devoted to expressing the psychological state of the speaker and the attitude or feelings of the speaker towards others. Paradigm cases would be 'congratulating', 'censuring', 'apologising' and 'criticising'. Instances of 'congratulating' in disk jockey talk are utterances such as the following:

Ex. 18 well done clever plugs

Ex. 19 anyone who's a typist in a hospital and has to read that
writing by doctors
congratulations

Despite the clear reference to *congratulation* in the latter example, it does in fact have much in common with the following instances of what might be called 'commiserations':

Ex. 20 Leo
(oh dear)
Uranus in Sagittarius
(please please)
is is urging and even compelling you to sever a few ties
(*oo that could be painful couldn't it*)
life each day as it comes must be faced

Ex. 21 a listener for ever is Marjorie Bunting
(*ah you must have suffered with that name*)
in Woodlands in Doncaster

Ex. 22 er Lisa
(heh)
Lisa Counter
(*poor dear with a name like that*)
er Lee Wildem

In contrast to congratulations and commiserations (which are positively predisposed towards their recipient) are a group of acts which might be classified (again loosely) as 'deprecations'. They are not as common as the other types of expressives and are as likely to be self-directed as other-directed (and see Coupland 1985 for the possible phonological consequences of self-deprecation, and other socio-psychological orientations upon D-J talk). The following is an example of self-deprecation:

Ex. 23 I think Andy by the way
who's on the road for the next two weeks
(and heheheh let's face it
you need a rest from me (sniffle))
er will be keeping the official listeners thing going

An example of other-deprecation would be:

Ex. 24 it's plagiarism fellas come on that's a two-day-old story

This latter example is addressed to Fleet Street journalists who ran, as if it were up-to-date, a story that had been carried two days previously by the disk-jockey.

Singling out a named individual for deprecation is rare, unless they can answer back in some way — so other disk-jockeys are fair game. When an ordinary member of the audience is deprecated, or subjected to a 'put-down', they are usually quickly given some kind of countervailing 'build-up'. Otherwise, deprecations are more likely to be directed at groups for whom clear stereotypes exist, operating along well-defined axes: journalists, doctors and traffic-wardens are more likely to be deprecated than nurses, firemen and typists.

Concluding remarks on foregrounding the interpersonal

The interpersonal dimension of the discourse is thus foregrounded in a variety of overlapping ways. The audience is presented with a range of participatory possibilities. It varies from being a direct addressee to being an overhearing recipient; and it is alternatively congratulated, deprecated and invited to respond. The alternatives may be represented schematically as follows:

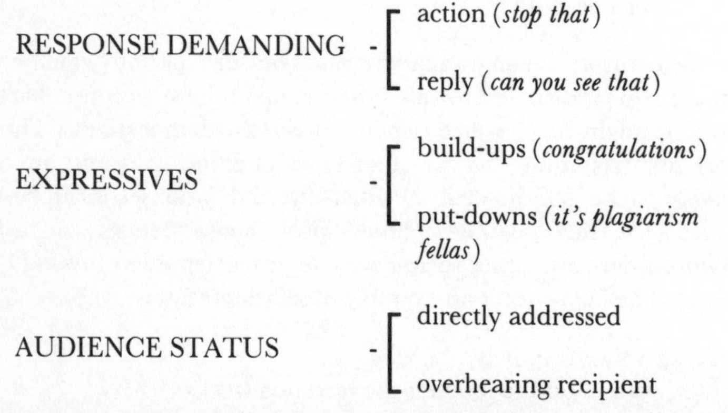

In this way it may be seen that the audience is not treated in D-J discourse as a homogeneous mass or as a unitary subject (it is not really the case, as is sometimes claimed, that D-Js speak to 'a single imaginary listener'). Programmers (and of course D-Js) are quite self-consciously aware of the audience. A recent interview with the Controller of Radio 1 confirmed the way in which they tend to see the listeners as a set of communities to be catered for:

> What the target audience is changes at different times of the day. For instance, in the early morning you've got whole

> families able to listen in until 9 to 9.30. Afterwards, Simon Bates is targeting to people listening in their own houses — that has to be generically housewives. At lunchtime Gary Davies can broaden it out a bit more as the youngsters can listen to it in their school break. (Johnny Beerling, Controller Radio 1, *Observer*, 23 February 1986)

These adjustments, however, are understood in terms of fairly large spans of broadcast time ('before breakfast', 'afternoons', 'evenings', etc.) into which different categories of music are placed. What remains unrecognised in comments such as the above is the ongoing character of the adjustments made to the alignment of the utterance. The participatory framework for the differing constituencies is constantly altering. The audience is treated on a moment-by-moment basis as a complex, internally differentiated phenomenon.

Speaker alignment

The relationship of the D-J to the talk is also one of variable alignment. On occasions, the D-J is animating pre-scripted materials such as 'Horriblescopes', letters from listeners (e.g. 'Our Tune'), interest items about celebrities, announcements about future events, and so on. Sometimes the D-J supplies his/her own scripted materials; sometimes, I presume, the production team has supplied them; and sometimes the audience itself has supplied them. And sometimes, of course, they are extemporising, playing off one or other of the different kinds of scripted materials. Building on Goffman (1981), we can summarise the possibilities as follows:

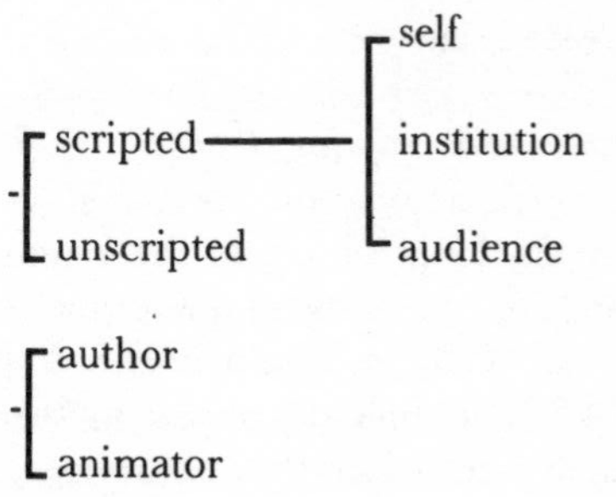

Hence, just as there is a variety of audience positions with respect to the discourse, there is also a variety of positions available to the D-J.

For the purposes of this chapter, I would wish to assert no more than that these possibilities seem to constitute an intuitively plausible set. I leave on one side the question of what specific textual criteria might be used to identify or recognise one alignment rather than another: for the moment, *what* precisely the specific alignment is at any time is possibly less interesting than the *way* in which such shifts occur. (Or maybe it is just easier to spot cases *where* shifts of alignment take place than it is to specify precisely between *what* it is that the shifts occur.)

Interpolation

The most obvious cases of shift involve instances of insertion. The following may be seen as paradigm cases:

Ex. 25 Leo
(*oh dear*)
Uranus in Sagittarius
(*please please*)
is is urging and even compelling you to sever a few ties
(*oo that could be painful couldn't it*)
life each day as it comes must be faced

Ex. 26 all the papers picked up the piece we ran two days ago on this programme
(*I noticed*)
that Bob Geldof
(*surprise surprise*)
will not be announced today as a winner or a loser of the Nobel Peace Prize

Both *please please* and *surprise surprise* may be considered as 'insertions' inasmuch as they do not actually constitute a component or element of the syntax of the clause that they occur within. They are not operating as any of the syntactic elements Subject, Predicator, Object, Complement, Adjunct, as may be seen in Figure 4.2. The difficulty of placing them syntactically is reinforced by their intonation: they occur as separate tone units,

Figure 4.2

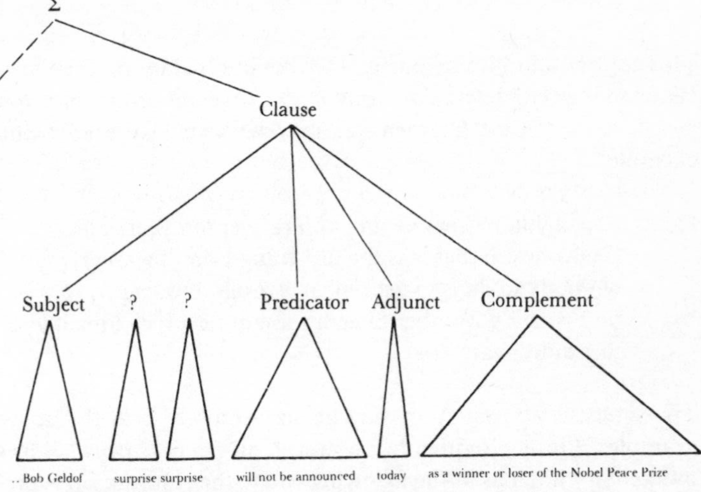

and this helps further to separate them off from the surrounding structure. Additionally, each of the paradigm cases consists of a repeated word; and this very reduplication supports the separation of the interpolated fragment from the surrounding discourse, by helping to limit or reduce possible structural ambiguities. Thus, the repetition of the item in *surprise surprise* undercuts a candidate interpretation at the moment of listening which brackets *surprise* and *Bob Geldof* together, hearing *surprise* as 'head' to a 'noun modifier' *Bob Geldof* by analogy with such structures as *strawberry surprise*, *peppermint delight*, etc. Similarly, the reduplication of *please please* helps to separate it off from *Uranus in Sagittarius*, thus excluding interpretations which mistake it for a structure analogous to *John, by the window please*, or *Ian, to bed please.*

Not only is the interpolated item not part of the syntax of the discourse into which it is inserted: it is also quite commonly the case that the syntax of the surrounding discourse resumes after the interpolation as a straight continuation of the point reached immediately prior to it. Thus:

Ex. 27 a listener for ever is Marjorie Bunting
(ah you must have suffered with that name)
in Woodlands in Doncaster

Ex. 28 you are now
(Marjorie)
the official Radio One listener for Princess Street

This continuation immediately after the interpolation of the syntax from immediately before it may occur even after the insertion of a fairly extensive fragment, as may be seen in the following example:

Ex. 29 now if you're healthy and you're over ten years old
(I emphasise that 'cos the one thing I don't wan er
anybody to do is to get sick as a result of doing it)
on Friday November fifteenth might be a nice idea if you
just didn't eat

The syntactic continuation may be very smooth as in the above example. Quite frequently, however, it may involve some momentary hitch as in the following where the resumption is prefaced by *er*:

Ex. 30 I think Andy by the way
who's on the road for the next two weeks
(and heheheh lets face it
you need a rest from me (sniffle))
er will be keeping the official listeners thing going

The momentary hitch in resumption may also be manifest in such features as reduplicating the initial item at resumption:

Ex. 31 Uranus in Sagittarius
(please please)
is is urging and even compelling you to sever a few ties

Whereas all the foregoing examples involve cases of insertion into an ongoing syntactic unit, it is also possible to find many cases where the insertion seems better understood as the interpolation of one kind of discourse into another. In such cases there is no syntactic link between the discourse after the interpolation and the discourse that preceded it. Instead, resumption of the discourse is marked by — for example — precise repetition at the onset of resumption of the lattermost item prior to interpolation. Thus:

Ex. 32 *Libra*
(oi! Libra stop that it's dirty)
Libra
let partners procrastinate and argue

or:

Ex. 33 er *Lisa*
(heh)
Lisa Counter
(poor dear with a name like that)

The onset of interpolation is sometimes associated with the occurrence of expressive particles such as laughter, *oh*, *ah*, *oo*, *oi*, as may be seen in the last two examples and in the following:

Ex. 34 Leo
(*oh* dear)
Uranus in Sagittarius

and:

Ex. 35 a listener for ever is Marjorie Bunting
(*ah* you must have suffered with that name)
in Woodlands in Doncaster

One curious feature about interpolations in general in D-J talk is their tendency to occur in the environment of a proper name. Clearly in some cases, this is mainly in order to comment semi-facetiously on some characteristics of the name itself, as may be seen in the last three examples above. But this is by no means the only use of interpolations in the environment of a proper name, as may be seen from the following:

Ex. 36 okay *Fleet Street*
(they're all awake now)
I have news of a rock star

or:

Ex. 37 *Bob Geldof*
(surprise surprise)
will not be announced today as a winner or a loser

Indeed, the particular operation of interpolation in these cases seems to cast light on their role in general, for they commonly seem to operate as a kind of reactive comment which may be oriented to the discourse itself:

Ex. 38 ... compelling you to sever a few ties
(*oo that could be painful couldn't it*)
life each day as it comes must be faced ...

or it may express an attitude to the topic of the discourse, as in the Bob Geldof example; it may express an attitude to the audience; it may even include some comment on the speaker himself, as in:

Ex. 39 I think Andy by the way
who's on the road for the next two weeks
(and heheheh let's face it you need a rest from me (sniffle))
er will be keeping the official listeners thing going

It is not merely the case, therefore, that the discourse constitutes differing recipient positions for its audience. As this section illustrates, it also varies quite significantly in the kinds of compositional orientation adopted by the D-J. This latter kind of variation is reflected in the frequent interpolations that register the shifting stance of the D-J to the talk. At the same time, then, as the discourse projects itself in relation to its audience in continuously changing ways, so also does it carry inscribed within itself differing compositional tendencies, switching to and fro between — for instance — the scripted and the extempore.

Conclusion

In manifold ways, therefore, the discourse eludes characterisation as some seamless, integrated unity authored by a stable subject to a homogeneous, unitary audience. Despite issuing — in its monologic aspects, at least — from a single vocal source, it is maintained as a thing of many 'voices' addressed to many 'audiences'. Even as monologue, it is an unstable mode. But its very instability lends to it a special kind of dynamic. On the one hand, it is continously inclusive with respect to diverse constituencies within the audience in a personalising, familiar, even intimate, manner. (Quiz-spots, readers' letters, phone-ins, and so on, may be seen as developments of this strategy.) On the other hand, although the discourse may constitute the audience in fragmentary terms, it also manages simultaneously to dramatise the relation of the audience to itself: as listeners we are made constantly aware of other (invisible) elements in the audience of which we form a part. At the same time, however, the discourse does not speak from a single authoritative position. It is sutured out of fragments which allow one 'voice' to put itself at a distance from, or call into question, the other 'voices' present in its composition.

This kind of fragmentariness constitutes an important dimension in the analysis of talk. For one thing, it provides in the phenomenon of interpolation a route into the isolation of unit boundaries in the compositional structure of monologue. Perhaps more significantly, however, it throws a more complex and variegated light on the study of language and ideology. Accounts of the ideological role of language in the media give particular attention to its representational function. And yet the process of constructing or reproducing a reality typically implies particular kinds of recipient or audience. Indeed, in D-J talk it is the construction and dramatisation of the respective relationships of D-J and audience to the discourse that receives particular emphasis. I would not wish to imply that D-J talk is thereby empty of ideology, but rather that a proper account of its role has inevitably to go beyond the study of its linguistic structures as a means of representation. What we need to recognise is that (to use Althusserian terms) the interpellated subject of ideology can be addressed in discursively discriminated ways. Indeed, if forms of direct and indirect address share some degree of correspondence with Althusserian notions of interpellation, then we can see in the particular instance of D-J talk how manifold are the forms that interpellation can take, in as much as D-J discourse differentially identifies its audience and prepares different positions from which to receive it. This conclusion, however, emerges — in part, at least — from close examination of the fine texture of the talk itself. The very details of the talk provide a crucial resource for more richly specific and empirically grounded, even if more densely complicated, accounts of the reproduction of social life by language in the media.

Notes

1. In preparing this paper I have benefited from discussions with, or written comments from, Bryan Crow, Paul Drew, Nigel Fabb, Alan Durant, Andrew Tolson and Paddy Scannell. I have not as yet been able to make the best use of their comments, so its faults remain very much my own.
2. This chapter appeared, in almost identical form and under the same title, in *Media, Culture and Society*, 8 (1986), pp. 421-40.

References

Atkinson, J.M. (1984) *Our master's voices*. London: Methuen

Atkinson, J.M. and Heritage, J. (eds) (1984) *Structures of social action*. Cambridge: Cambridge University Press

Bauman, R. and Scherzer, J. (eds) (1974) *Explorations in the ethnography of speaking*. Cambridge: Cambridge University Press

Coulthard, M. and Montgomery, M. (eds) (1981) *Studies in discourse analysis*. London: Routledge and Kegan Paul

Coupland, N. (1985) '"Hark, hark, the lark": social motivations for phonological style-shifting'. *Language and Communication*, 5, 3, pp. 153-71

Fowler, R., Kress, G., Hodge, R. and Trew, T. (1979) *Language and control*. London: Routledge & Kegan Paul

Goffman, E. (1981) *Forms of talk*. Oxford: Basil Blackwell

Halliday, M.A.K. (1978) *Language as social semiotic*. London: Edward Arnold

Hartley, J. (1982) *Understanding News*. London: Methuen

Hartley, J. and Montgomery, M. (1985) 'Representations and relations: ideology and power in press and TV news'. In T. Van Dijk (ed.) (1985) *Discourse and communication: new approaches to the analysis of mass media discourse and communication*. Berlin: Walter de Gruyter

Montgomery, M. (1986) *An introduction to language and society*. London: Methuen

Sacks, H. (1974) 'An analysis of the course of a joke's telling in conversation', In R. Bauman and J. Scherzer (eds) *Explorations in the ethnography of speaking*. Cambridge: Cambridge University Press

—— (1978) 'Some technical considerations of a dirty joke'. In J. Schenkein (ed.) *Studies in the organisation of conversational interaction*. New York: Academic Press

Schegloff, E. and Sacks, H. (1973) 'Opening up closings'. *Semiotica*, 8, pp. 289-327

Schenkein, J. (ed.) (1978) *Studies in the organisation of conversational interaction*. New York: Academic Press

Searle, J. (1978) *Speech acts*. Cambridge: Cambridge University Press

Sinclair, J. and Coulthard, M. (1975) *Towards an analysis of discourse*. Oxford: Oxford University Press

Trew, T. (1979) 'Theory at work'. In R. Fowler, G. Kress, R. Hodge and T. Trew, *Language and control*. London: Routledge & Kegan Paul

Van Dijk, T. (ed.) (1985) *Discourse and communication: new approaches to the analysis of mass media discourse and communication*. Berlin: Walter de Gruyter

5

Talking in Silence: Ministry in Quaker Meetings[1]

Alan Davies

Protestantism and the control of the WORD

> Any social setting [should] be viewed as self-organizing with respect to the intelligible character of its own appearances. Any setting organises its own activities to make its properties as an organized environment of practical activities, dateable, countable, recordable, tell-a-story-aboutable, analysable, in short accountable. (Garfinkel 1967, p. 33)

Speaking in a public setting, speaking in the sense of having the floor, represents control of a scarce resource. When that public setting is religious, control becomes more valued because the speaker is in some sense God's representative, i.e. priest. The distance between priest and non-priest is the scene of a major Reformation argument, and that distance is both symbolised and indicated by the relative claims for the legitimacy of religious speaking. The seventeenth-century mystic Jacob Boehme writes (*Apology to Tilken*, ii, p. 298) 'If I had no other book except the book which I myself am, I should have books enough. The entire Bible lies in me if I have Christ's spirit in me. What do I need of more books?' Radical Protestants agreed that there was no need for an interpreter: 'there is something nearer to us than Scriptures, to wit, the Word in the heart, from which all Scriptures come' (Penn 1726, p. 782). Since the Word was immanent it could literally mean all things to all men: 'the new way of Faith meant many and discordant things according to the preparation of the ears of those who heard. It spoke, as all Pentecosts do, to each man in his own tongue.' (Jones 1914, p. xxxix) Religion provides the channel between God and man. The more reformed the religion the more public participation there is in the speaking roles during the rituals. Christianity in its reformed mode insisted that Logos, the Word, was within, not out there. It was inevitable, therefore, that the extreme seventeenth-century radicalism of the Seekers and later the Quakers should lead both to extreme positions: first, that everyone equally may speak in worship (i.e. not only the priest or other official) and, second, that nobody (at all) really should speak because saying, speaking, is creaturely, it removes us from God, and because speaking usurps (or lays claim to) the hierarchical priestly separation.

As a result, Quakerism has always had a tension between speaking and silence (Bauman 1974, p. 145; Maltz 1985, p. 123). Speaking can be seen to be the prerogative of a special group, the 'ministers'. Walker (1952) argues that the authentic Quaker tradition is for a ministry (i.e. a separated group of ministers). He concludes: 'There has been a conception of the ministry present in Quakerism from the very beginning' (p. 271). Bauman (1974) sees it as a general problem and considers that there has always been a tension in Quakerism between silence (the 'norm' of the worship) and speech (or 'ministry'), that the tension between the natural and the spiritual faculties — between speaking and silence — is a necessary component of the Quaker experience. 'For the Quaker ministry ... the tension took on an added dimension because the role demanded that the minister depart from absolute silence by speaking in the very conduct of a fundamentally religious experience' (pp. 159-60).

In order to clarify the place of speaking and not speaking in the Quaker tradition, I provide a brief history of Quakerism and a longer discussion of the nature of worship within that history.

Quakerism

Quakerism grew out of several traditions, one the general Protestant Reformation and Puritan revival in Western Europe, another the semi-mystical beginning in Germany and the Low Countries in the fourteenth century among the 'Friends of God' who experimented with united silent worship and were influenced by Meister Eckhart. Later, in the fifteenth century, the movements (though hardly institutionalised) of the Familists (Family of Love) and the Seekers developed, the former in the Isle of Ely, the latter in various parts of England. William Penn described them:

> They sometimes met together, not formally to pray or preach, at appointed times and places, in their own wills, as in times past they were accustomed to do, but waited together in silence and as anything rose in any one of their minds that they thought favoured a divine spring, so they sometimes spoke. (Penn 1694)

The leaders of the early Quakers, the first Publishers of Truth, as they were later called, were convinced of their own direct revelation; they had experience of mystical revelation themselves and they sought ways of tapping this resource and making it known to others. The best-known is George Fox, the founder (or perhaps a founder) of Quakerism, certainly the one who made the organisation of the Society of Friends of Truth (Society of Friends or Quakers) possible and still today very much his creation.

Here is a typical description of his experience:

> When all my hopes in men were gone so that I had nothing outwardly to help me, nor could tell what to do, then, O then, I heard a voice which said, 'There is one, even Christ Jesus that can speak to thy condition', and when I heard it my heart did leap for joy. I knew experimentally that Jesus Christ enlightens, gives grace and faith and power. I now knew God by revelation, as He who hath the key did open. (Fox 1694)

The key word here is *experimentally* or as we might say, experientially, i.e. in the light of one's own experience. Quakerism grew up as an assertion of the centrality of individual experience in the religious life and as continuing evidence of the validity of that experience. It works, was what the Seekers and later the Quakers were saying and what they still say.

We may feel that in their emphasis on experience and on the common interpretation of that experience by one another, Quakers were primitive ethnomethodologists of a kind, recognising and interpreting the rules of experience in the process of that experience. Of course, their emphasis on individual experience had its own built-in heresy in that there seemed no way to prove the value of priority of anyone's experience, a heresy that the greatest of the Quaker preachers, James Nayler, fell victim to in 1655 in his triumphal entry into Bristol, certain of his reincarnation as a second Christ. Nayler was disowned and Fox provided, through his hierarchical organisation of the meetings of the Society, that individual experience would always in the future be subject to group doubt and group judgement. Again, the intuition of individual members is only meaningful if it relates to a knowledge shared by other members, a good ethnomethodological precept. In rejecting all outward forms and ceremonies early Quakers ran the risk (not always avoided, as with Nayler) of extreme nativism or naturalism. Quakerism was not anarchism and it required the sadness and the shock of Nayler's disgrace to make it come to terms with the necessary measures taken.

The full title of Quakerism is the Religious Society of Friends. As with other religious bodies, worship is at its heart and the vehicle for worship is the religious church service known as the Meeting for Worship. As present (1986) there are several traditions of Quakerism across the world in the autonomous Yearly Meetings, in some cases, as in the USA, a pastoral ministry replacing the British tradition of the priesthood of all believers; but even the pastoral tradition retains something of the unprogrammed nature of the fully silent meetings, with short periods given over to silence. It is, of course, the silent meeting that is firmly associated with Quakers. Charles Lamb wrote, 'although frequently the meeting is broken up without a word having been spoken, ... the mind has been fed. You go away with a sermon not made with hands ... you have bathed in silence' (Lamb 1800). But it is not clear that the silent meeting was a deliberate policy; indeed it had been suggested that Quakers stumbled upon it by accident (in that they were *waiting* on God) and that it is this accident that has really been the only Quaker contribution to worship; i.e. that silence is creative in worship; all else including the belief of that of God in everyone is either normal Christianity or radical puritanism. Certainly silence was at first deeply disturbing and could be used as the engine of revivalism (as no doubt it is when used by charismatic movements today).

One account describes the visit of Thomas Parrish to Leominster in 1655:

> And after some time he spoke 'Keep to the Lord's watch'. These words being spoke in the power of God had its oper-

> ation upon all or most of the Meeting so that they felt some great dread or fear upon their spirits ... So after a little time he spoke again saying 'What I say unto you, I say unto all, Watch', then was silent again. (Penny 1907)

And so on. One of the most powerful accounts is that of Richard Davies, a Welsh hatter, who went first to a Quaker meeting in Shrewsbury in 1657. The meeting though 'silent from word' was, said Davies,

> as a hammer and a fire, it was sharper than any two-edged sword, it pierced through our inward parts, it melted and brought us into tears that there was scarcely a dry eye among us, the Lord's blessed power over-shadowed our meeting and I could have said that God alone was master of that assembly. (Davies 1771, p. 34)

Formalism and spontaneity, tradition and experience vie with one another in religion. Both are necessary but the very nature of custom and the social process is to conventionalise. Quaker Meetings for Worship are not always, not often, spontaneous happenings — but let me compare the ideal and the real views of the Meeting for Worship.

The ideal is that the Meeting for Worship begins as soon as one member is present in the Meeting House, preferably a hollow square arrangement. As other members join in, the Meeting for Worship gradually centres down, becomes a 'gathered' meeting, and out of the deep silence will eventually come, in spoken contributions, examples of ministry which will be 'in the life', i.e. relevant to that occasion, that meeting, and will speak to the condition of all present. The ministry may be prayer or invocation but will always arise out of the first-hand experience of the speakers. Thus the Meeting worships because it has opened itself to God, the speakers are transmitters of God's voice. In this view the Meeting for Worship is an end in itself, a poetic mystic experience that does not lead back into everyday life.

The real view of the Meeting for Worship is that the silence is not always quiet, that the meeting is not always gathered, i.e. become a unity, that for at least part of the meeting there may be small children present who are not primarily interested in silence, that members may not distinguish deep thought from light sleep, that the spoken ministry can be irrelevant to many, sometimes trivial, often repetitive because of the tendency of the same members to minister, and occasionally quite inappropriate, so often beginning in music hall fashion — 'As I was on my way to Meeting this morning '..., or offensive — as when one member will address another directly. And when it is acceptable, it is often repetitive or narrow. So often the same key words and references are used, triggering off stock responses and indicating the ritual foundation underlying all religious observance. And yet all this may be 'in the life'; though what is said may not speak to *my* condition, it may meet someone else's, and though the freedom to minister will sometimes lead to abuse, it is a freedom that is of too great value to limit, and rarely if ever leads into anarchy — it is the freedom of the public meeting at which all may speak. And here we must distinguish the two senses of 'member', the member of that Meeting for Worship, i.e. all present, and the member of the Society of Friends, i.e. those who have actually applied for membership, been accepted and are listed as members. At all Meetings for Worship it is members in the first sense, i.e. the *more* inclusive sense, who may speak.

And in spite of the noise of reality, the realistic view of the Meeting for Worship says that the end of the Meeting for Worship is always served: its purpose is to reflect life and to relate back to life, 'to make you', as William Penn said, 'fit for His service'. The Meeting for Worship is not an end in itself, but a recharge so that all life can be lived as worship. It brings members together in a context where all (and note the shaky 'member' distinction here) can agree that the conditions are present for a holy dialogue. And because of the insistence that God is in everyone, there is nothing special about who are in the Meeting and where it is taking place; the only thing special is the readiness for dialogue in a setting of silence. From being an accident, the silence has become a discipline that makes worship possible — in Barclay's words 'though there be not a word spoken yet is the true spiritual worship performed, and our souls have been greatly edified and refreshed, and our hearts wonderfully overcome with the secret sense of God's power and Spirit which without words have been ministered from one vessel to another' (Barclay 1678, p. XI.6).

My quotations have all been from the seventeenth century. Here are two moden ones, if only to show that the tradition continues unchanged. The first is Hubbard (1974):

> Now there is no programme at all for a Quaker Meeting and so there is no guarantee that anything at all will happen. What usually happens is that the silence remains unbroken for some 15 or 20 minutes. Then someone — anyone, for this is unarranged and unpremeditated — stands and speaks for a few minutes and then sits down. The silence continues. After another 10 minutes or so another person may stand and speak and so on. An hour's Meeting without any ministry is unusual, but not unknown; an hour's Meeting in which more than about six people offer ministry for a total time of more than 15 minutes is also unusual but not unknown. (p. 189)

The second is by Gorman (1973), who makes some suggestions about the 'normal' pattern of a Meeting for Worship and then goes on about the

> problem of writing about the content and timing of spoken contributions in a Meeting for Worship. It is so easy to fall into the trap of appearing to suggest that there is a proper sequence which every Meeting should follow. Because of the essential spontaneity of Quaker worship there can be no such sequence. (p. 106)

The Religious Society of Friends has always given a high profile to ministry. Up till 1924, London Yearly Meetings recognised 'public Friends' or 'Recorded Ministers', i.e. Quakers who were recognised as having a facility for speaking in the ministry. But after that date the practice was discontinued, underlining the recognition by modern Quakerism of the importance of spoken contributions and the importance of encouraging as many members as possible to contribute. The 'Advices', a set of recommendations to members, say

> Remember that to everyone is given a share of responsibility for the Meeting for Worship whether the service be in silence or through the spoken word. Do not assume that vocal ministry is never to be your part. If the call to speak comes, do not let the sense of your own unworthiness, or the fear of being unable to find the right words, prevent you from being obedient to the teaching of the Spirit ... Pray that your ministry may rise from the place of deep experi-

> ence, and that you may be restrained from unnecessary and superficial words Faithfulness and a sincerity in speaking, even very briefly, may open the way to fuller ministry from others. Try to speak audibly and distinctly, with sensitivity to the needs of your fellow worshippers. Wait to be sure of the right moment for giving the message. Beware of making additions towards the end of a Meeting when it was well left before ... Receive the ministry of others in a tender and understanding spirit and avoid hurtful criticism ... remembering that ministry which to one may seem to have little value, to another may be a direct word from God. (Advices 1964)

L.V. Hodgkin (1919) points to the greater danger of over-speaking, greater than over-silence: 'each Friend who feels called upon to rise and deliver a lengthy discourse might question himself — or herself — most searchingly, as to whether the message could not be more lastingly given in the fewest possible words or even through his or her personality alone, in entire and trustful silence' (pp. 77-8).

Of course, as Hubbard wryly suggests, there is lots of material waiting to be incorporated in that to-be-written 'Objections to Quaker Belief', objections from the orthodox that a priest/minister is needed to distinguish God's voice and the devil's, from the man in the street that it is all imagination anyway, and from the psychologist that it is all the subconscious. But these objections are irrelevant, irrelevant to Quakers who have always avoided talking *about* belief, avoided theology and talk about religion (notions to Quakers are what theory may be to ethnomethodologists) because belief is second hand, secondary to experience. Irrelevant too to us because we are not in this discussion concerned with whether Quakerism is true or right, only or partially, but only with what its members do; real or fiction, the discourse of the Meeting for Worship is something we can observe.

Hubbard (1974) continues about his own handling of the silence:

> To seek for the true silence, in which God may be heard, is an intensely personal but not a lonely quest. One is not conscious in the usual sense of other people in Meeting. Their breathing, the odd cough, the rustling in a handbag

> for a handkerchief, the turning of the pages of a book; these are not noises which disturb. Somehow, as the Meeting centres down, the silence becomes more palpable, so that noises make little impact on it. It is stronger than they are ... Most of us are agreed that the spoken contribution comes best from resistance overcome; one tries to stay silent but fails. (p. 196)

He continues that there is nothing wrong about bringing a text to read as long as one waits for the right moment to read it, a moment which, of course, may not come.

> Sitting quietly, working inwardly to find the centre, the stillness, listening for the voice of God, which may bring a concept into your consciousness either as a thought, a word or a visual symbol, one does not want to speak. Then the idea comes and grows. One has to say something, it must be said. One stands and starts talking. The words seem to arrange themselves; not me, but God in me for a brief while. Then suddenly the idea is expressed, the words stop, one becomes conscious of oneself again and sits down. (pp. 196-7)

Hubbard considers that there is a 'logical and associative' link in the sequence of contributions to ministry, and Gorman agrees: 'as a general rule ... it is usually helpful if later ministry can build on and develop what has come earlier ... if the spoken contributions tend to drift aimlessly over a variety of unconnected topics, then the meeting has not been truly gathered even if each may have been good in itself' (p. 12).

Hubbard has strong feelings against the activity we are presently engaged in: 'it would be wrong to set down a record from an actual Meeting ... Ministry is of God, it exists in its proper context, of words before and after and of ready hearers, and should not be transplanted out of that context' (pp. 199-200). I have given prominence to Hubbard because he seeks Quakerism as a learner, having become convinced (a 'convinced' Friend is one who joins the Society as an adult) in middle age; he is thus able to objectify his experience and the Society of Friends itself in a satisfying, contemporary and accessible way. Two further points from his account are of help here.

First he mentions that phenomenon of ministry in which one

person's perplexity is answered by another's ministry. Certainly this phenomenon is well attested. The second is the lack of distinction between speech and non-speech. 'It is the essence of the Meeting for Worship that the distinction between spoken ministry and silence is not significant, that the two elements are understood as variations on the same theme, so that we can speak of silent ministry' (pp. 200-1).

Gorman (1973) disputes the significance of physical characteristics such as trepidation, pounding of the heart as being the necessary sign for when to break silence. They can, he argues, be all too often self-induced. 'The first Quakers', he points out, 'did not see in this a call to speak, but rather the response to the awesome presence of God' (p. 117).

In all religion language acts as a control and operates in favour of tradition and conservatism — e.g. the static language situation in regard to Arabic in Islam, the continuing explications of the Vedar, the religious dismay over the final vernacularisation of the Roman Catholic Church — and the arguments over the Anglican Prayer Book (Doody 1980). Religion is linguistically ritualised and for many believers, since God does not change, therefore the language that interprets him must not change. The universality of the Church is curiously one of space and not time in that past changes are ignored; instead the emphasis is on a homogenised present.

Silence and speaking

'Quaker silence', says Evelyn Underhill (1936, pp. 307–8),

> goes beyond all expressive worship to that which inspires it, and makes a direct metaphysical claim to communion with God in the inner deeps. The primitive, charismatic strain in New Testament religion, its realistic dependence on the 'Leadings of the spirit' is here brought back into the foreground and set over against all rites and sacraments as the very essence of the Christian worshipping life . . . These peculiarities set Quaker worship apart from all other types of Christian cults, Catholic or Protestant . . . Here the mystical and inspirational element in Christianity which had faded out of the public life of the Church, . . . is powerfully reasserted. Historically, Quakerism may be regarded as the mystical wing of the Puritan movement.

If silence is the unmarked form, the norm, why must it ever be broken? If God speaks in the silence to every worshipper, why is ministry ever necessary? As we have seen, the point of ministry is that it should always be the particular speaking for the general. And Steere (1972) reminds us of the social dynamism of ministry: however desirable full silence may be, it is quite literally death to a Meeting:

> Meetings that have turned completely silent almost inevitably wither away. Something is missing in the corporate relationship ... an occasional completely silent Meeting may ... be one in which great things have happened within the hearts of those who attended. But the practical experience of the Society of Friends, historically, knows the fate of a Meeting that is habitually mute. (p. 6)

Steere also points to some of the humdrum problems over speaking: too frequent (or too long) from the same member, or too personal. But he also points out that a strong Meeting can absorb irrelevancies and take them down into the silence. And he reminds us of the traditional manner of recognising that one's ministry is appropriate, that one should give it because it is 'in right ordering'.

Kelly (1966) gives supreme value to silence. 'Outwardly, all silences seem alike, as all minutes are alike by the clock. But inwardly the Divine Leader of Worship directs us through progressive unfoldings of ministrations and may, in the silence, bring an inward climax which is as definite as the climax of the Mass when the Host is elevated in adoration' (p. 84). He continues:

> Brevity, earnestness, sincerity — and frequently a lack of polish — characterise the best Quaker speaking. The words should rise like a shaggy crag, upthrust from the surface of silence, under the pressure of river power and yearning, contrition and wonder. But on the other hand the words should not rise *up* like a shaggy crag. They should not break the silence but continue it. For the Divine Life who was ministering through the medium of silence is the same life as is now ministering through words. And when such words are truly spoken 'in the life', then when such words cease, the *uninterrupted* silence and worship continue: for silence and words have been of one texture, one piece. Second and

> third speakers only continue the enhancement of the moving Presence, until a climax is reached, and the discerning head of the Meeting knows when to break it. (pp. 85-6)

Trueblood (1960) appears to prefer an American tradition of pastoral Meetings, each with its own 'minister'. The reason he gives is his abhorrence of a general ministry:

> Many of us groan inwardly when, in such a Meeting, we hear the familiar opening reference 'As I looked out of the car window on the way to meeting' ... this highly personalised approach is often superficial and it is superficial because it does not rest on any serious and sustained effort. It is shoddy because it is fundamentally easy.

Beamish (1967) reminds us there was a popular anti-intellectual strain in early Quakerism; 'it came to be understood that no preaching or public prayer could be undertaken without a moving of the Spirit, which was undeniably supernatural and with which any attempt to study a subject must inevitably interfere'.

Edward Grubb, discussing modulation in the delivery of the message, becomes comically prescriptive:

> the practice of sing-song in Quaker ministry is happily almost extinct and it will be well to guard against any tendency to fall into it. Have you ever noticed [*sic!*] that the various dialects that distinguish different parts of our islands are very largely due to differences of modulation. Be on your guard here: some dialects are actually pleasing to the ear, but others are mere 'graceless modes of noise-making'. If you come from the North of Ireland, please pay special heed [*sic!*]. (n.d., pp. 6-7)

And Zielinski (1975) reminds us that silence is a partner in a Meeting for Worship, along with, second, 'communion, a spiritual unity of the whole Meeting', and third, the message. 'Provided that the two other factors, silence and communion, are present there is no need to control or evaluate the content of a message. It is a part of the collective spiritual experience.'

This collective spiritual experience seems to mean in more contemporary terms having a channel open to God, or being on line to God. What is said is less important than the fact that communication is taking place. For it has always been clear among Quakers that the message in a Meeting for Worship comes from God (or is indeed God 'speaking'). Early Quakerism saw the role of the speaker as entirely passive, as a conduit or mouthpiece or 'oracle' for God the speaker. A *motion* was the term used for the impulse to the act of speaking; an *opening* for the clearing of the channel for God's words to be spoken forth (Bauman 1974). 'I was taught to watch the pure opening and to take heed lest, while I was standing to speak, my own will should get uppermost, and cause me to utter words from worldly wisdom and depart from the channel of true Gospel Ministry' (Woolman 1910, p. 25).

The relation between silence and speaking also has a linguistic commentary. Tannen and Saville-Troike (1985) present a range of interactions:

> at one pole are the functions of pausing in cognitive processes, impression formation, and as part of communicative style partly responsible for cultural stereotyping, at the other pole are the functions of silence as the background against which talk has meaning, or as the nonverbal activity which structures interaction. Furthermore, we see that silence can itself be a communicative device in interaction; either obstructor or facilitator of divine inspiration; and a means of emotion management and display. (pp. xvii, xviii)

Maltz (1985) compares the role of silence in Pentecostal and Quaker worship. Noisiness is, he says, the defining characteristic of Pentecostal worship. 'There is no such thing as a silent Pentecostal' (p. 135). He refers to comments in Samarin (1973) that what distinguishes one variety of Protestantism from another is mainly different rules for the use of speech in religious contexts (p. 118). In other words, as we have already seen, changes in modes of worship are primarily changes in conceptions of when and where speech and silence are appropriate, what kind of speech acts are appropriate in what contexts, who should speak when and who should remain silent. Quakerism and Pentecostalism thus appear as different solutions to the same problem, that of the relation between speaking and God's word and the Holy Spirit, or between speaker and hearer. 'In general', Maltz says,

> Quakers look inward while Pentecostals look outward. Quakers see the spirit within each individual, they contrast an inner spiritual self with an outer actual one; they stress the silent wait for inspiration over the inspired utterances which result; and they have an ambivalence about the preaching necessary to evangelize among outsiders. (p. 134)

Pentecostals and Quakers have different methods for reaching the same solution, that of waiting on the Holy Spirit, Pentecostals through inspired noisiness, Quakers through silent waiting. Both have the same dilemma, how to distinguish the methods they use from human self-indulgence.

Bauman (1974) takes up the recurring theme of the legitimacy of religious speaking among early Quakers. 'The point at issue', he says, 'between the Quaker ministers and their priestly counterparts was fundamentally one of the legitimacy of religious *speaking* and the source of legitimate religious words' (p. 35). Bauman makes it clear that what is at issue is again not the content of the message but the control of the channel.

> [George] Fox's extensive resort to parallelistic constructions and to repetitions and recombinations of key words and phrases (power, life, gospel, order, need, government) are all devices that enhance fluency in spontaneous oral composition as demonstrated in research on the formal devices that make possible the improvisational composition of oral poetry in the act of performance by contrast with the performance of ready-made oral forms. (Bauman 1974, pp. 76-7)

Silence and speaking for Quakerism are in tension, then. Both are necessary but the unmarked form is always silence and therefore to speak is an effort (hence perhaps the attested psychological stress and physical strain that precede it). Speaking arises out of silence and is a means to the end of even deeper silence. The holding of a Meeting for Worship as a felicitous speech event requires that participants maintain this delicate balance between speaking and silence.

In the second half of this chapter I address the question of the Meeting for Worship as a language learning activity. In particular, I will ask how it is that members learn to act as members and demonstrate in their language performance, both in speaking and in being silent, that they are indeed members.

Learning the language of ministry

In terms of *language learning*, three models suggest themselves as descriptions of a Quaker Meeting for Worship (M/W): (1) the conversation; (2) formal settings; (3) continuing states of incipient talk. Let us examine each in turn. My argument will be that the M/W approximates most closely to the third, the continuing state of incipient talk, but that it also borrows from the other two models; that, in fact, it is *sui generis*, a unique case.

First, conversation. The 'rules' usually suggested for informal conversational settings are: 'Conversation is verbal and non-verbal interactivity realised by reciprocal behaviour between at least two people who alternate in the role of addresser and addressee' (Myers, 1979, p. 2). The two basic features of conversation are 'at least and no more than one party speaks at a time in a single conversation, and speaker change recurs ... it is within any current utterance that possible next speaker selection is accomplished ... we shall speak of this as the transition relevance of possible utterance completion' (Schegloff and Sacks, in Turner 1974, p. 236). Add to this the unifunctional nature of many of the performatives used in ministry such that many may be treated as reports or descriptions, then it becomes unclear to what extent the Meeting for Worship is a conversation. We cannot speak of alternate addresser/addressee, nor of distribution of speaker's rights — unless each item of ministry is treated as a single utterance in terms of challenge and response. That is quite unacceptable on Quaker grounds — a Meeting for Worship is *not* a debate. Sequential properties, yes; ministry does, it is claimed, follow some sequence (and it would be odd if it didn't). But ministry does not seem to allow for turn-taking in the formal sense of built-in transition probabilities.

Second, formal settings. I quote from Edmundson (1981 p. 8):

> In larger gatherings in which it is desired that purposeful talk take place, there are often special conventions which hold for organisational turntaking. It is clear that different turn-taking conventions hold for different settings — e.g. in the classroom, the formal debate, the public lecture. Often in such formalised settings there is one participant who has

> a privileged role position, whereby he controls turn-assignment at the conventionally determined transition points. He has, for example, authority as teacher, Speaker (in the House of Commons), judge (in a court of law), or chairperson. Such special conventions are relatively easily observed and described.

Clearly this cannot directly apply to the M/W since there is no 'one participant who has a privileged role position, whereby he controls turn-assignment', nor indeed are there 'conventionally determined transition points'. At the same time, the Meeting for Worship *is* a formal setting, a larger gathering in which it is desired that purposeful talk take place. It could perhaps be maintained that the group itself is doing being its own privileged role position in the same sense as in rejecting a separate and specialised priesthood — what is manifested in its place is the priesthood of all believers. None the less, in spite of the reality of group control — which is often spoken of as existing in the so-called 'gathered Meeting' — allocation of turn-taking remains inexplicit.

Third, the continuing state of incipient talk. Goffman and others have pointed out that speech is not necessarily central to an event, that there are 'other arrangements' in which, for example, people who are on familiar terms with one another may be engaged together in an ongoing activity, and while so engaged occasionally speak aloud. Examples suggested (e.g. by Schegloff and Sacks in Turner 1974) are

> members of a household in their living room, employees who share an office, passengers together in an automobile ... In such circumstances, there can be lapses of the operation of what we earlier called the basic features: for example, there can be silence after a speaker's utterance which is neither an attributable silence, nor a termination, which is seen as neither the suspension nor the violation of the basic features. These are adjournments and seem to be done in a different manner from closings. Perhaps in such a continuing state of incipient talk need not begin new segments of conversation with exchanges of greetings, need not close segments with closing sections and terminal exchanges. (Turner 1974, p. 262)

This is more like the Meeting for Worship, but there remain inadequacies: silence after a speaker's utterance is needed as termination in a meeting for Worship, and while silence is an adjournment, the attribution (or non-attribution) of exchanges of greetings as openings are just not relevant; no piece of ministry begins with greetings, not even the first, and there are no adjacency pairs and therefore again the notion of terminal exchange does not appear to be relevant.

What is, however, crucial to the categorisation of a Meeting for Worship as a continuing state of incipient talk is precisely — as Goffman says — that speech is not central to the event: what is central is silence, or, to be more precise, what is claimed to be central is 'celebration', 'baptism' or worship. That is what the Meeting for Worship is for, the silence is the ground on which worship becomes possible and the speech is in some sense heard silence, meditation breaking through, making itself heard.

The Quaker (theological) view is that ministry/speaking reveals and at the same time deepens the silence by breaking it. Like buoys in a river channel, night lights or stars across a wide and dark sky, speaking in a Meeting for Worship is the negative correlative of what it illuminates. Perhaps for that reason *what* is said in a Meeting for Worship is not often remembered well, it is socially phatic and religiously ritualistic. And yet this is still not an adequate account. What is said does have content, what is developed in a M/W does have themes, the speaking is (often) focused in a way that family talk in the living room, colleagues' talk in an office, passenger talk in a car is not.

So, what sort of speech event is the M/W — or to put it another way, what is it that members know, how do they exhibit their competence, in what sense can they be said to have accomplished language learning? I will consider this question under the five headings of religious language, content, cohesion, context and pausing. I will again argue for the centrality to the speech event of silence, of members being silent, and I will add a comment on norms and prescriptions.

Data of fifteen meetings

To illustrate my argument, I want to look at some data of ministry. First, the statistics. About 60 different Meetings were approached with the request to allow me to make an audio recording of the Meeting for Worship. In the event, 15 meetings agreed to permit recording and in due course I visited the majority (two were recorded by associates) as set out below. The 'willingness' response of *c.* 25 per cent was disappointing. The reasons given by Meetings for non-participation were varied, but two reasons recurred: first, that the M/W is an intimate, personal experience which is easily disturbed by an intruder, especially if he is deliberately 'observing'; second, that an audio recording does not capture the 'whole' of the religious experience. While sympathising with these views, I noted wryly that they are typical of objections to social science investigators and observers and lead, of course, to the unsolvable 'observer's paradox', viz. how do I know that the Meetings for Worship I have taped are 'natural', 'normal' or 'representative'? The answer of course is that I don't: what I do is to take up the 'common sense' position that on the basis of my own previous experience of Meetings for Worship they are not untypical; and, further, note that participants in the Meetings for Worship I did record commented that those Meetings for Worship occasions were no different from other non-observed M/W occasions.

In view of the unease expressed in so many Meetings about tape recording and the likely distraction from worship caused by wired recording apparatus, equipment was kept to a bare minimum: basically one BASF cassette recorder and a directional microphone. The cassette player is battery-operated and so it was possible to give the recording equipment a very low profile. The cassettes were extended play (e.g. TDK AD 120).

The 15 tapes were transcribed by hand, with careful timing notation and attention to speech features. Inevitably, there are certain words and phrases that cannot be distinguished however often the tape is repeated. It is possible that more accurate recording procedures would have produced a better, more accurate quality of sound recordings.

A quantitative overview reveals the following:

1. Fifteen Meetings for Worship were audio recorded: five in Scotland, five in England, three in the USA and two in Ireland. Each Meeting for Worship lasted one hour. (Hereafter data are quoted for only 14 meetings since one in England was a special half-hour Meeting for Worship.)
2. The total number of speakers in the 14 Meetings was 72; a

mean average of 5.1 per Meeting occasion with a range from four to seven.

3. The total amount of speaking time in the 14 Meetings: 197.25 minutes: a mean average of 14 minutes of spoken 'ministry' (and 46 minutes of silence) per Meeting occasion. The range of filled time: 20.25–7.5 minutes.

4. The mean average length of each piece of ministry or spoken contribution was 2.75 minutes; a range of 0.25–10.25 minutes. Of the spoken contributions 70 per cent were three minutes or less.

5. Of the 72 spoken contributions, 41 were by men, 31 by women.

6. Most Meeting occasions started ministry in the first 15 minutes but late on in that period. There was great variability in the timings of the last spoken contribution. There was some tendency for Meeting occasions with late first ministry also to have late final ministry.

Meeting for Worship no. 7: spoken ministry

I choose as illustration Meeting no. 7 and present below the complete texts of the six speakers on this occasion (A-F); thereafter, in abbeviated note form some of the key words and phrases used by the six speakers. In so far as certain styles of ministry are valued, it is probably the case that simple and brief contributions of an almost gnomic variety are preferred. Thus, as a preliminary example, the following extract from Meeting no. 2 (the whole of a speaker C's ministry on that occasion; as in the case of all data to be reproduced below, the transcription is very broad: orthographic, with minimum of punctuation added. Dots (. . .) indicate failure to make sense of what is said. Slant lines are used to indicate my interpretation of sense-groups):

> religious experience seems to be such an individual thing . . . I like to think of it as a pearl of great price that each one carries about with us . . . that glimpse of the whole that stays with us always, and gives us comfort and faith and hope. (M/W 2: Speaker C at 52 minutes: 0.5)

Now the texts of M/W 7. Speakers are indicated by letter and sex. Times of speaking in the Meeting for Worship and length of ministry are indicated (as above) in minutes, thus: 10.50: 0.5, i.e. at 10.50 minutes into the Meeting, a contribution lasting 0.5 minutes).

A. (Woman) A reading of the third Query for serious consideration. Do you gather together at Meetings for Worship in expectant waiting on God prepared to share experiences and insights / are these Meetings occasions when, by the help of the Holy Spirit you are enabled unitedly to worship God / are you open to the promptings of the spirit and sensitive to one another's needs whether your response be in silent worship or through the spoken word (10.50: 0.5)

B. (Woman) I telephoned to my daughter in Brussels this morning and before she hung up she said pray for Mrs Gandhi and I said what because this was my daughter's birthday and I was surprised that she mentioned it and she said it was a special EEC broadcast Saturday that requested that people in Europe to pray for Mrs Gandhi pray for her son pray for the people of India and to try to pray to try to stop the horrible violence in the world (11.50: 0.5)

C. (Man) In recent discussions about violence whether in writing or in speaking we have got ourselves into logical absurdities / in the UK in discussions about the miners' strike it is almost as though anything that stops people doing what they want to do is violence violence then becomes really rather a trivial sort of idea / it's almost as though not giving up your seat up on the bus or refusing to do the washing up at home is a kind of violence / that leads into a useless kind of distinction or definition / it's better it seems to me to restrict violence quite simply to what hurts other people physically and if we want to extend that into psychological damage then that no doubt is measurable also and can do physical harm / but what all sorts of violence whether physical or these other more structural kinds that people worry about quite properly what they all have in common is a negative attitude to others / they all represent an attempt to solve problems too simply they all represent a lack of the reconciling approach that we know is right but often takes such a long time (33.00: 2.0)

D. (Man) The Query has started me thinking the worship of God is far more than such things as the enjoying and being awe-inspired by the view of K— B— and the mountains beyond and perhaps the realisation that they've all been there longer than mankind has been there and they will be there long after we've departed this earth / or a smaller edition of it to admire the sun as one should say playing on the sides of H— H— as you journey from M— to B— R— or even the autumn colourings that many of us saw on our way here and on other short or long journeys / they all point that there is a being that we call God who arranged all these things both in the large extent and in the very minute extent / but when we come to worship God together we bring into far more we open up more stages / we each of us can help the other to realise the worthy-ship of God we may all emphasise slightly different attributes of the Godhead but they are all needed for us to successfully worship God together in a Meeting such as this (44.00: 2.25)

E. (Man) At the beginning of our Meeting we were . . . the Query asking us whether we joined here to worship God in proper spirit and help each other do so and then later we were reminded about all the violence and dreadful things that have happened have been happening in India at this time and we were asked to pray that people there might be helped and then we were reminded that violence of the sort that is afflicting in India and in our own country and in other places well results from having negative views of other people that . . . the basis of it / and I was wondering how all those things fitted together and it seems to me that when we think of God we do think of his positive attitude to . . . call it / we say God is love and somehow we feel that Jesus embodies this kind of attitude now we don't worry as Quakers very much as to why or how this is that Jesus has this particular involvement . . . here in this part of the world but we I think accept this / and I think that the value of coming to Meeting is that by thinking even if it's only once a week about this God who embodies this positive attitude that makes it easier for us to have the same attitude / now the natural thing so often I think is to have negative attitude to people this is your first reaction very often it's mine certainly first reaction and I hear about certain things and people have done this and that I feel negative but if we have had this sort of idea about God in connection with God even if it's only once a week then I think that after having the negative feelings and feelings might come that surely that's not right surely I should have had a positive feeling and so that negative feeling is it would of course be much better if we could think of God and think about Meeting and so forth more than once a week but it's true even once a week / I think this is the real value that it helps us later on to have the right attitude to the various things that happen to us every day (53.50: 3.75)

F. (Woman) I have a favourite poem by Francis Thompson in which he speaks of being chased by those feet following after and finally accepting God in his life and it seems to me that this is the ultimate fear of being swallowed up by something and ruled by something other than ourselves / and it is one of the reasons we need each other to support each other in acknowledging God as part of ourselves / and when we look at the world this week the ineptitude that is all round us becomes so apparent that without God we cannot do anything right / only with his help can we resolve war only with his help can we prevent famine / and it's that ineffectualness that ineptitude that I think we have to recognise I pray that his his reign will become apparent to us so that we can do things better in future (59.25: 2.0)

M/W 7: Keywords and phrases

1. A. … third query … gather … Meetings for Worship … expectant waiting on God …
2. … are … Meetings … help … holy spirit … worship God … open … promptings …
3. … spirit … one another's needs … silent … spoken …
4. B. … pray … Mrs Gandhi … pray … on … pray … people … India … pray … stop … horrible …
5. …violence in … world
6. C. … violence … miners' strike … violence … hurts other people … negative attitude …
7. … solve problems too simple … reconciling approach …

8\. D. ... query ... worship ... God ... autumn colourings ... God ... worship ... together ... help ...
9\. other ... worthy-ship ... God ... together ... Meeting ... this ...
10\. E. ... Meeting ... query ... worship God ... spirit ... help ... each other ... violence ... India ...
11\. ... own country ... negative ... God ... love ... Jesus ... attitude ... things ... every day ...
12\. F. ... favourite poem ... accepting God ... fear ... need each other ... support ...
13\. ... acknowledging God ... without God ... anything right ... resolve war ... famine ... pray
14\. ... better ... future

Religious language

There are obvious points to make. The language used is religious in the sense defined by Crystal and Davy (1969): 'The interesting thing about the semantic structure of theological language is the way in which there is a clear linguistic centre to which all lexical items can ultimately be referred, namely the term "God"' (p. 165). Admittedly they are writing of written religious texts, but they claim 'religious English is formally very different from all other varieties of the language. It is probably the most clearly marked variety of all' (p. 171). They point to the use of unspecific words: e.g. from M/W 7, above:

line	*unspecifics*
1	waiting on God
2	holy spirit worship God
	open promptings
3	spirit
4	pray
8	worship God
9	God
10	worship God spirit holy
11	God love
12	God
13	God pray

(and c.f. 'pearl of great price' in M/W 2, quoted above, p. 123)

Content

Ministry in all Meetings for Worship recorded ranges across a number of social and spiritual issues, but the tendency is to restrict the coverage on any one M/W occasion and also to relate the social issue commented on to an underlying religious theme. Thus the ground of all ministry (as the key-words suggest) is spiritual experience. The model both for the course of an individual ministry contributions and for the general discourse chain of ministry contribution on any one ministry occasion is to move from the personal to the divine. Since speakers sometimes also begin with the divine, we can summarise the ministry (both individual and group) direction as:

(God) → Me/Experience → God

As a self-styled 'experimental' or experiential religious body, it is appropriate perhaps that the move in Quaker ministry is from personal experience to God in order to return to and validate that personal experience.

Among the issues addressed in the ministry I recorded are:

> Violence, war, famine, strikes, nature, children, trust, forgiveness, change, brotherhood, redemption, the local Meeting itself and its problems

Their own personal experiences were referred to by 75 per cent of the speakers. Reading aloud was rare and on only two occasions was there singing, once a hymn (with all members joining in — a very unusual occurrence) and once a song as part of a spoken contribution.

Praying was common as a mode of ministry, but the manner tended to the general rather than the specific. That is to say, the style was very rarely of the traditional prayer variety with second-person address to God forms. That did occur, but rarely. Far more common were the prayers which used the statement as a form of indirect address, *declaratives* for *imperatives*. The old-style prayer of Quaker ministry when the speaker would kneel is long gone. But praying continues to be common, if in this more informal style. Such prayers are concerned with adoration, praise, and above all petitions, asking God, indirectly, for help. Of course we could, in a reductionist way, say that *all* Quaker ministry is prayer since it all takes place in a religious/worship context, and all, as we have suggested, comes back to God. That is true, but less helpful as an analysis.

There is topic placement in ministry chains. In particular, there is seizure of first topic as a lead into subsequent contributions. Thus, in M/W 7 the reading of the Query (a set Quaker text occasionally read aloud) leads with being open to one another's needs. This is made concrete by the reference to Mrs Gandhi's assassination and to violence, a theme which is taken up by speakers C, E and F. Speaker D goes back to the Query (read by A) and E links the Query (A) to the violence theme. Speaker F sums up that 'we need each other', the reconciling through caring (first theme) of violence.

Cohesion

As in any discourse there is cohesion within any one speaker's contribution. What is striking here (and M/W 7 is typical) is the extent of the cohesion across speakers. No doubt this can be explained in part by the accommodation model (Giles and Powesland, 1975); lexical repetition, synonymy, pronominal substitution and repetition are very evident, e.g. for M/W 7:

line	*line*	*line*	*line*
1 query (A)	8 query (D)	10 query (E)	12 God (F)
1 God (A)	8 God (D)	10 God (E)	
2 spirit (A)	10 spirit (E)		
5 violence (B)	6 violence (C)	10 violence (E)	
1 worship (A)	8 worship (D)	10 worship (E)	
4 pray (B)	13 pray (F)		
3 needs (A)	12 need (F)		

and:

negative attitide (C) — positive attitude (E)
sensitive to one another's needs (A) — need each other (F)
gather together at Meeting (A) — coming to Meeting (E)

Context

The discourse is firmly located in the here and now. It is in our world and in our time that God speaks and acts, not in some historical or idealised state. Fifty-four of the total 72 speakers in all Meetings for Worship studied used some reference to hereness and nowness, e.g. (data from all Meetings for Worship, not just from M/W 7):

> in this room — 40 years ago — a week ago — the radio this morning — Saturday — the view of K— B— — this Easter — sitting here (×2) — last year — this time of year — last Fall

Forty-eight of the 72 speakers use the first-person pronouns *I* or *me* and in M/W 7 five of the six speakers use first-person singular or plural pronouns. And in terms of the discourse model suggested above: (God) → Me/Experience → God, there is constant reference to God in M/W 7 — 18 mentions by four of the six speakers, providing a constant ground to the whole discourse of: I → God.

Pausing

Walker (1985) suggests that a pause of 0.5 seconds can be regarded as a long pause. She distinguishes switching pauses (at the margins of speakers' turn) from inturn pauses (during single speaker utterances). 'Normal' switching turns are 1.5 seconds' duration, 'normal' inturn pauses are 1.0 seconds' duration. Anything longer, in either case, is likely to be regarded as an invitation to someone else to take over the present turn (in the case of inturn pauses) or the next turn (in the case of switching pauses). In M/W 7, inturn pauses far in excess of the normal 1.0 seconds are found. Speaker F, for example, has a pause of 5 seconds — thus: '... support each other (5 secs) in acknowledging God ...'; of 6 seconds — thus: '... as part of ourselves (6 seconds) and when we look at the world ...'; and 7.5 seconds and another 5 seconds — thus: '... can we prevent famine (7.5 secs) and it's that ineffectualness and that ineptitude (5 secs) that I think ...' Chafe's reasons for hesitation, finding or clarifying an initial focus, moving to next focus, the need to verbalise something low in codability, may be of relevance here (Chafe 1985).

Doing being silent

The paper 'Notes on the art of walking' (Ryave and Schenkein 1974) provides a descriptive style for Meetings for Worship. A 'togethering', for example doing being silent together, is a 'settinged' activity. By that we mean the propriety and relevance of a togethering is a function of such factors as time, place and participants. There are, clearly, proper and/or expectable occasions for a togethering. This observation is rather fundamental in a consideration of recognition work, for such factors as time, place and participants are invoked by members to see, notice and account for some others as a togethering without having to approach them to determine by interview if such is, in fact, the case. Plainly, being silent together cannot be properly done any time, anywhere, with anybody.

We are now in a position to argue that the Meeting for Worship has a limited set of degrees of freedom. It is not open-ended (it has a fixed termination), it does not encourage frequent speaking in concert or questions requiring answers — or answers to rhetorical questions in earlier ministry, or many forms of speaking that are entirely normal in other situations. Thus among the non-mentionables are vocative invocation in order, e.g. to insult or to make arrangements or propose marriage, and reference to some informational data which do not have overt general significance (thus 'Civil War began today in North Korea' would even without some relation to life in general or the group in particular be acceptable, while 'Cod was cheaper this morning' would probably be as unmentionable as 'This is no longer a one-way street' or 'I've got a puncture in my front tyre.' Or of course dyadic asides, e.g. 'What's on television this evening?') Of course, these examples are not strictly unmentionables. They are just not among the mentionables, they don't get said. If they did, then our normal semantic sponge or one of Grice's maxims of conversation (Grice 1975) would at once assign meaning to them and accept them as relevant or not to our own condition at that time. Again, among the constraints are that the same person does not speak more than once, nor does s/he speak for the whole of the Meeting for Worship.

The recognition of others doing being silent: what confirms this is through conformity to the constraints of *mentionable* (what is legitimate for members to talk about to one another, assuming a shared background and an agreement as to present context);

members (members possess 'knowledge in recognising the activities that participants to interaction are engaged in', Turner 1970); *topic* (given what gets talked about, i.e. mentionables, their sequency is relevant, and in particular the position of first topic in a single conversation); *placement* (crucial for certain sequences, possibly less so for the non-conversation of ministry).

What language learning can we say has taken place in a M/W event? Members recognise one another by keeping to the (linguistic) rules of (a) silence, by doing being silent together and (b) when speaking some combination of religious language and first-person reference, the (God) → I → God linearity. Of course we do not know about the competence of those who do not speak (the majority rarely if ever do). What is remarkable is the language success of those who do speak; disfluencies very rarely occur (in my data only two occurrences of double speaking, i.e. the same person speaking twice).

What do occur are flawed performances, e.g. too frequent speaking by one actor, speaking at too great length, occasionally too intimate a revelation (usually about the self but also about others). Not that these flawed performances are dismissed as having no value. The Meeting for Worship has a group strength which can absorb and build on highly flawed performances.

The event of speaking and being silent in Quaker Meetings

My concern has been descriptive, not prescriptive, in what is a competent performance, not a perfect, polished one. Members are amateurs rather than professionals. Norms do enter since there are certain more highly valued performance styles, typically those of the more laconic, distanced, even gnomic, that at the same time fit directly into the discourse, into the developing meditation. Examples would be the 'pearl of great price' contribution or the following complete contribution:

> The philosopher von Hugel was once asked what was the essence of Christianity and he replied Christianity is caring / caring matters most / we've heard some examples of caring this morning / and caring is the way in which we can all share in being part of the answer to each other's prayers. (M/W 12)

The performance of a Meeting for Worship is not professional but community, folk, family, not unlike taking part in a folk dance. The novice ('attender' is the name often used for a non-member who attends Meetings for Worship) becomes part of the group, an acknowledged performer, admitted through the combination of open invitation to speak and the constant repetition within and across Meetings of a heavily marked style and content.

What sort of speech event is a Meeting for Worship? First, it *is* an event, a religious event and a learned religious event. It appears to be more a 'continuing state of incipient talk' than a conversation or a formal occasion. We have suggested ways in which members learn to behave as members and how we recognise learned behaviour. Members of a Quaker Meeting, no less than members of a family, office group or friends travelling in a car, have been socialised into appropriate linguistic behaviour.

In what sense can the Meeting for Worship be considered a single conversation? The answer is probably that it cannot (no closures, no adjacency pairs, no turn-taking sequences, not inexplicit, not random, probably not normally non-fluent). But it is open to all, only one speaks at a time, there is a sequence leading from first topic. It is a repeated event in the social process, like family meals, journeys, games, committee meetings on the one hand, and seminars with set papers on the other. Yet it is still special because it is not made up of single conversations, unlike the first group (family meals, etc.), and it is spontaneous, unlike the second group. Further, and perhaps most important, it contains so much silence. The silence is not that described by Basso (1970) among the Western Apache: 'keeping silent among the Western Apache is a response to uncertainty and unpredictability in social relations' (p. 83). It is not that. Given that the Meeting for Worship is a social occasion, the boundaries are presumably social ones — e.g. time, arriving, departing, formal ending, announcements — not linguistic ones.

I want to suggest that the Meeting for Worship is both a social occasion and a speech event. Certainly that is how members see it. As in other speech events such as single conversation, there are forward and back references (e.g. 'last week in Meeting'); but to members a Meeting for Worship is also a social occasion in which ministry is normal and in which items of ministry interrelate. Perhaps a better analogy than a family meal is a performance (music, singing, stories) and there is therefore a strong link with oral narrative.

But where does that leave Protestantism and the control of the WORD? We began by suggesting that Quakerism was located in its origins at the radical end of discourse propriety, the least ritualised, seizing and sharing language control among all members. Where is that vision now in the light of 300 years and such data as we have presented?

The answer seems to be a partial triumph for democracy: the sharing of control still continues, ministry is open to all, though it is probable that a few 'ministers' dominate in frequency of turns. But the style and content of the discourse remain substantially 'high' style and religious, even semi-ritualised. As Weber remarks, 'it is the fate of charisma to recede before the powers of traditions ... after it has entered the permanent structures of social action' (1978, pp. 1148-9). Such receding took place early in Quakerism. The early-seventeenth-century unfettered, spontaneous (neo-Pentecostal) speaking became constrained and conventionalised into an incantatory and catechetical style by the end of the century. Continuous charisma, like continuous revolution, is rare if indeed possible, perhaps that is the strength of Pentecostalism. But what Quakerism does bear witness to is that although the event is religious (and therefore the message never changes and the manner of proclaiming it must tend toward ritual) there is no special ministry, no separate messengers; those who open up the channel of worship between God and his people with God's message are no priestly elect.

Although all this may seem to detract from the delightful spontaneity thought (by outsiders) to characterise a Quaker Meeting for Worship, the premise of open ministry does remain: anyone may speak, all may learn. 'Remember that to everyone is given a share of responsibility for the Meeting for Worship, whether that service be in silence or through the spoken word. Do not assume that vocal ministry is never to be your part' (Advices 1964). Like other forms of discourse, it must be learned: 'my understanding became more strengthened to distinguish the language of the pure spirit ... and taught me to wait in silence, sometimes many weeks together, until I felt that rise which prepares the creatures to stand like a trumpet, through which the Lord speaks to his flock' (Woolman 1910, pp. 159-60).

As in all spheres of life some learn better than others: our evidence suggests that in spite of the recurring attempts to open up access to ministry to the membership as a whole (such as the laying down of 'recorded ministers' by London Yearly Meetings in the 1920s), Bauman's contrast between the structural dimension and the expressive holds good (1974). While the prophetic ministry remains open to all, the legitimacy of religious speaking is controlled through learning. Quaker ministry like all other forms of speaking is constitutive of the social life of its own domain.

Notes

1. The author wishes to acknowledge the support of the Leverhulme Trust which awarded him a research grant during the period 1983-5 for the purpose of pursuing research in this area.

References

Advices (1964) 'Advices and queries'. In *Church government.* London: Society of Friends

Barclay, R. (1678) *Apology for the true Christian divinity.* London

Basso, K.H. (1970) 'To give up on words: silence in Western Apache culture'. *Southwestern Journal of Anthropology*, 26, pp. 213-30

Bauman, R. (1974) 'Speaking in the light: the role of the Quaker minister'. In R. Bauman and J. Sherzer (eds) (1983) *Let your words be few.* Cambridge: Cambridge University Press

Bauman, R. and Sherzer, J. (eds) (1974) *Explorations in the ethnology of speaking.* Cambridge: Cambridge University Press

Beamish, L. (1967) 'The silent century'. *Friends' Quarterly*, January.

Boehme, J. (1764) 'Apology to Tilken'. In *Theosophia revelata*, vol. 2. English trans. by Sparrow, Ellitone and Bunden. London

Braithwaite, W.C. (1912) *The beginnings of Quakerism.* London: Macmillan

Chafe, W.C. (1985) 'Some reasons for hesitating'. In D. Tannen and M. Saville-Troike (eds) *Perspectives on silence.* Norwood, NJ: Ablex, pp. 77-89

Crystal, D. and Davy, D. (1969) *Investigating English style.* London: Longman

Davies, R. (1771) *Life.* Quoted in W.C. Braithwaite (1912) *The beginnings of Quakerism.* London: Macmillan

Doody, M.A. (1980) 'How shall we sing the Lord's song upon an alien soil?: The new Episcopalian liturgy'. In L. Michaels, and C. Ricks (eds) *The state of the language.* London: University of California Press, pp. 108-24

Edmundson, W. (1981) *Spoken discourse: a model for analysis.* London: Longman

Fox, G. (1694) *Journal.* London (Revised edn, London: London Yearly Meeting of the Society of Friends, 1975)

Garfinkel, H. (1967) *Studies in ethnomethodology.* Englewood Cliffs, NJ: Prentice-Hall

Giles, H. and Powesland, P.F. (1975) *Speech style and social evaluation.* London: Academic Press

Gorman, G. (1973) *Introduction to Quakerism.* London: Society of Friends

Grice, H.P. (1975) 'Logic and conversation' In P. Cole and J. Morgan (eds) *Syntax and semantics 3: Speech acts.* London and New York: Academic Press

Grubb, E. (nd) 'The delivery of the message'. *Preparation for service,* no. 10. The Yearly Meeting Committee on Ministry and the Friends' Fellowship Union

Hodgkin, L.V. (1919) *Silent worship.* London: Allen & Unwin

Hubbard, G. (1974) *Quaker by convincement.* Harmondsworth: Penguin

Jones, R. (1914) *Spiritual reformers in the 16th and 17th centuries.* London: Macmillan

Kelly, T. (1966) 'The gathered meeting'. In R. Kelly (ed.) *The eternal promise.* New York: Harpers

Lamb, C. (1800) 'A Quaker's meeting'. In C. Lamb, *Essays of Elia.* London (also Oxford University Press, London, 1946)

Maltz, D.N. (1985) 'Joyful noise and reverent silence: the significance of noise in pentecostal worship'. In D. Tannen and M. Saville-Troike, (eds) *Perspectives on silence.* Norwood, NJ: Ablex

Myers, T. (1979) *The development of conversation and discourse.* Edinburgh: Edinburgh University Pess

Penn, W. (1694) 'Preface' to George Fox's *Journal.* London

——— (1726) *Works,* vol. 2. London

Penny, N. (ed) (1907) *The first publishers of truth.* London: Headley

Ryave, A.C. and Schenkein, J.N. (1974) 'Notes on the art of walking'. In R. Turner (ed.) *Ethnomethodology.* Harmondsworth: Penguin, pp. 265-74

Samarin, W.J. (1972) *Tongues of men and angels: the religious language of Pentecostalism.* London: Macmillan

——— (1973) 'Protestant preachers in the prophetic line'. *International yearbook for the sociology of religion,* 8, pp. 243-57

Schegloff, E. and Sacks H. (1973) 'Opening up closings'. *Semiotica,* 8, 4, pp. 289-327. Reprinted in R. Turner (ed.) (1974) *Ethnomethodology.* Harmondsworth: Penguin

Steere, D. (1972) 'On speaking out of the silence: vocal ministry in the unprogrammed Meeting for Worship'. Pendle Hill Pamphlet no 182, Philadelphia

Tannen D. and Saville-Troike, M. (eds) (1985) *Perspectives on silence.* Norwood, NJ: Ablex

Trueblood, D.E. (1960) 'The paradox of the Quaker ministry'. Quaker lecture, Indiana Yearly Meeting

Turner, R. (1970) 'Words, utterances and activities'. In J. Douglas (ed.) *Understanding everyday life.* Chicago: Aldine. Reprinted in R. Turner (ed.) (1974) *Ethnomethodology.* Harmondsworth: Penguin

——— (1974) (ed.) *Ethnomethodology.* Harmondsworth: Penguin

Underhill, E. (1936) *Worship.* London, James Nisbet and Co.; (1962), Fontana

Walker, A.G. (1985) 'The two faces of silence: the effect of witness hesitancy on lawyers' impressions'. In D. Tannen and M. Saville-Troike (eds) *Perspectives on silence.* Norwood, NJ: Ablex

Walker, H.E.(1952) 'The conception of a ministry in the Quaker movement and a survey of its development'. Unpublished PhD thesis, University of Edinburgh

Weber, M. (1978) *Economy and society.* 2 vols, Berkeley and Los Angeles: University of California Press

Woolman, J. (1910) *The journal and essays.* A.M. Gunmore (ed.) London: Dent (first published 1774)

Zielinkski, S. (1975) *Psychology and silence.* Pendle Hill Pamphlet no. 201, Philadelphia

6

The Interaction of Discourse and Lexis: a Stylistic Analysis of 'Vertue' by George Herbert

Michael Hoey

Literary discourses are unusual among written discourses in that they frequently repay a second reading. There are many reasons why this should be so, but amongst them is the fact that they are often more complexly and/or more elegantly organised than their non-literary equivalents. The organisation that attracts the reader by its complexity or elegance may be phonological, graphological, lexical, grammatical, or discoursal in nature, or any combination of these; typically, a stylistic analysis of a particular work will concentrate on one of these to the exclusion of the others. While this is frequently a rewarding strategy, it can result in descriptions of literary works that are less convincing than might have been the case, had a more eclectic approach been adopted.

This chapter attempts to demonstrate the value of an eclectic approach to stylistic description, despite the risks attendant on such an approach. Some attention is paid to phonological (metrical) matters, and passing reference is made to grammatical features; the main thrust of the chapter is however to integrate lexical and discourse descriptions. The lexical description adopted is that traditionally undertaken by literary critics and involves identification of multiple meanings and lexical relations across the work. The discourse description adopted is probably less familiar to most readers and is that developed by Winter and his associates and usually referred to as clause-relational analysis.[1]

The chapter divides into two uneven halves. In the first, I attempt to show how clause-relational analysis is used to describe written discourse. This survey of the approach is neither technical nor detailed, and the reader should look to the works mentioned in the References for a fuller account of this approach to the analysis of discourse. It is, however, meant to provide sufficient detail to allow the reader to follow the stylistic analysis provided in the second half of the chapter. The purpose of this stylistic analysis is not to demonstrate the efficacy of the clause-relational approach but to show how an adequate stylistic account of a poem requires that one integrate the insights gained from the clause-relational description with those gained from lexical (and phonological and syntactic) description. This end will be incapable of achievement unless the analysis says something interesting about the literary discourse chosen. Thus the second purpose of this analysis is to cast light upon the literary discourse in question: 'Vertue' by George Herbert.

Part 1: The clause-relational approach to discourse analysis

Clause-relational analysis starts from the assumption that when two or more sentences (or groups of sentences) are read together, their interpretation takes into account their juxtaposition. In other words, the meaning of sentences placed together is not exhausted by a description of their meaning in isolation. Consider the following trio of sentences:

1. (A) His mother said, 'I am going up to London for a day, with Mr Hooper.'

   (B) Kingshaw's heart thumped. (C) He knew he would not have another chance like it.[2]

An adequate reading of these sentences, which begin a chapter of a modern novel, requires that the reader make a connection between the sentences. Most readers would identify sentence (B) as supplying information about the *effect* of what his mother said, and would see sentence (C) as supplying the *reason* for Kingshaw's heart thumping. These relations are imputed to the passage by the reader; there are no overt signals of the relations between the sentences. However, a reader could justify such an imputation by converting the passage into dialogue, thus:

2. *Discourse.* His mother said, 'I am going up to London for a day, with Mr Hooper.'
   Questioner. What effect did this statement have?
   Discourse. Kingshaw's heart thumped.

Questioner. Why?
Discourse. He knew he would not have another chance like it.

If the questions so inserted seem to other readers to do no more than spell out the relation already perceived, then they may be taken as grounds for imputing such a relation. Another way of checking the validity of inferred relations is to insert some explicit labelling of the relations, as in:

3. The *effect* of his mother's saying 'I am going up to London for a day with Mr Hooper' was to *make* Kingshaw's heart thump, *because* he knew he would not have another chance like it.

If such labelling is already present, inference is unncessary. The writer is in such cases making the relation explicit for the reader, though there may be other inferrable relations between statements in addition to those signalled by the writer. Examples of the explicit signalling of relations are the following *highlighted* items; not every signal has been picked out:

4. (A) The one *drawback* is that a mother leaves her offspring unguarded and *therefore* liable to be eaten by another female in the group. (B) *On the other hand,* the risk may be worth it *because once* a female loses her own infants, she is unlikely to kill. (C) *Therefore* the practitioner of infanticide reduces the danger of her own offspring becoming victims. (D) She *also* reduces the size of the coterie and *thus* cuts down competition for food.[3]

Relations may be of two kinds: Matching and Sequence.[4] Most of the relations we have so far considered have been sequence relations. They occur whenever two or more (groups of) statements are presented by the writer or perceived by the reader as belonging in a particular order. Thus two sentences may be read as describing events that follow one after the other in time and/or as presenting propositions that follow one after the other in logic. These sequences may be characterised more precisely, if necessary, e.g. cause–consequence, instrument–purpose. In example 1, there is both a temporal and, by inference, a logical sequence between sentences (A) and (B), with sentence (A) being prior to sentence (B). There is a logical sequence also between sentences (B) and (C), in this case the latter sentence being logically prior. Logical relations are being signalled by *therefore* (× 2), *because, once,* and *thus* in example 4.

Matching relations occur when two or more statements or groups of statements are considered in terms of what they do (or do not) share. In Matching, what is important is how each statement casts light on the other. An example is the following:

5. (A) They could hear the sound of an axe in the distance and thought it was their father felling trees. (B) (i) But it was not an axe that they heard; (ii) it was a branch the wind was blowing against a tree.[5]

Sentence (Bi) denies the hypothesis in sentence (A); sentence (Bii) corrects it. We can check this by projecting it into dialogue, thus:

Discourse. They could hear the sound of an axe in the distance and thought it was their father felling trees.
Questioner. Were they correct?
Discourse. It was not an axe that they heard.
Questioner. What was it?
Discourse. It was a branch the wind was blowing against a tree.

Unlike example 1, however, the relations here are not simply imputed by the reader; they are signalled by the writer, by repetition. We can set out each of the pairs as follows:

They	could hear	the sound of an axe
They	heard	not an axe

where *the sound of an axe* is contrasted with *an axe*;

They thought	it was their father felling trees	[that they heard]
[I, the author know]	it was not an axe	that they heard

where their thought is contrasted with the author's certainty; and finally:

It was	not an axe	that they heard
It was	a branch the wind was blowing against a tree	[that they heard]

where what it wasn't is contrasted with (and replaced by) what it was.

Matching may also be signalled in a manner similar to Sequence relations, by conjuncts, subordinators, and lexical signals. Instances in example 4 above are *on the other hand* and *also*. In the latter case, it will be noticed that *also* supports a pattern of repetition similar to that just described.

Matching and Sequence relations may occur simultaneously; there may be more than one relation explicitly signalled, e.g.

7. (A) Richard pulled a face to scare her away. (B) But the only result was that she pulled a face as well.

(concocted example)

where *result* signals a cause–consequence relation and the repetition patterning and *as well* signal a compatibility relation. More commonly, perhaps, one or both of the relations may be inferrable only, e.g.

8. Unemployment rose and inflation fell.

(concocted example)

Here the parallelism (x rose / y fell) tells us we have a Matching relation, but we do not know whether the writer perceives it as a contrast or compatibility relation. In addition it is possible to impute a cause–consequence relation to the clauses, but the writer has not made his or her intentions clear on the matter. Context will often determine whether or not a relation can reasonably be inferred.

Another feature of relations is that they nest. Consider the following passage:

9. (A) From the culinary point of view, [apples] divide into four groups of which the first two are the most important. (B) Cooking apples are sharply flavoured and are therefore never eaten raw. (C) They quickly form pulp when cooked. (D) The second group is dessert apples, sweeter in flavour and mainly eaten raw. (E) These may be cooked, when they will hold their shape.[6]

Sentences (B) and (C) are in a Matching relation; both sentences provide compatible detail for cooking apples. Sentences (D) and (E) are in the same relation, providing detail this time for dessert apples. But what is important from our point of view, and indeed more noticeable to the reader, is that the two pairs of sentences are in a Matching relation; their detail is matched in respect of their difference. Thus *sharply flavoured* is contrasted with *sweeter in flavour*, *never eaten raw* with *mainly eaten raw*, and *form pulp* with *will hold their shape*. Thus the pattern of the passage is as shown in Figure 6.1, where the Contrast between the two groups of sentences is signalled by repetition and parallelism between the

Figure 6.1

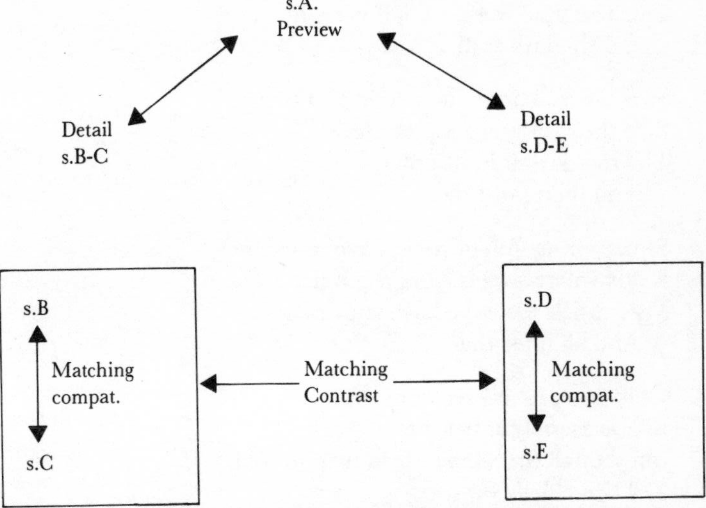

details of the clauses. In other words, the large discourse Contrast is built out of a series of lexical contrasts. This we will return to in our discussion of 'Vertue', to which we now turn.

Part 2: A stylistic analysis of 'Vertue' by George Herbert

There have been a number of applications of clause-relational description to literary discourse with stylistic intent,[7] and it is not the intention of this chapter,[8] as noted earlier, to demonstrate the validity of this kind of stylistic analysis. Rather, we repeat, the aim is to show how each type of analysis (phonological, grammatical, lexical and discoursal) needs the other in a stylistic description (particularly, in the case in question, lexical and discoursal), and in so doing to produce a valid account of the poem 'Vertue'. It will be argued that in many cases, including the one we shall be considering, to apply only one of these kinds of analysis without the other is to threaten the utility of the analysis, at least from a stylistic point of view. The poem to which I seek to apply this combination of clause-relational and lexical descriptions reads as follows.

Vertue

Sweet day, so cool, so calm, so bright,
The bridall of the earth and skie:
The dew shall weep thy fall to night
    For thou must die.

Sweet rose, whose hue angrie and brave
Bids the rash gazer wipe his eye:
Thy root is ever in its grave,
    And thou must die.

Sweet spring, full of sweet dayes and roses,
A box where sweets compacted lie:
My musick shows ye have your closes,
    And all must die.

Only a sweet and vertuous soul
Like season'd timber, never gives:
But though the whole world turn to coal,
    Then chiefly lives.

Even on a superficial reading of this poem, there are a number of problems of interpretation. To begin with, we have the title: the difficulty here is not so much *why* it is called 'Vertue' (though that is not entirely transparent) as what 'vertue' is considered to be. Then there is the emphasis on sweetness — the word occurs six times in 16 lines. As with 'vertue', the difficulty is determining what constitutes sweetness. Thirdly, there is a grammatical oddity in verse 3: Spring is addressed and yet the third line uses the plural form *ye.* Finally, line 12, *And all must die*, is both unexpectedly universal and contradicted by the following verse. It is not unreasonable to expect an adequate stylistic analysis to square up to at least some of these problems.

Before, however, we analyse the poem's organisation in terms of clause relations, we first consider what insights we can gain from an examination of the metre of the poem, in other words, from a consideration of an aspect of the poem's *phonological* organisation. This is in keeping with our aim of demonstrating the interrelationship of the different kinds of stylistic analysis. There is a conflict between the regular iambic metre (⏑ –) and the natural stress required for the lexis. If we superimpose a naturally stressed reading,[9] marked by / , onto an iambic stressing, marked by \ , we note several lexical items that are thereby given unusual emphasis because caught in the tension between the two stress systems. In the 'transcription' that follows, any lexical item so emphasised (one is tempted to pun on *stressed*) is marked accordingly and highlighted in bold type. Grammatical items are ignored, as are instances of syllables that would receive stress if a rigid iambic metre were adhered to but would not in a natural reading; the latter have bracketed markers. In summary, then, X above an item indicates harmony between natural stress and metre; \ indicates metrical expectation of stress not fulfilled by natural stress; / indicates natural stress not expected by the metre.

```
 /   X    X     X     X
Sweet day, so cool, so calm, so bright,

    X   (\)    X      X
The bridall of the earth and skie:

    X     X     X   X
The dew shall weep thy fall to night

     X      X
  For thou must die.


 /   X      X  /  \     X
Sweet rose who hue angrie and brave

 /  (\)  /   X   X    X
Bids the rash gazer wipe his eye:

    X    X (\)   X
Thy root is ever in its grave

      X     X
  And thou must die.


 /    X    / (\)  /   X     X
Sweet spring, full of sweet dayes and roses,

  X      X     X   X
A box where sweets compacted lie;
```

In the verse lines above, these words are printed in bold: **Sweet**; **Sweet**, **angrie**; **Bids**, **rash**; **Sweet**, **full**, **sweet**.

X X X X
My musick shows ye have your closes,

X X
And all must die.

/ \ X X X
Only a sweet and vertuous soul

X X X X
Like season'd timber, never gives;

X X / X X
But though the whole **world** turn to coal,

X X
Then chiefly lives.

We notice that *sweet* receives emphasis on four of the six occasions of its occurrence; this confirms the concept's centrality in the poem and the need for an analysis to account for it. We will also now expect our analysis to show why *angrie*, *bids*, *rash*, *full*, *only* and *world* receive emphasis in a normal reading of the poem.

With the questions raised by this analysis and the problems listed earlier before us, we now at last turn to considering the poem's organisation in terms of clause relations. We begin by noting that the first three verses can be shown to be in a Matching compatibility relation: verse 2 answers the question 'How does the rose compare with the day?' and verse 3, 'how does the spring compare with the day and the rose?' We do not have to rely on projection into dialogue however. The relation is signalled by repetition and parallelism. All three verses take the form:

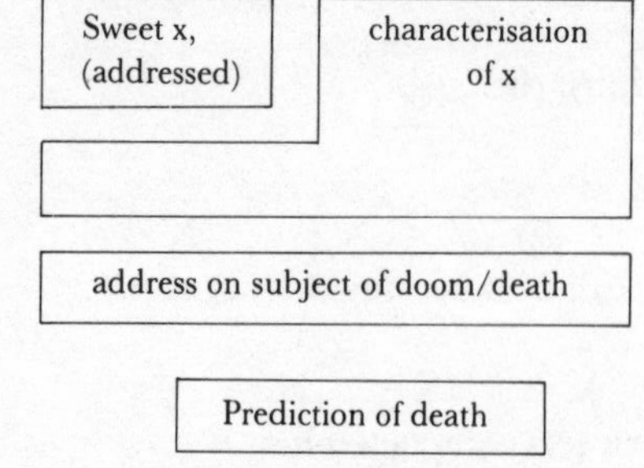

This parallelism of verse structure is further supported by repetition at the beginning and end of each verse:

Sweet	day	For	thou	must die
Sweet	rose	And	thou	must die
Sweet	spring	And	all	must die

The first of these picks up the item *sweet* that we noted as emphasised metrically.

Encouraged by this evidence of Matching compatability, we consider more closely the relationship between verses 1 and 2, and find further, less obvious, parallels between the two instances of address on the subject of death, in lines 3 and 7. To begin with, both lines contain a second-person singular possessive indicating particular address. More interestingly, perhaps, there are parallel paradoxes in the two lines. *The dew* is characteristic of the beginning of the day, *thy root* of the beginning of the rose. *Night* and *grave* are fairly self-evidently the end of the day and the rose respectively. Thus the beginning of the day weeps for the end of the day, and the beginning of the rose is found where the end of the rose will be. The night precedes (and gives rise to) the dew, but it also succeeds it, because the dew is at the beginning of the day. Likewise the rose's grave precedes the rose's root and also succeeds it. Without the grave, there could be no root and no rose; without the night there could be no dew and (for lack of contrast) no day. It should perhaps be made clear that I am not claiming for these comments the status of linguistic analysis; rather, I am claiming that the Matching relation between verses 1 and 2, linguistically signalled by repetition and parallelism, motivates literary observations of this kind.

We noted earlier the repetition at the end of each verse. But along with the repetition of *thou must die*, verse 2 shows the replacement of *for* by *and*, a change confirmed in verse 3:

v.1:	For	thou	must die
v.2:	And	thou	must die
v.3:	And	all	must die

The change indicates a difference between verses 1 and 2 in respect of the way the last line relates to the rest of each verse. In verse 1, *for* signals that *thou must die* is in a reason relation with line 3 (*the dew shall weep* ...); the lines can be projected into dialogue as follows:

Poem. The dew shall weep thy fall to night
Questioner. Why?
Poem. [For] thou must die.

In verse 2, however, *and* appears to rule out interpretation of the last line as *reason. And* emphasises the expectedness of this prediction; it is also compatible with an inferred relation of *consequence*, e.g.:

Poem. Thy root is ever in its grave
Questioner. What is the consequence of this?
Poem. [And] thou must die.

Notice that *thus* could be inserted between *and* and *thou* in the original. An interpretation of this change might be that death is the natural consequence of the rose's situation, a claim not made for the day.

Are there any other points of contrast between the first two verses? It is useful at this juncture to consider again the lexical items that were shown to be emphasised by the tension between the natural and metrical stress pattern. In verses 1 and 2, these were *sweet* (which since it occupies the same place in both verses we ignore), *angrie*, *bids* and *rash. Bids* indicates a clear difference between the day and the rose, and secondarily, between the dew and the gazer. *The dew* is agent[10] of *weep*, and *day* is experiencer of *fall.* But the roles are reversed (though without symmetry) in the second verse: *rose* (or more accurately its *hue*) is agent of *bids* and *the ... gazer* is experiencer of *bids.* Thus the rose is active whereas the day is passive.

In both verses, weeping is described, but it takes place for very different reasons:

Poem. The dew shall weep
Questioner. What will it weep in response to?
Poem. ...thy fall

Poem. ...the rash gazer wipe[s] his eye
Questioner. What does he weep in response to?
Poem. [thy] hue angrie and brave.

Here then is a second aspect of the same contrast. The weeping in the first verse is in response to what has happened to the day, while in the second it is in response to what the rose is like. This allows us to account for the emphasis given to *rash.* In the first case, the dew weeps because the day has suffered: in the second, the gazer weeps because *he* has suffered. He has been *rash* enough to gaze. Thus, we might say, the rose is aggressive while the day is the victim of aggression.

This interpretation is suggestive enough to encourage a careful look at the lexical item *angrie,* also singled out in the stress analysis, since anger and aggression are easily associated. We find that *angrie* has three possible meanings[11] here:

(i) It may mean 'enraged', in which case it contrasts with one of the meanings of *cool* (line 1), namely 'self-controlled'. It contrasts with *calm* (also line 1) in the same way.
(ii) It may mean 'red' in which case it contrasts with a second meaning of *cool,* namely as an attribute of colours. A *cool* colour is blue, green, or occasionally violet.
(iii) It may mean 'inflamed' in which case it contrasts with a third sense of *cool,* i.e. that of not being hot.

Thus *angrie* and *cool* are opposed in a variety of ways, an opposition supported by that between *angrie* and *calm.* There is, however, no contrast between the remaining adjectives in lines 1 and 5: *bright* and *brave.* Indeed one of the senses of *brave* is very compatible with that of *bright,* namely the sense (no longer current but available to Herbert) of making a fine display.

Summarising our discussion so far, we have the relations between the verses shown in Figure 6.2. It will be noticed that line 2 does not participate in this pattern of alternating compatibility and contrast; we will return to it later. Apart from that, however, the pattern is regular and may be seen as showing that the day and rose, though they differ in a number of respects, share two more fundamental properties: they are both sweet and they will both die. In the final analysis, therefore, according to this interpretation, the verses are in a relation of compatibility.

We have so far only discussed the first two verses. We must now look at verse 3 and see whether its relation to the first two is more complex than our initial characterisation of compatibility suggested. The answer is that it is. The third verse is in two relations with all that precedes it: the relation of compatibility

Figure 6.2

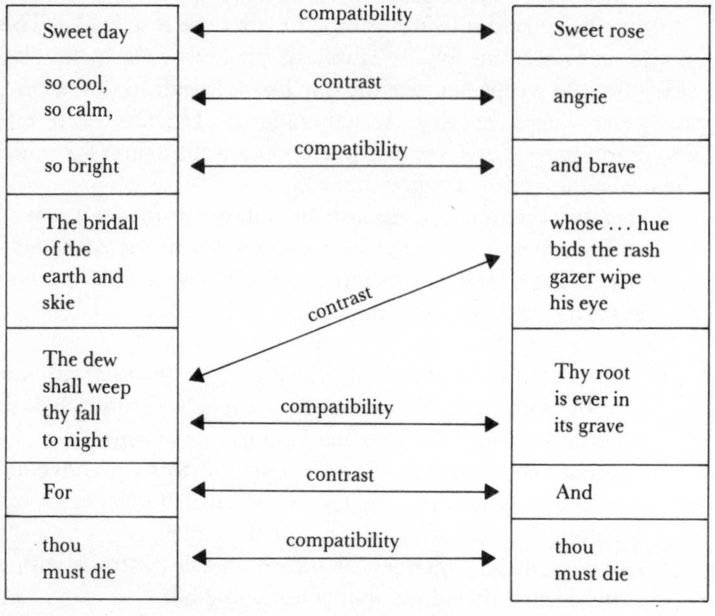

and the relation of generalisation to particulars (whether examples or exhaustive details is not clear). The grounds for identifying the relation of compatibility have already been given. The grounds for identifying the relation of generalisation–particulars are as follows:

1. The verse can be seen as answering the questions 'How does the spring subsume the day and the rose?' and 'What generalisation can be made about death that covers the particulars given?' These questions, and the relation they indicate, are quite congruous with the questions used to indicate the compatibility relation earlier; there is nothing to prevent the verses being in both a compatibility and particulars–generalisation relation. We do not, however, have to rely on intuited questions to identify the latter relation any more than we had to with the former.

2. *Sweet spring* is at the same level of particularity as *sweet day* and *sweet rose*, but the characterisation that follows is of a different type. Instead of the spring being evaluated in terms of its typical properties, it is described as *full of sweet dayes and roses*, a phrase emphasised (as we noted earlier) by the tension betwen natural

and metrical stress. This may be understood as meaning either that *spring* is a composition made up of *dayes* and *roses*, in which case the properties of the latter are subsumed within the former, or that *spring* embraces *dayes* and *roses*, in which case the properties of the latter will remain separate from that of the former. Either way, although literally at the same level of particularity, we interpret *spring* as more general than *dayes* and *roses* because more comprehensive; this interpretation is reinforced by our awareness that *spring* is more vaguely defined.

3. Line 10 provides support for both the interpretations given in (2), and thereby provides further support for the generalisation–particulars relation. *Box* and *compacted*, in the sense of *pressed together*, support the interpretation of *full of* as embracing *dayes* and *roses*. Perhaps more interestingly, however, *compacted* may also mean *bound together in a system*, which supports the interpretation of spring as subsuming dayes and roses.

4. *My musick shows* ... in line 11 suggests a summarising function, indicating as it does the regularity of the pattern already established by the poet's *musick*. If the pattern is that reliable, it is ripe for generalisation, which we get in the last line (see 6 below).

5. The choice of the plural form, *ye*, in line 11, instead of the singular form found elsewhere, indicates that what is being said covers a greater number of cases than what was said in the equivalent lines in earlier verses. *Closes* likewise indicates a generalisation; previously, each death has been predicted singly. The generalising function of this line is not however sufficient to account for the grammatical conflict between the singular vocative, *Sweet spring*, and the plural addressee of this line. We will return to this point below and in so doing will reinterpret the line in a way that makes the generalisation rather different in kind from that which we are considering.

6. Perhaps the single most compelling piece of evidence for regarding verse 3 as Generalisation to verses 1 and 2's Particulars is the final line: *all must die*. Here the particular *thou* of the previous two verses has been replaced by *all*, the ultimate generalisation. We cannot entirely dismiss a more restricted reading of *all* as *all ZERO* with *springs* or *dayes and roses* elided, but even read thus the line strongly supports the recognition of a generalisation–particulars relation. The all-embracing reading must be regarded as the more plausible, because the following verse offers an apparent exception to the generalisation that would be inexplicable if only *dayes*, *roses* or *springs* were doomed. The all-

embracing reading clinches the relation.[12]

We can represent the relationship of the parts of verse 3 to what preceded it as shown in Figure 6.3; the terminology is non-technical.

Figure 6.3

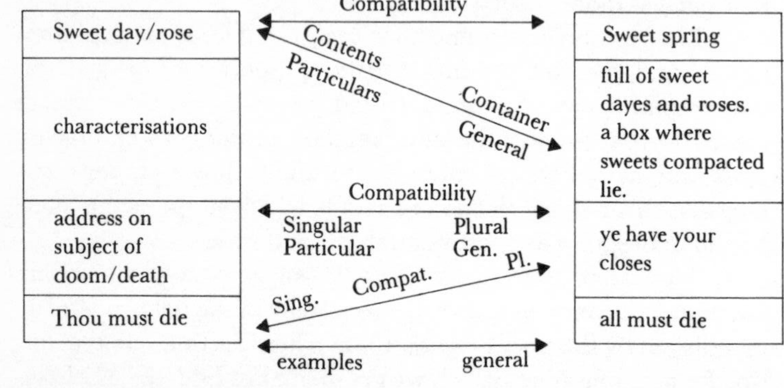

Simplifying somewhat (in particular ignoring the contrastive element in the relation between verses 1 and 2), we can represent the relations between the verses as a whole as in Figure 6.4.

Figure 6.4

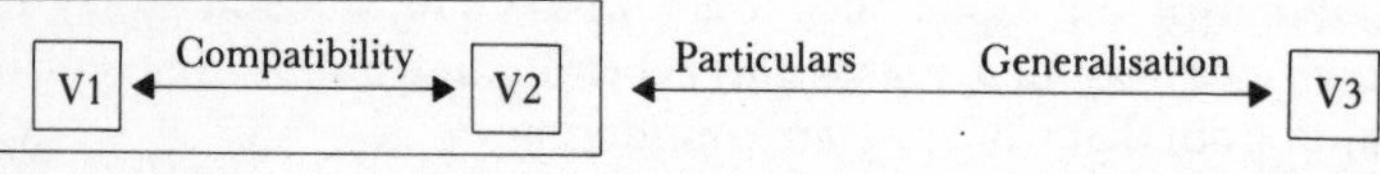

We must now return to the problem we left unresolved in line 11; the choice of the plural form *ye* to refer apparently to a singular addressee. The first possibility to be considered is that it does not refer to *Spring* — but this has to be dismissed, since there is no other second person referent to which it could refer in the verse, unless one argues, somewhat implausibly, that the *dayes and roses* inside the Spring are being addressed. A second possibility is that the real readers are being addressed, that there has been a switch from apparent addressee to real addressee(s) — but this leaves the address to the Spring without a main clause, a clearly unsatisfactory state of affairs. So we are left with the conflict of singular/plural still unresolved. We might note in this connection that the singularity of the Spring is stressed rather than otherwise by the use of the singular *box* to characterise it in the previous line. So how do we square this circle? Furthermore, if we accept that Spring is the only possible reference for *ye*, why should *closes* be plural as well? A thing can only die once.

A clue to the answers to these questions can be gleaned from the one line we have yet to consider from the earlier verses — line 2, but to make use of it we shall have, Worzel Gummidge-style, to doff our linguistic head and don a literary one instead. The day is described as 'the bridall of the earth and skie'. 'Bridall' introduces a sexual element into the verse, supported by *fall* in the moral sense and *die* in its common, seventeenth-century denotation. What typically follows a bridal union is children; what always follows the fall to night is a new day. Procreation is cyclical: the process repeats itself. Likewise the day 'falls' only to rise anew after night. In the same way, the death of the rose feeds the 'grave'; in fact, the rose recycles from the root (as suckers demonstrate). Thus we have three cycles — the day, the rose, and the spring, the last of which binds the others into a single system or cycle. In these terms it becomes perfectly acceptable to address Spring as singular, since there is only one spring at any time, but since at the same time Spring is part of a larger world cycle and will come to an end year after year, it can be referred to as plural and can be said to have plural deaths.

The day's cycle is shorter than the rose's. The rose's shorter than the Spring's, and the Spring's shorter than the world's. The *world* is, however, only mentioned in the last verse and there it is not its cycle but the end of its cycle that is in focus. We must now don our linguistic head again and consider this verse's relation to the previous verses.

Verse 4 is in a contrast relation with verses 1–3, where the contrast is one of generalisation–exception between verses 3 and 4. There are a number of clear signals of this. *Only* straightforwardly signals exception. *Sweet* is replaced by *sweet and vertuous*, and in the context of sameness, the addition of *vertuous* is sufficiently striking to set up a contrast. Most obviously, perhaps, *die* is replaced by *lives* in the final line. All this is sufficient by itself to establish the contrast relation. But there are further points of contrast. Syntactically the last verse is quite different from its predecessors, being made up of two main clauses with a shared subject. Also, there is no overt addressee; the verse is a statement about the soul, not addressed to it. From the point of view of the tension between natural and metrical stress, it is the only verse that does not emphasise *sweet*; instead it is the marker of exception, *only*, that is emphasised.

The discourse pattern to the poem as a whole can be represented as in Figure 6.5.

Since sweetness is shared by all the things mentioned, what makes the soul an exception is that it is *vertuous.* We can now account for the poem's title but have still to discover what it is to be *vertuous.* One of the ways we can define an adjective is to place it in an indefinite nominal group with an appropriate head and to use the predicate to comment on it. The result is not usually a full definition but is nevertheless helpful in understanding what the word means, e.g.:

A deciduous tree loses its leaves in winter.
or An honest man never lies.

In the first case, *loses its leaves in winter* is a useful shorthand definition; in the second, *never lies* is a guide to the kind of meaning *honest* has, even though it does not accurately define the word. Applying this to the poem, we are told:

Only a . . . vertuous soul . . . never gives

Thus the meaning of *never gives* will offer us a guide to the meaning of *vertuous* for Herbert.

There are in fact a number of relevant meanings for the phrase, all of which connect with crucial lexis in earlier verses. The first we consider is that of 'attacks';[13] this picks up the feature of aggression we noted regarding the rose. The soul 'never attacks' whereas the rose is 'angrie' and 'bids the rash gazer wipe his eye'. Thus being 'vertuous' has to do with not attacking, being peaceful. A second sense to *gives* is that of 'succumbs, yields to pressure', which would appear to connect with the sexual connotations noted in verse 1. While the soul 'never succumbs', the day falls to night. Thus being 'vertuous' has also to do with behaving chastely and constantly.

The third, most striking, sense of *give* that we consider is the following, which I quote verbatim from Webster, not becaue there is anything talismanic about a dictionary definition but

Figure 6.5

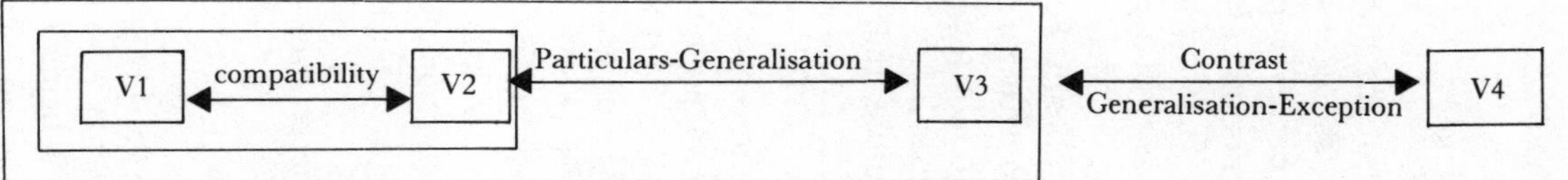
V1
compatibility
V2
Particulars-Generalisation
V3
Contrast
Generalisation-Exception
V4

because if I put it in my own words, it might be felt that it was too neat to be truthful; I have added points of comparison in square brackets:

> to become affected by weather conditions, specif.
> (a) to fade, as colour [cf. the rose];
> (b) to become soft or moist [cf. the day];
> (c) to shrink, as timber;
> (d) to thaw [cf. the spring].

So the soul never fades, but the hue of the rose does. The soul never becomes moist, but the dew weeps for the day. The soul never thaws, the thawing occurs as part of the process of Spring. In other words the soul is not part of the cycles that the rose, day, and spring are all part of. Thus being *vertuous* would appear also to have to do with the property of not being subject to the cyclical process of birth and decay.

This last sense poses problems. For the first two senses of *never gives* it is not difficult to construct a meaning of 'vertue' that fits. Thus in the first case, it might mean 'peacefulness' or possibly 'charity', in the second, 'chastity' or 'constancy'. But what meaning might be given to 'vertue' that would fit with the sense of being outside the cycles of life? And where does it come from, this 'vertue'?

The contrast between the verses helped us identify *vertuous* as crucial. We then used the meanings of *never gives* to help us pin down what Herbert means by 'vertue'. We now need something to help us define *vertuous* further, and the only possibility left us is the simile *like season'd timber.* At first sight, this seems unpromising, because too remote from the word we are trying to define. However, there is an interesting parallel between this simile and part of the definition of *give* quoted from Webster above:

> Like season'd timber, never gives
>
> shrink, as timber

In the definition, timber is used to illustrate the meaning of 'give'; in the poem, *season'd timber* is used to illustrate the meaning of *never gives.* Clearly then it is being *season'd* that makes the difference between timber 'giving' and 'never giving'. We can set this out thus:

Only a sweet and virtuous soul never gives	A sweet soul gives
season'd timber never gives	(timber gives)

(The brackets indicate that this statement is not directly made within the poem.) It is clear from the above that *vertuous* is to the soul what *season'd* is to timber. It is therefore to *season'd* that we must look to answer our questions about *vertuous.*

There are five interpretations we can give *season'd* that are of direct relevance to our understanding of 'Vertue' (both the word and the poem). The first of these is 'matured, experienced'. Thus the soul acquires its *vertue* through experience of life, not by avoiding it. The second sense is closely related; *season'd timber* is timber that has been through the seasons. A direct link is therefore made between season'd (= vertuous) and Spring, one of the four seasons. The soul to be 'vertuous' must pass through the seasons; if 'vertue' is connected with being outside the cycle, it is because the soul has broken through the cycles, not missed them out. It might be noted that *seasons* and *cycles* are closely related in meaning. But this only accentuates our earlier worry that we have in line 12 an all-embracing generalisation and in verse 4 an apparent exception to it. For if the soul passes through the seasons, the cycles of life, why does it not die?

A third sense of *season'd* is *salted*, which places it in direct contrast to *sweet* found everywhere else. *Sweet* and *salted* are both pleasant flavours, but 'sweetness' is natural to fruits and the like, whereas *seasoning* is something added to food to give it extra flavour and, more importantly, in Herbert's time, to preserve it. Thus we may interpret sweet as the natural, inherent quality of life, while *season'd* is something added from outside. Further, meat that is *season'd* has its life extended beyond the natural cycle; but for this to happen, the animal from which it is taken must first die, a breaking of the natural cycle indeed, but only to hasten death, not circumvent it. According to this sense of *season'd*, then, 'a . . . vertuous soul' is one that has passed through death, not avoided it; and 'vertue' is something given to the soul, not inherent to it.

The same interpretation is forced upon us by the fourth sense of *season'd*, and perhaps the most natural in the context. *Season'd timber* is timber that has been treated and preserved. Again, something has first to die; timber can only be treated if cut from the tree. The cycle is again broken, not by the timber but by an outside agent; death is introduced unnaturally early. The word *season'd* is related to the passive 'was seasoned' and assumes an agent to do the seasoning. So a 'vertuous soul' is one that has been through death and, again, has been treated from outside — to preserve it. A knowledge of Herbert suggests strongly who the agent of seasoning might be. As a small linguistic clue, however, we might note that *seasons* can refer not only to the natural seasons but to the ecclesiastical seasons — Lent, Easter, and so on. Thus a 'vertuous soul' is one who has passed through the Church year!

We can now see that the apparent contradiction between line 12 and verse 4 is no contradiction at all. To be 'vertuous', the soul has first to conform to the generalisation that 'all must die'. Within verse 4, a contrast is made between two states of dead wood — *coal* (charcoal, useless dead wood), which the world may turn to, and *season'd timber* (useful dead wood). Thus each cycle ends in one of two ways, with the world turned to coal or, prematurely, with the timber/soul *season'd.*

World was one of the words given emphasis in our analysis of the stress system. We can see now why. A contrast is being set up between the soul (unworldly) and the world, between unnatural life and the natural world; even the world as the all-embracing context for cycles 'must die'. In such a context, though season'd timber does not seem to have life when compared to the day and rose, it comes to seem like life when all else is uselessly dead; this accounts for the odd time reference of *then* in the final line, and for the equally odd adjunct *chiefly*. Season'd timber is not chiefly living now.

So *vertue* is not a natural property like sweetness but is the result of treatment from outside (real world knowledge of Herbert tells us, from God). The process can only take place if death is undergone prematurely; it involves changing the nature of what was alive (animal to meat, wood to timber) and preservation beyond the natural term of life. Above all, it can only be God's doing, not the soul's. Such an interpretation is theologically consistent with Christian doctrine which, given Herbert's beliefs and vocation, we would expect it to be:

'By our baptism, then, we were buried with him [Christ]

> and shared his death, in order that, just as Christ was raised from death by the glorious power of the Father, so also we might live a new life. For since we have become one with him in dying as he did, in the same way we shall be one with him by being raised to life as he was.' (Romans 6: 4-5; Good News Bible translation)

We have now answered all of our questions. We have found an interpretation of 'vertue' that makes sense of the poem, and have related the property of *sweet*-ness to the property of being *season'd* which was crucial to our understanding of 'vertue'. The grammatical oddity of *ye* was explained by reference to other verses' allusions to cyclical events, while the universal generalisation *all must die* was found not to be contradicted by the final verse. As we went, we also explained why some words have been emphasised by the tension between a natural stress and metrical stress. All were shown to have a central part in the configuration of meanings of the discourse. And that brings us back to linguistic matters.

We began with two purposes for this chapter — to provide an acceptable interpretation of a poem, and to show how each type of analysis needs the others in stylistic analysis. Whether or not the interpretation reached is felt to be satisfactory is for others to judge. It is, however, important to the other purpose of this chapter that we reflect upon the process just completed, not least because it is hoped that it may be generalisable to other poems. The simplest way of doing this is to represent the stages of our argument in a diagram (Figure 6.6); the arrows can be glossed as 'led us to consider/investigate'. The diagram is necessarily simplified but not to the point of falsification. It will be seen that we have shifted from one kind of analysis to another over and over again. Discourse observations were supported by lexical, phonological, and syntactic observations, lexical ones by discourse, phonological and syntactic, and so on. Intermingled with these were literary and theological observations necessary to make sense of the linguistic evidence. An analysis for purists it is not, but an analysis for students of literature I believe it is. The future of stylistics lies not in the meticulous application of a single descriptive apparatus, insightful though that can be on occasion, but in the eclectic marshalling of observations from all branches of language study and beyond. I hope the analysis I have offered provides modest support for this prophecy.

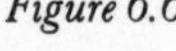

Figure 6.6

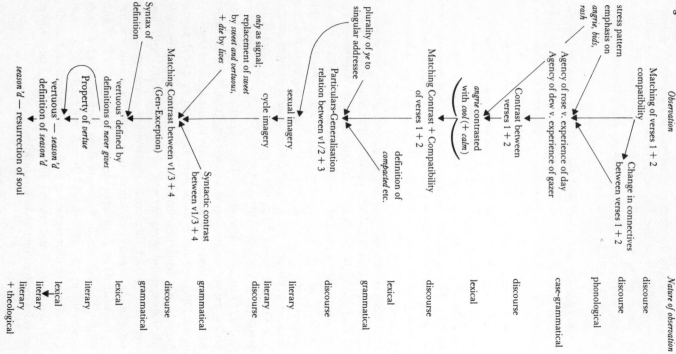

Observation	*Nature of observation*
Matching of verses 1 + 2 compatibility	discourse
Change in connectives between verses 1 + 2	discourse
stress pattern emphasis on *angrie, bids, rash*	phonological
Agency of rose v. experience of day Agency of dew v. experience of gazer	case-grammatical
Contrast between verses 1 + 2	discourse
angrie contrasted with *cool* (+ *calm*)	lexical
Matching Contrast + Compatibility of verses 1 + 2	discourse
definition of *compacted* etc.	lexical
plurality of *ye* to singular addressee	grammatical
Particulars-Generalisation relation between v1/2 + 3	discourse
sexual imagery	literary
cycle imagery	literary discourse
only as signal; replacement of *sweet* by *sweet and vertuous*, + *die* by *lives*	
Syntactic contrast between v1/3 + 4	grammatical
Matching Contrast between v1/3 + 4 (Gen-Exception)	discourse
Syntax of definition	grammatical
'vertuous' defined by definitions of *never gives*	lexical
Property of *vertue*	literary
'vertuous' — *season'd* definition of *season'd*	lexical literary
season'd — resurrection of soul	literary + theological

Notes

1. For detailed accounts of clause relational work, see Winter 1971, 1977, 1979; Hoey 1979, 1983a; Hoey and Winter 1986; Jordan 1980, 1985. This approach has close affinities with work done by Beekman and Callow, 1974; Graustein and Thiele 1979; Grimes 1975; Longacre 1972, 1983; and Crombie 1985.

2. From *I'm the King of the Castle* by Susan Hill, published in Penguin Books, Harmondsworth, 1974, Chapter 5, p. 58. In this and all subsequent prose examples, sentences are lettered for ease of reference.

3. From 'Dog eat pup' in 'Nature' section of *BBC Wildlife*, 4,2 (Feb. 1986), p. 61.

4. A third class of relations relating to Speech Act Theory and exchange structure had recently been posited (Hoey 1986; cf. also Crombie 1985a), but this does not affect the stylistic analysis of poetry.

5. From 'Hansel and Gretel' in *Fairy tales* retold by Bridget Hadaway, 1974, Cathay Books, London, p. 23.

6. From *Home growing* (edited by Ann Bonar), Marshall Cavendish, London, 1977, p. 12.

7. See for example Hoey and Winter 1981; Hoey 1982, 1984; and Mahoney 1985.

8. This chapter is the product of long maturation. The earliest analysis was done in conjunction with Eugene Winter and Winnie Crombie at the Hatfield Polytechnic as part of a course in stylistics. A later version was presented to a Staff Seminar at the University of Birmingham; comments from colleagues, particularly from Marcus Walsh, led to my incorporating into the analysis the observations on the lexis and its relationship to the discourse organisation. In a form recognisably like the one before you, the analysis was then given to Birmingham University students, and then finally to a Workshop on Language Teaching, Translation and Literature held at the University of Diepenbeek under Professor Rene Dirven, as part of a series of papers and discussions given in conjunction with Malcolm Coulthard. I am grateful to all the named people and many more unnamed who have prevented this chapter from being any worse than it is.

9. I am not suggesting that there is only one natural reading, but I would assert that the one given is natural if no effort is being made to reinforce any of the poem's meanings.

10. The case grammar terminology is drawn from Longacre 1976; he prefers the term 'role' to 'case'.

11. Definitions are throughout taken from Webster.

12. It is worth noting in passing that the line is yet again in a different relation with its predecessor. Whereas in Verse 1 it offered *reason* and in verse 2 *consequence*, in this verse it offers a *compatible* conclusion with that in line 11.

References

Beekman, J. and Callow, J. (1974) *Translating the word of God.* Grand Rapids, Mich.: Zondervan

Crombie, W. (1985) *Process and relation in discourse and language learning.* Oxford: Oxford University Press

Grustein, G. and Thiele, W. (1979) 'An approach to the analysis of English Texts'. *Linguistische Studien,* A55, pp. 3-15

Grimes, J. (1975) *The thread of discourse.* The Hague: Mouton

Hoey, M. (1979) *Signalling in discourse.* Discourse Analysis Monographs no. 6. Birmingham: English Language Research, University of Birmingham

——— (1982) 'Discourse-centred stylistics: a way forward?' In W. Gutwinski and C. Jolly (eds) *The Eighth LACUS forum, 1981.* Columbia, SC: Hornbeam Press, pp. 401-9

——— (1983) *On the surface of discourse,* London: Allen & Unwin

——— (1984) 'Crabbe's *Dumb Orators* as detail tree: an analysis of a narrative poem in terms of its discourse organisation'. *MALS Journal,* 9, pp. 87-116

——— (1986) 'Overlapping patterns of discourse organization and their implications for clause-relational analysis of Problem-Solution texts'. In C.R. Cooper and S. Greenbaum (eds) *Studying writing: linguistic approaches; written communication annual 1.* Beverley Hills, Calif.: Sage, pp. 186-214

Hoey, M. and Winter, E. (1981) 'Believe me for mine honour'. *Language and Style,* 14, 4, pp. 315-39

Hoey, M. and Winter, E. (1986) 'Clause relations and the writer's communicative purpose'. In B. Couture (ed.) *Functional approaches to writing.* Norwood NJ and London: Francis Pinter

Jordan, M. (1980) 'Short texts to explain problem–solution structures — and vice versa'. *Instructional Science,* 9, pp. 221-52

——— (1985) 'Towards an integrated theory of textual cohesion'. *MALS Journal,* 10, pp. 8-40

Longacre, R. (1972) *Hierarchy and universality of discourse constituents in New Guinea languages.* Washington, DC: Georgetown University Press

——— (1976) *An anatomy of speech nations.* Lisse: Peter de Ridder Press

——— (1983) *The grammer of discourse.* New York: Plenum Press

Mahoney, D. (1985) 'Hamm's anti-narrative: a static tale'. *MALS Journal,* 10, pp. 70-95

Winter, E. (1971) 'Connection in science material: a proposition about the semantics of clause relations'. In *CILT papers and reports,* No. 7, pp. 41-52. London: Centre for Information on Language Teaching and Research for British Association for Applied Linguistics

——— (1977) 'A clause-relational approach to English texts: a study of some predictive lexical items in written discourse'. *Instructional Science,* 6, 1, pp. 1-92

——— (1979) 'Replacement as a fundamental function of the sentence in context'. *Forum Linguisticum,* 4, 2, pp. 95-133

7

Degrees of Control: Stylistics and the Discourse of Children's Literature

Peter Hunt

> The question is: in what ways are presentational process, presented world, and implied reader functions of one another? (Ruthrof 1981, p. 123)

> All literary works contain ... sub-texts, and there is a sense in which they may be spoken of as the 'unconscious' of the work itself. The work's insights, as with all writings, are deeply related to its blindnesses: what it does not say, and *how* it does not say it, may be as important as what it articulates; what seems absent, marginal or ambivalent about it may provide a central clue to its meaning. (Eagleton 1983, p. 178)

The problem of children's literature

The realisation of a text, and especially of a text for children, is closely involved with questions of control, and of the techniques through which power is exercised over, or shared with, the reader. Many of the confusions over the status and quality of children's books and literature stem from the assumption that they must necessarily be, in Barthes's terms, *lisible* rather than *scriptible*, readerly rather than writerly (Brooke-Rose 1981, p. 41), 'closed texts' which the skilled reader reads 'below capacity'. By attempting to control the text in certain ways, writers 'require' readers to read only within both implied and defined limits, and texts become, in Bakhtin's terms, 'monological' rather than 'dialogical' or 'polyphonic' (Seldon 1985, p. 17). Generic expectations are consequently self-fulfilling: children's books are as they are because writers assume, from what they write, that that is how they should be. Hence children's books are very frequently perceived as being of poor quality by definition, because the mode or genre is primarily defined unconsciously by the textures of implication within the text (most clearly seen in the stylistic features which this chapter will examine), and consciously by content items or overt relationships with the audience. Texts which challenge these assumptions commonly find themselves in the no-person's land between writings for adults (so-called) and writings for children (so-called).

In peer texts, the adult reader (ideal or otherwise) can adjust to the degree of control which the author appears to be exercising. As an adult reader, my selection of a text may, in part, be governed by the amount of effort I wish to bring to it, and by a judgement of how much effort is warranted. With books 'for' children — or for 'unskilled' readers — because of the status of the audience, the author–reader (or narrator–narratee) relationship is a more than usually unbalanced power-relationship. The audience is 'created' by the writer much more directly than with a peer text, in the sense that the text does more than display its codes, grammar, and contracts, suggesting what the reader should choose to be to optimise the reading of the text. Drawing on the power-codes of adult–child, book–child, and written–oral relationships, it *prescribes* what the reader *must* be, and indeed, because there is both an authoritarian and educational element involved, what the reader *can* be. The exercise of such power is by no means inevitable, although it is so characteristic as to define the children's book for many readers. Very often, a deliberate attempt seems to be made to limit the child reader's interaction with the text. This may seem to be malevolent — if one believes that the 'open' text is fundamental to literary development, or, as some censors clearly suppose, benevolent, or, as Jacqueline Rose suggests, merely a fact of life for the 'impossible' category of children's fiction (Rose 1984, pp. 1-2).

It is commonly assumed that control is efficiently exercised by modifying (that is, restricting) content, vocabulary, plot-type and so on. I would like to suggest that, simply because such modifications *are* obvious, they are not as significant in their potential effect as the stylistic features that convey them. Furthermore, stylistic features may well reveal convert attitudes in the author: the syntagmatic structures of language can be a remarkably accurate reflection of the paradigms they express. That is, style can show not only 'conscious' choices, but also unconscious prejudices.

The very fact that readers 'know' when they are reading a children's book (even when given an anonymous extract) suggests that there may be an identifiable lexical set for children's books (Hunt 1978, p. 146), which in itself defines, and is defined by, the theoretical presuppositions of writers, and a characteristic mode of narration. Together, they constitute a 'register' which may expose a sub-text rhetoric which is actually *anti*-child and which exploits the assumption that children cannot distinguish good writing from bad. Debased writing demonstrates a debasing attitude: far from regarding only (in De La Mare's phrase) 'the rarest kind of best' as good enough for the innocent, developing audience, it seems that adult readers of children's books (parents, teachers, reviewers) are themselves unable or unwilling to detect the limited and limiting in prose. As a result, the primary audience is not given the opportunity to compare original with unoriginal, unfamiliar with familiar, challenging with confirming, or, it might be said, 'fresh' with 'stale'. (If this seems to be unjustifiably judgemental, it will be seen that the first item in each of these pairs represents the declared preference of most writers of and about children's books; it also represents the most efficient means of information-transfer, and perhaps a working definition of 'literature'.) As a consequence of the doublethink that declares a practical and ideological preference for one type of language use, and yet perpetuates its antithesis, confused standards flourish in and around children's books.

The briefest glance at what passes for criticism in the field of children's books suggests that the fundamental problem is in merely perceiving what is on the page. Reading a text intended for a non-peer audience is a complex act, involving generic, educational, social and literary preconceptions, and, for many children's book 'practitioners', honest doubts as to the validity of their own judgements in the face of the Leavisite literary/educational establishment (Hunt 1984). What is needed is an accessible technique for identifying significant features, which does not appeal to some mythic 'trained intuition' (as Leavis put it), and which triggers, supports, and sharpens perception: for all its philosophical shortcomings, such a technique can be provided by stylistics.

Children's literature, style and stylistics

What part do style and stylistics play in the overall communication process? To begin with, we cannot isolate stylistics from the act of reading. Reading is an interaction, and we make sense of texts in terms of the codes of the text and the codes we bring to it. The reader fills the 'gaps' in the text, thus reducing its indeterminacies (although there is also the paradox that the more information the text provides the more indeterminate it can become: far from clarifying, each additional word may widen the possible range of connotation). This contribution by the reader means, for Wolfgang Iser, that 'the most effective literary work is one which forces the reader into a new critical awareness of his or her customary codes and expectations' (Eagleton 1983, p. 79), and this process will begin with a perception of stylistic deviation. However, Eagleton observes that this rationale implies a liberal humanist ideal of reading (that the mind should be open to influence by the text), and also masks a power structure, in that the reader becomes no more than a mechanic, 'recouping the "meaning" of the text according to a kind of "do-it-yourself kit" of cues provided by the author' (Eagleton 1983, pp. 79-80).

The relevance of this to children's literature is striking. Can, for example, Eagleton's criticism of liberal humanist readers be applied to the implied readers of a text 'for children', when they are exploring and discovering text codes, and when the indeterminacies are part of a much more fundamental learning process? And if Iser (despite what Eagleton detects) is at pains to support the 'open' text, what can we make of a situation in which, for children, limitation and restriction are seen as a virtue by some critics? It may be correct to assume that child-readers will not bring to the text a complete or sophisticated system of codes, but is this any reason to deny them access to texts with a potential of rich codes? Equally, the argument that the child-reader does not understand complex indeterminacy would be more convincing if what is commonly subsituted for it could be 'simple': 'simplicity' (cf. J. Coupland 1983) often equates with unoriginal phrasing and a tendency to summarise thought or action. While this may derive from a residual attempt to build the oral storytelling situation into the written text, the summary, and the allusion which provides the semantic content of the unoriginal phrase, are both quite sophisticated devices in terms of the decoding needed. Paradoxically, although they require considerable input by the reader, they remain reductive, rather than interactive. An example from a characteristic text:

> By good fortune they encountered Uncle John himself cutting up a felled tree as an offering of gratitude to the good brothers who had given him hospitality. He stuck his axe into the wood when he saw them and invited them to sit down on the trunk. (Harnett 1951, p. 211)

The summarising clauses 'they encountered' and 'when he saw them' are so placed as to impose the narrator's authority from the point of view of information transfer. The qualifier 'as an offering ... hospitality' cannot be related to the 'they/them' characters, while any dialogue is only implied ('and invited them') by a formal choice of lexis. Similarly, the preliminary clause 'By good fortune' is not only precise judgement, restricting interpretive alternatives, but its relationship to the characters who are the 'consciousness-focus' of the text is — partly because of its structural place in the sentence — ambiguous; significantly, it is also a cliché requiring a complex decoding through generic sets of various kinds.

Textual limitations are in direct opposition to both the theory and practice of teaching and producing children's texts (Bolt and Gard 1970, p. 25; Meek *et al.* 1977, p. 180; Haviland 1975, p. 306; Applebee 1978; Chambers 1973; Trelease 1984), and the central attitudes and propositions have been summed up by a distinguished British librarian, Peggy Heeks, who quotes *A language for life* (1975): 'Literature brings the child into an encounter with language in its most complex and varied forms', and comments that this rightly emphasises

> the engagment with words that is at the heart of the literary experience. It is style which, ultimately, decides the quality of a story ... Style may be enjoyed by children without being identified by them ... but it is essential that we, the adult selectors of books for children should train ourselves to be sensitive to the words which carry the story. (Heeks 1981, p. 50)

Thus, although it is generally agreed by authors and teachers that there is no need to restrict language in texts designed for children (Cameron 1969, p. 90), or for that matter to change the coinage of criticism (Lanes 1971, pp. vii-viii; Egoff *et al.* 1980, p. xv), the fact that these agreed-upon ideals are not maintained in practice once again returns us to the sub-text. (In one notable instance, a major British award-giving committee actually questioned whether 'literary' standards were at all relevant in choosing a 'good' children's book (Fox *et al.* 1976, p. 139; Hunt 1980, p. 225).) The association between language and thought, language and education and language and socialisation are recognised: why, then, in this context, a neglect of language itself? To some extent, it seems, the interests of critics lie elsewhere; at root, textual studies are not popular.

This may seem surprising in view of the legacy of 'Practical Criticism' which has dominated literary education in the USA and the UK for the last 50 years, but three influences have been at work. The first is the emphasis placed on the *use* of children's literature. This has led to concentration on affect, which has led in turn to some very simplistic models of the reading process, and a concentration on thematic analysis. Secondly, the point of stylistic analysis has rarely been made clear. Early 'formalist' stylistics shared with 'practical criticism' the danger that, as Ian Watt put it, 'its air of objectivity confers a spurious authority on a process that is often only a rationalization of unexamined judgements' (1960, p. 59), and its relation to affect has been frequently challenged. Consequently, it has come to be seen as an arid exercise in comparison with the thrust and interest of narrative itself. And thirdly, the main drive of critical thought over the last 20 years has been towards contextual studies, reader response, plurality of readings, and the philosophy of the text (perhaps, a sceptic might say, more portable concepts for students).

However, if we agree on the relevance of the study of style, what methodology is available to us? Stylistics, or linguistic criticism, has had a chequered history. Its early claims to be the area where linguistic and critical exegesis overlap (Leech 1969, p. 225) or that it provides 'a basis for aesthetic appreciation by bringing to the level of conscious awareness features of the text accessible only to trained intuition' (Widdowson in Allen and Pit Corder 1973, p. 204) have been questioned. As style cannot be related directly to response (Fish 1980, pp. 68-96) the study of stylistics was seen for some time only as a 'pre-critical' activity, a mechanical act, endorsing, as Fowler puts it, 'a complacent and unprogressive ideology of literature' (Fowler 1981, p. 19). However, as

Cluysenaar (1976, p. 16) and others have noted, the selection of both text and analytic method is in itself a critical act: to describe form is to make a critical statement. Stanley Fish's argument that, because the analytic method dictates what is perceived, stylistics is a 'closed' system, is only a stumbling block if stylistics pretends to be definitive rather than suggestive. The recent work of Fowler (1981) and the revival of interest in Bakhtin and others (Selden 1985, pp. 16-19), who provide ideological correlatives for stylistics, place it once more in the mainstream of critical techniques.

Methods of stylistic analysis, like the analysis of narrative acts, are open to the objection that if they are seen 'as merely technical operations, leaving the construction of meaning to other studies, they leave us empty-handed if not empty-headed' (Ruthrof 1981, p. 123). Nevertheless, the 'technical operations' are vital, and useful taxonomies have been developed, usually working back from the particular to the general (Crystal and Davy 1969, pp. 15-19; Leech and Short 1981, pp. 75-82). Typical is the scheme of Cummings and Simmons, who progress from phonology and phonetics to graphology, grammar (clause, group, unit-complexes and rank-shift), lexis (collocations and sets), context, and varieties of language. In themselves, of course, these operations have scant critical meaning, but as Cummings and Simmons observe 'stylistic analysis is ultimately a study of context and situation ... Items in literary texts ... mutually define their meanings' (1983, p. 218). Similarly Fowler notes:

> Linguistic structure is not arbitrary but is determined by, or motivated by, the function it performs ... Within a given community, particular ranges of significance tend to be conventionally attached to specific types of construction. (Fowler 1981, p. 28)

The interrelationship between the style and discourse of children's books is clearly complex, and in the remainder of this chapter I will deal with two central aspects of it: the implications and realisation of authorial stance, and the power-structures and controls implied by the style of dialogue presentation.

Control in narrative

Criticism, perhaps especially of children's literature, is controlled by perception of genre; is children's literature identified by lexical items, grammatical structures, higher level narrative units, or an overall tonal strategy? For example, what cues the 'implied audience' for this extract?

> He woke up with a jerk, shivering with cold. He began to stretch his cramped legs but they hurt. Opening his eyes, he looked around in the darkness. He knew immediately where he was. He had been locked under the stairs. He peered through the crack at the side of the small door. It was pitch black. (Magorian 1983, p. 192)

It could be that phrasal 'woke up' (rather than 'woke' or 'awoke') and the economical syntax (and lack of punctuation) of the second sentence are intended to link to discourse to the mind of the character. Unfortunately, the stylistic simplicity of the passage (that is, its lack of deviation or variety) merely points up the logical and referential anomalies. (How could he 'peer through' a 'crack' (is it really a 'crack', or a 'gap'?) which he could not see (as it was 'pitch black')? Indeed, how could he know that he was under the stairs if it was so dark — and if he knew by some means other than sight, why are we not informed about it?) The summarising mode is so pervasive that it constantly shifts towards implicit authorial control, which in turn becomes a marker (or an assumed marker) of the genre of children's literature. And this is quite apart from the grammatical features: five of the seven sentences have the same structure (six if we discount the clause 'opening his eyes . . .'). Michelle Magorian's *Goodnight Mr. Tom*, from which the scene above was taken, not only won the British Library Association's Carnegie Medal, but also (ironically enough), the International Reading Association's Children's Book Award (1982). As this extract is characteristic of the novel, we may have here some indication of the relative stress laid by judges upon content and style.

Magorian's text tells rather than shows, explicates rather than demonstrates, and books which retain this dominating narrational presence — the residual or 'transferred' storyteller — are a textual echo of storying as an event, which the storyteller essentially controls. It seems, in general, that this control is only reluctantly relinquished (which may say something about the adult–child relationship) — and this can scarcely be for so simple a reason as that the reading audience cannot understand the text without a built-in prompter. Indeed, the voice of the storyteller, addressing the audience 'directly', is difficult even for a skilled reader to account for in the 'two-dimensional' printed text. It is an accepted definition of 'literature' — from a linguistic point of view — that its messages are 'text contained'. However, as the history of the early novel demonstrates, the act of storying involves a narrative voice or stance, an implied narrator or author or quasi-storyteller (or a device to replace it) — and this produces a grammatical and psychological situation of immense complexity (see, for example, Rimmon-Kenan 1983, pp. 86-116). When, as in texts designed to be read *to* children (or, indeed, any audience) there is a first-person marker, there can be problems. Hugh and Maureen Crago, in their longitudinal study in 1983, cite the antepenultimate text page of Potter's *The tale of Tom Kitten.* Where, as far as the readership is concerned, does the message emanate from? 'And I think that some day I shall have to make another, longer book, to tell you more about *Tom Kitten*' (cf. Hunt 1984, p. 52).

One of the most complex instances is the opening of Milne's *Winnie-the-Pooh.* The narrative begins with a direct address to the implied reader, marked by second-person form: 'Anyhow, here he is . . . ready to be introduced to you.' It then moves to a situation where the 'I' narrator describes how s/he tells a story to Christopher Robin, who now becomes both a character *and* an addressee: 'You aimed very carefully at the balloon, and fired. "Did I miss?" you asked . . .' (Milne 1926 (1970 edition), pp. 16-17).

The problems confronting a reader of this text and a listener to that reader are formidable — not least because the reader implied (and thus required) by the text is not the actual receiver. Hence the linguistic needs are different. There is an entertaining paradox here. The storyteller's summaries, intended to make things easier for the *listener,* are quite likely when they appear in a text being read silently, to make things more difficult for the *reader.* They have not sprung from a genuine need (on the part of the reader), and as a result they require an artificial convergence of text-codes and reader-codes, rather than, as in the case of the 'given' text, allowing an exploration of codes which *may not* cohere, *and may not need to.* The implications of this can be seen in Leeson's recent account of the history of children's literature (1985, pp. 15-109) which emphasises the interplay of oral and written patterns in a socio-political context (a view that recalls both Ong's work on orality and the arguments over Saussure's 'phonocentric approach' to language (Norris 1982, p. 42ff).

These features of control — summary and the quasi-storyteller's voice — can be seen in an example from Ruth Park's novel, *Playing Beattie Bow* (which won the Australian Children's Book of the Year Award in 1981):

> As she stood there, looking up at the askew, rusted pulley, and the edge of the roof above it, a small patch of the sky suddenly lost its stars.
>
> Someone was lying on the warehouse roof looking down at her.
>
> *Chapter 7*
>
> When Abigail realised that she was being spied upon . . .
>
> (Park 1982, pp. 96-7)

Here we have three renditions, or variations, of the same essential semantic set, which progressively 'close' the text. 'A small patch of the sky suddenly lost its stars' requires a considerable interpretive effort by the reader — and it carries several possibilities. 'Someone was lying on the warehouse roof' restricts these possibilities. 'Looking down on her' and 'realised that she was being spied upon' similarly move from 'sharing' to 'telling', from 'open' to 'closed'. Of course, it could be argued that this progression reflects the deductions made by Abigail, so that Park holds to the contract of narration through a single consciousness. However, the progression from stylistic deviation (the adverb in an adjectival position — 'askew, rusted pulley') to cliché ('being spied upon') reassumes control. This is further corroborated by the explanatory work of the first sentence in the new chapter, and of course we need not assume that the presence of a chapter-division requires a break in the flow of reading.

Control in speech and thought

The residual storyteller tends to direct responses, telling rather than showing (Booth 1961, p. 2ff.; Rimmon-Kenan 1983, pp. 106-8), and in his/her absence we have seen that various stylistic devices may be substituted. In the case of the narration of 'speech' and 'thought', a reasonably sophisticated stylistic apparatus has been developed for distinguishing the strength of the narrational intervention. The description of thought and speech presentation has produced a variety of terminologies, of varying degrees of subtlety (for example, Chatman 1975, p. 230, 1978, p. 201; Bonheim 1982, p. 51; Fowler 1977, p. 102ff.; Rimmon-Kenan 1983, pp. 108-16; and cf. in particular the discussion by Young, in Chapter 1 of this volume, of 'projection' and 'focusing' in narrative). Very broadly, a distinction is made between 'tagged', 'free', 'direct' and 'indirect' representation. 'Tagged' refers to speech or thought represented in inverted commas, usually with a 'tag' (or reporting clause, or inquit) — for example, 'she said'. 'Free' representation does not have a tag. The distinction between 'direct' and 'indirect' is the traditional one between 'showing' and 'telling': in Chatman's example, 'I have to go' as opposed to 'She said she had to go.' Of course, there are many instances where tagging is by implication, or where the narrational summary is so abstract that it removes itself into another category — what Leech and Short call the Narrative Report of Speech Acts (1981, pp. 323-4) — or it becomes Free Indirect Discourse. This mode 'gives the impression of combining direct discourse with indirect discourse' and includes 'not only the co-presence of two voices but also that of the narrator's voice and a character's preverbal perception or feeling' (Rimmon-Kenan 1983, pp. 110-11) Fowler calls this 'mind style' — 'any distinctive linguistic presentation of an individual mental self' (1977, p. 103). The more sophisticated the readership is assumed to be, the more easily the transition can be made away from control and towards Free Direct or Free Indirect Thought.

There are further very interesting gradations within these broad categories of 'speech' and 'thought' when the lines between perception and feeling, and between thought and expression, are blurred (Bonheim 1982, p. 51). Leech and Short posit a cline from the mode in which the narrator seems, intrusively, to be into total control (Narrative Report of Speech Acts), through stages of progressively decreasing control: Indirect Tagged Speech, Indirect Free Speech, and Direct Tagged Speech, to the point at which control seems to have been relinquished, with Direct Free Speech (p. 324). They also suggest that 'the norm, or baseline for the presentation of thought is indirect tagged, whereas the norm for speech is direct tagged' (p. 344). Both of these norms represent *acceptable* illusions. Whereas we are used to perceiving speech verbatim, 'a direct perception of someone else's thought is not possible' (p. 345). Thus Indirect Free Thought occupies the middle ground between showing and telling, while Direct Tagged Thought is the most artificial form, the most governed by the reductive narrative voice.

Let us take two examples, from different ends of the 'quality' spectrum. The first is a mass-market, syndicate-produced, formula novel for adolescents, *The invisible intruder*:

> 'By the way, an octopus is pretty lucky — it has three hearts.' 'O-oh,' said Bess. 'What does it do with them all?'
>
> Mr Prizer chuckled. 'I suppose they provide a better circulatory system to get the blood to all the eight legs.'
>
> As the man paused, Bab remarked that an octopus exudes an inky smoke-screen when it is confronted by an enemy.
>
> 'The moray eel is the natural enemy of the octopus.'
>
> Bab asked Mr. Prizer if she might see the rest of his collection of shells.
>
> 'It's not unpacked yet. But I've got some beauties.'
>
> The elderly man did not sit down again and the visitors took this as an indication that the interview was at an end. They all thanked him for his interesting talk, but Nancy and Ned noticed that he did not invite them to return. They mentioned this to the others as the group trudged up the hill to the road. (Keene 1972, pp. 32-3)

The fact that this is the most elementary kind of formula writing is marked by the lexis ('chuckled', 'trudged') and by the obvious insertion of 'improving information' with its appropriate forms. More importantly, the implied audience is 'marked' by the strong control of dialogue presentation. Of the nine speech acts, only two are presented directly (both, interestingly enough, spoken by the adult); of the rest, one is 'tagged' ('said Bess'), while the following two are tagged by implication. The remaining four are either reported indirectly ('Bab asked'; 'Bab remarked') or absorbed into the narrative as summary ('they all thanked him'; 'they mentioned this'). This mode of reporting seems to imply that the audience will *need* to have things explained and deductions made on its behalf. This may seem to be helpful for developing readers, but it in fact defines them reductively and limits their involvement. This may be convenient for an author who has nothing to say, but many educationalists would see this as deleterious from an educational point of view, and probably from a literary point of view as well. At the other extreme is dialogue in which the authorial voice is absent, or appears to have relinquished control. (There is a paradox here, too, in the relationship between writer and oral storyteller. The written 'tag' has to substitute for the change in voice tone or colour which may distinguish orally imitated speakers. These tags draw attention to the artificiality of the written medium, but to dispense with them may increase the awareness of artificiality through the effort required to assign roles.) While it is not possible to make any correlation between open/closed texts and the amount of tagging, because texts which imitate other media (such as those deriving from television scripts, or using the ready-made characterisation of television and film) have similar characteristics to 'open', 'text-contained' pieces, texts with a predominance of 'free' elements generally make more demands on the reader.

The potential effect of judicious control of dialogue can be seen in the next example. In a key scene from Alan Garner's *Red shift*, Jan is sunbathing in her bikini, and her boyfriend Tom is finding the situation very frustrating (especially as he has recently discovered that Jan has slept with someone else):

> 'Listen to me,' said Jan. 'Being together: OK? That's what I mean. That's what's new, important. The silences. OK? The bikini was a mistake: but only because I didn't understand. Don't cane ignorance. Please. I love you.'
>
> 'Understand what?'
>
> 'Please, Tom.'
>
> 'Understand that intelligence isn't the same as finesse? ... You're tearing me. You're tearing me. Bikini!'
>
> 'I'm trying to be honest! I don't understand! It's my fault. I love you. I love you like nothing else.'
>
> 'Bikini!'
>
> 'I love you.'
>
> 'Bikini!'
>
> 'It's hurting you too much,' said Jan. 'I'll get rid of it.'
>
> 'Have you caught up?' said Jan.
>
> 'Don't.'
>
> 'I only want to know.' (p. 130)

Red shift is only arbitrarily on the 'juvenile' lists (which, in itself says something about the rhetoric which controls the production of children's literature), and it demonstrates the dependence upon 'open' reading and reader-deduction which is a mark of the *scriptible* text. These two facts may not be unconnected. Neil Philip (1981) has pointed out the subtletly of Garner's technique, and part of this may well be due to the restricted tagging:

> What is interesting about this technique is how much it enables Garner to communicate without ever expressing it in words. The whole of Tom and Jan's sexual relationship, for instance, is contained in pauses between sentences. It is quite clear, but it is neither described nor mentioned. (p. 106)

In fact, Garner brackets the implied sexual act with the two tagged speech items ('said Jan') — a positive use of the device, as compared with the arbitrary (although perhaps unconsciously revealing) use of a far wider range of devices by the author(s) of *The invisible intruder.*

The choice of mode, then, can make a considerable difference (at least in theory) to the perceived status of the narrative. As Chatman observes, the use of 'indirect forms in narratives implies a shade more intervention by a narrator, since we cannot be sure that the words in his report clauses are precisely those spoken by the quoted speaker' (Chatman 1978, p. 200). Conversely, 'free' dialogue entails 'more inference than other kinds of narrative. To a greater degree than normal, the reader is required to interpret the illocutionary force of the sentences that are spoken by the characters ... to infer what they 'mean' in context ... to supply, metatextually, the correct verb tag' (Chatman 1975, pp. 244-5). Of course, we are dealing only in possibilities, and there is no statistical method for proving that one form is more common than another in any particular kind of text, nor of judging affect. None the less, Leech and Short's ideas are highly suggestive. Are children's novels more prone to tagging? Can the process be reversed: if we perceive control of speech and thought presentation, do we deduce that we are reading a children's book?

An example from the 'second golden age' of British children's books (conventionally taken as the period 1950–70) may make the point. It seems to me that this aspect of style clearly identifies both the period and the implied audience for *When Marnie was there* (Robinson 1967):

> Anna smiled. 'Yes, you were painting on the marsh.' She would have liked to add that she had remembered her ever since as if they had been friends, but felt this would be too extravagant.
>
> The Lindsays were delighted and amazed, wanting to know how and when the two could possibly have met. And why hadn't they been there, they demanded. Miss Gill told them. It was the last time she had come down to Barnham for a few days' sketching. (p. 200)

Even the projected thought is heavily tagged ('she would have liked to add') and placed within authorial control by the omission of 'she' in 'but felt this would be too extravagant'. The point here is that once an author employs indirect reporting, summary words ('delighted', 'amazed') and graphic tags ('demanded') replace in the first instance a deduction by the reader, and in the second the purely functional (and hence more or less invisible) tag. For this reason, the text may seem, to peer readers, to be simplistic, and, possibly, patronising.

If we were to characterise children's literature stylistically, then, we might expect to find a relatively high proportion of dialogue ('"and what is the use of a book," thought Alice, "without pictures or conversation?"') and of highly organised dialogue at that; where 'thought' items occur, we might expect to find tagging, and indirect presentation (and, possibly, Direct Tagged Thought, as this is clearly the most simplistic mode). In addition, authors whose status is ambiguous — that is, between writing for children and writing for adults — may show significant differences in these stylistic patterns. (Of course, individual style may run counter to these large generalisations, as in the case of Garner. Malcolm Bradbury's later style, for example in *The history man* (1977), and *Rates of exchange* (1984), is much given to relentless tagging which deliberately emphasises — or over-emphasises — the overbearing narrative voice.) Impressionistic sampling suggests that children's books are likely to have about half as many Direct Free Speech items, and twice as many Indirect Tagged Thought items, as adult texts. Both Direct Tagged Thought and (to a lesser degree) Direct Free Thought items are far more common in children's texts. Unfortunately for those who would claim that similar evaluative standards can be applied to both children's and adult's texts, tagging tends to be more common in 'popular' as opposed to 'serious' adult novels (with, of course, individual variations).

There may well be a correlation between the perceived status of a writer and the extent to which these generic tendencies are resisted. For example, we have seen that the impression that may have been gained from *When Marnie was there* was one of strong control by a residual storyteller. In Garner's *The stone book* (1976), the reported perceptions tend to paraphrase the consciousness of the central character, and the status of many of the sentences is somewhere between Direct Free Thought, Narrative Report of Speech and Free Indirect Discourse. Consider the opening:

> A bottle of cold tea; bread and half an onion. That was Father's baggin. Mary emptied her apron of stones from the field and wrapped the baggin in a cloth.
>
> The hottest part of the day was on. Mother lay in bed under the rafters and the thatch, where the sun could only send blue light. She had picked stones in the field until she was too tired and had to rest. (p. 11)

The revealing lexical items are the unqualified 'Father's' and 'Mother' — as opposed to 'her father's' or 'Mary's mother'. Hence 'Mary' in the third sentence qualifies retrospectively 'Father', and, in effect, implies a tag to the first sentence, which is seen as a thought emanating from the character, rather than an observation by the narrator. The same applies in the second paragraph, although the comparative remoteness from the controlling noun 'Mary' may suggest a certain ambivalence of status of some of the sentences. The success of 'The Stone Book' Quartet, both critical and popular, points up the fallacy of prescription in this stylistic area.

Conclusions

Stylistics tends to prove what it sets out to prove, because it follows its 'hunches' with analytic equipment designed for each hunch — as Fish points out:

> Formal patterns are themselves the products of interpretation and therefore there is no such thing as a formal pattern, at least in the sense necessary for the practice of stylistics (as an absolute science), that is, no pattern that one can observe before interpretation is hazarded and which

> therefore can be used to prefer one interpretation to another. (1980, p. 267)

Consequently, the most rewarding applications of stylistic analysis will be those which confirm or refute a perception which itself has a socio-political origin. In the case of children's literature, a field without a canon, such perceptions, confirmations and refutations have a much more direct influence on the development of the discourse than in most discoursal areas.

A controlled narrative decreases the possibilities of interaction, and, ultimately, proscribes thought. By reducing the distance between teller and tale, it makes the narrative contract more specific; when this is placed in tension with the authoritarian mode of the implied narrator, then that contract becomes a very fragile one. This is especially the case when the implied emotional capacity of the audience (signalled by the 'content' items and the structure of the text) is perceived to be at variance with that of the controlling mode. What may be then perceived is an inappropriate simplification; an intrusive violation of the narrative contract. (This may account for why so many 'teenage problem' novels appear to the adult reader to be unsatisfactory — and, conversely, why so many 'children's books' seem to be unsatisfactory to children.)

The cliché, the 'standard phrase', may well be an automatic identifier of children's literature because it tends to occur where summaries are demanded: and summaries are demanded by the choice of level of control — which is in turn based upon assumptions about what the readership is, and what it should be allowed to be. The guiding voice of the storyteller has itself become an ominous cliché in a narrative relationship, a rhetoric which overtly encourages freedom while covertly suppressing it. Didacticism (in the sense of deliberate indoctrination or specific pendantry) is far from dead in modern children's literature, and it may be that because it is ineffective when it is obvious, it tends to disguise itself in modes of telling and control.

The wide acceptance of restrictive texts not only limits what readers think about, but also their ability to think. The neglect of this problem is part of the general neglect of children's literature by socio- and psycholinguistics, and it reflects the immense influence that unsophisticated readers have on the production of children's literature. Most readers can feel superior to material written for children, and can therefore feel free to prescribe and criticise, where they might be more hesitant with other genres. (The problem is compounded by the constant appeal to 'use' of children's books by several professions with different aims.)

Stylistic demonstration of how certain modes of thought and writing may operate in relation to children's literature suggests links between hidden and/or unconscious rhetorical strategies and the way in which they surface in language use. This is, inevitably, a matter which involves ideology and politics. Children's books are commonly seen as an 'innocent' area of writing, but because of their position as part of the process of education (linguistic and textual, as well as social) their linguistic characteristics have a direct social significance. This is, perhaps, why both analysis and text-production tend towards the prescriptive and judgemental, both consciously and, as we have seen, unconsciously. But from linguistic and critical points of view (supposing that these can be momentarily separated from ideology) the most interesting characteristic of children's books is that they are about *themselves*, about the conditions and presuppositions that generated them. They not only tell stories about others, they tell stories about their own rationales of telling, and the circumstances of the telling, through their stylistic devices.

References

Allen, J.B.R. and Pit Corder, S. (1973) *The Edinburgh course in applied linguistics*, vol. 2. London: Oxford University Press

Applebee, A.N. (1978) *The child's concept of story*. Chicago: University of Chicago Press

Bolt, S. and Gard, R. (1970) *Teaching fiction in schools*. London: Hutchinson Educational

Bonheim, H. (1982) *The narrative modes: techniques of the short story*. Cambridge: D.S. Brewer

Booth, W. (1961) *The rhetoric of fiction*. Chicago: University of Chicago Press

Bradbury, M. (1977) *The history man*. London: Hutchinson–Arrow

—— (1984) *Rates of exchange*. London: Hutchinson–Arrow

Brooke-Rose, C. (1981) *A rhetoric of the unreal*. Cambridge: Cambridge University Press

Cameron, E. (1969) *The green and burning tree*. New York: Atlantic Little Brown

Chambers, A. (1973) *Introducing books to children*. London: Heinemann

Chatman, S. (ed.) (1971) *Literary style: a symposium*. New York: Oxford University Press

—— (1975) 'The structure of narrative transmission'. In R. Fowler, *Style and structure in literature.* Ithaca: Cornell University Press, pp. 213-57

—— (1978) *Story and discourse: narrative structure in fiction and film.* Ithaca: Cornell University Press

Cluysenaar, A. (1976) *Introduction to literary stylistics.* London: Batsford

Coupland, J. (1983) 'Complexity and difficulty in children's reading material'. Unpublished PhD thesis. University of Wales, Cardiff

Crago, H. and Crago, M. (1983) *Prelude to literacy.* Carbondale, Ill.: Southern Illinois University Press

Crystal, D. and Davy, D. (1969) *Investigating English style.* London: Longman

Cummings, M. and Simmons, R. (1983) *The language of literature.* London: Pergamon

Eagleton, T. (1983) *Literary theory: an introduction.* Oxford: Blackwell

Egoff, Sheila A., Stubbs, G.T. and Ashley, L.F. (eds) (1980) *Only connect,* 2nd edn Toronto: Oxford University Press

Fish, S. (1980) *Is there a text in this class?* Cambridge, Mass.: Harvard University Press

Fowler, R. (1977) *Linguistics and the novel.* London: Methuen

—— (1981) *Literature as social discourse.* London: Batsford

Fox, G. *et al.* (eds) (1976) *Writers, critics and children.* New York: Agathon; London: Heinemann

Garner, A. (1975) *Red shift.* London: Collins

—— (1976) *The stone book.* London: Collins

Harnett, C. (1981) *The Wool-Pack.* Harmondsworth: Penguin

Haviland, V. (ed.) (1975) *Children and literature: views and reviews.* London: Bodley Head

Heeks, P. (1981) *Choosing and using books in the first school.* London: Macmillian Education

Hunt, P. (1978) 'The cliché count'. *Children's Literature in Education,* 9, 3, pp. 143-50

—— (1980) 'The good, the bad, and the indifferent'. In N. Chambers (ed.) *The signal approach to children's books.* Harmondsworth: Penguin, pp. 225-46

—— (1984) 'Childish criticism: the sub-culture of the child, the book and the critic', *Signal,* 43, pp. 42-59

Keene, C. (1972) *The invisible intruder.* London: Collins

Lanes, S.G. (1971) *Down the rabbit hole.* New York: Athenaeum.

Leech, G.N. (1969) *A linguistic guide to English poetry.* London: Longman

Leech, G.N. and Short, M.H. (1981) *Style in fiction.* London: Longman

Leeson, R. (1985) *Reading and righting.* London: Collins

Magorian, M. (1983) *Goodnight Mr. Tom.* Harmondsworth: Penguin

Meek, M. *et al.* (eds) (1977) *The cool web.* London: Bodley Head

Milne, A.A. (1921; 1970) *Winnie-the-Pooh.* London: Methuen

Norris, C. (1982) *Deconstruction: theory and practice.* London: Methuen

Ong, W.J. (1982) *Orality and literacy.* London: Methuen

Park, R. (1982) *Playing Beattie Bow.* Harmondsworth: Penguin

Philip, N. (1981) *A fine anger: a critical introduction to the work of Alan Garner.* London: Collins

Protherough, R. (1983) *Developing response to fiction*, Milton Keynes: Open University Press

Rimmon-Kenan, S. (1983) *Narrative fiction: contemporary poetics.* London: Methuen

Robinson, J.G. (1967) *When Marnie was there.* London: Collins

Rose, J. (1984) *The case of Peter Pan or the impossibility of children's fiction.* London: Macmillian

Ruthrof, H. (1981) *The reader's construction of narrative.* London: Routledge & Kegan Paul

Selden, R. (1985) *A reader's guide to contemporary literary theory.* Brighton: Harvester Press

Trelease, J. (1984) *The read-aloud handbook.* Harmondsworth: Penguin

Watt, I. (1960) 'The first paragraph of *The Ambassadors*: an explication'. In D. Lodge (ed.) (1972) *20th century literary criticism.* London: Longman

8

Telling the Case: Occupational Narrative in a Social Work Office

Andrew Pithouse and Paul Atkinson

Introduction

The perspective on discourse reflected in this paper derives from our sociological interests in work, occupations and organisations. Through the detailed investigation of a text drawn from social work we shall exemplify some features of 'case-talk' between professionals. There are many occupational contexts where case-talk is a major feature of everyday work. Doctors, lawyers, and others all have to present 'cases' to audiences of fellow professionals or other interested parties. The young doctor or medical student, for instance, is routinely called upon to recount the features of a case to colleagues and superiors; the senior clinician will also recount cases (at grand rounds and clinico-pathological conferences, for instance). The solicitor or barrister, of course, will have to 'present' and argue a client's case before legal and lay audiences (juries, judges, magistrates). In this paper we are concerned primarily with case presentations between co-workers within the same occupation and the same organisation. Presentations of this sort serve a number of purposes. As well as facilitating the transfer of information between colleagues, they accomplish the instruction of junior participants and the scrutiny of juniors' work by their seniors.

To varying degrees, much of the work of people-processing organisations is 'invisible'. Workers often enjoy high levels of autonomy and privacy in their dealings with clients. Surveillance and quality control are not maintained by direct and intrusive oversight by superiors. Rather, 'cases' are often inspected either through written case-notes and records, or through spoken presentations. These accounts are not the mere recapitulation of disparate 'facts', 'findings' and 'outcomes'. Typically, they are ordered into coherent narratives. The 'case' is shaped and ordered through the account. The narrative itself conveys — often implicitly — the workers' evaluative stance towards the work which is recounted, and the client(s) so described. The competence of workers may thus include the rhetorical skills of case-talk. Our understanding of people-processing work should therefore include some awareness of the 'ethnopoetics' of occupational and organisational cultures.

The term 'ethnopoetics' is used generally to refer to the narrative and rhetorical performances of given cultures (cf. Hymes 1977, 1978; Tedlock 1972). It is commonly restricted to the analysis of non-literate cultures, but there is no need to restrict its reference in that way. Even within the most literate of social milieux, there are many tasks and occasions which call for skills in oral narrative and recital, quite apart from everyday interactional contexts in which storytelling is an appropriate activity. In addition to the occupational contexts referred to above, one can instance political oratory (J.M. Atkinson 1984); religious preaching (Sherfey, Tilton and George 1977); street trading (Pinch and Clarke 1986); school teachers' staffroom talk (Hammersley 1984; Hargreaves 1981); academic lecturing (Goffman 1981) from within our own 'literate' culture. Indeed, many of the skills of even the most 'learned' professions are transmitted as part of an essentially oral tradition: medicine is a prime example, where word of mouth, validated by personal experience, is often preferred over published sources of knowledge. Case-talk is by no means the only genre of spoken narrative or recital between professional colleagues. Others include the sharing of 'experience' between novices (cf. Sudnow 1967; P.A. Atkinson 1981) and 'atrocity stories' (cf. Dingwall 1977). Even in those contexts, stories about 'cases' often feature prominently, as the subjects of cautionary tales, suspense stories, boasts, confessions and self-justifications. Talk of this nature establishes the boundary between one occupation and another, and embodies the members' everyday sense of their 'licence and mandate' (Dingwall, 1976).

Our exemplification of case-talk is not intended to adhere to any single theoretical or methodological orthodoxy. There is a convergence of interests among sociologists which directs attention to the significance of discourse, rhetoric and narrative. Theoretical orientations derive from ethnomethodology, discourse analysis and pragmatics, structuralist and post-structuralist analyses of texts. While these approaches differ in important particulars, they agree in the centrality accorded to language in constituting social reality and its orderly appearance. We have drawn on these perspectives eclectically in arriving at our characterisation of case-talk, without entering into detailed and explicit discussion of the various positions.

In general, we take it as axiomatic that the organisation of narrative is a fundamental resource whereby social actors give shape to their personal experiences, endow them with consequence and value, and render them available to other individuals (Labov and Waletsky 1966). Through narrative formats, tellers produce 'accounts' of their troubles, inviting sympathetic response, formulating blame and excuse. They render them dramatic, humourous or sentimental. Stories 'gain in the telling' not simply in the sense that we are prone to exaggerate and dramatise, but also in the sense that without 'the telling' the events and experiences of work and domestic life would lose their meaning.

Our own case-study is based on everyday work in a social work office, and addresses the topic of case-presentation by a social worker to her supervisor. We shall show how the social worker constructs an account of her work and her client. In doing so we shall illustrate the following themes. First, it is through case-talk that otherwise unobserved work is normally 'seen' and assessed. Second, 'good' work is observed when the worker provides a 'good account': that is, a narrative couched in the appropriate way, furnished with the 'right' sort of details and implying an apt evaluative stance. Third, the worker's 'diagnosis' of the problem and justification for action are implicit in the narrative presentation: they reside in a moral tale of family life rather than explicit theorising. In the course of presenting our own case-study we shall make a number of assertions about social work. We shall not interrupt this particular paper with detailed evidence and justification for these observations. The interested or sceptical reader is referred elsewhere (Pithouse 1984, 1985). Some of our remarks might possibly be read as criticisms of social work in general, or the particular workers whose words and actions are reported. We have no intention of being critical of social work. Similar remarks could be made about a wide range of occupations and occasions. The features we discuss are generic to organisational life (see, e.g. Manning 1971, 1977); social workers are not being singled out here.

These general observations are derived from an intensive ethnographic study of child-care social workers in a local authority social work office (see Pithouse 1984). The data collected include participant-observation field-notes, interviews with workers, and tape-recordings of supervisory meetings. It is one of the latter which provides the illustrative material for this chapter. The data are broadly transcribed. Our observations do not depend upon the detailed analysis of fine-grained features of the discourse.

A case in context

Detailed oral accounts of observed family life are the stock-in-trade of social work. They indicate to the social worker and to fellow professionals that a caring relationship has been struck with clients and that within this relationship the 'problem' can be identified and some solution attempted. While this case-talk maintains the 'family' as the boundary for discussion and future planning, it is never simply a conversation about a particular family or domestic situation. Rather, accounts are also located within the temporal process of a supervisory relationship, within which each learns of the other's expectations and abilities. The accounts that each provides are shaped in the light of those mutual perceptions. For example, where a worker has established her identity as the capable practitioner, then her accounts may well be truncated and 'filled in' by the supervisor. The latter draws on her background knowledge of the case in question and of the worker presenting it. The unfamiliar case and the worker who has yet to establish her competence may result in the supervisor requiring a more detailed account of events. Nevertheless, the supervisory encounter is a delicate blend of dependencies that demands a skilful approach by both parties.

The worker looks to the supervisor to endorse the core identity of a minimally regulated practitioner and support for her view of case requirements. The supervisor depends upon the worker for a frank statement of her unobserved activities: this entails a supervisory style free of an over-assertive or critical manner that would inhibit such open discussion. Supervision in this sense is very much a dance of interests that are managed within an ambience of careful consultation and subtle direction by both parties.

The experienced practitioner knows the supervisor's expectations and how they may fit with her own case requirements. Likewise, the supervisor knows the experienced practitioner will only accept a viewpoint that is framed in such a way as not to offend the image of the self-regulating, competent worker. As one social worker expressed it:

> ... supervision er its a bit of a game really. You know what the team leader thinks and how she'll react, so you sort of manipulate what you say. But then she knows me quite well and she's good at getting things out of me (*laughs*) by the way she asks questions. Er, generally I get what I want and she gets her point across.

Accounts are construed in relation to such contingencies and relationships, but they also present a further distinctive and regular feature. This addresses the meanings associated with those who receive the service; that is, the families or individuals that workers describe as their 'clients'. Typically, the clients are deemed recipients of the service that is delivered in their 'best interests'. They are rarely seen as eligible to participate fully in the definition and planning of the service, nor do they share fully in diagnoses, suspicions or assumptions that the worker holds about their domestic lives. It has to be remembered that while workers believe their practices to be guided by the best of motives, they nevertheless apply a technology that resists specification in terms of a standardised input and a predictable outcome. None the less the good worker persists in applying her particular style of caring intervention. Indeed, her ability to do so in the face of intractable problems marks out a key element of the approved occupational identity. Occupational failure is rarely looked for in the worker's own abilities or in the occupational mission itself. Demoralising failure is attributed to others. Frequently it is the clients themselves who are seen as the main cause of an intervention with little prospect of success. In this respect, oral accounts contain an element of moral assessment whereby the clients' departures from expected domestic conduct are cast as the culpable acts of unworthy sorts of people.

Workers' oral accounts embody their versions of commonsense theory. Like all 'everyday' theory it is neither consistent nor complete, yet it appears as sufficient and coherent for the practical purpose at hand. Within the work-setting, the actors' mundane theory is a contradictory amalgam of formal social work concepts, practice wisdom and the workers' understanding drawn from their participation in the wider culture beyond the work setting. This body of diffuse background knowledge is flexibly drawn on in order to resolve the inconsistencies and dilemmas of practice itself. As we shall show in the analysis of a case-presentation that follows, moral evaluations of family life, common-sense understandings, elements of formal theory and practical experience merge easily in case-talk.

In this chapter it will not be possible to set out a range of accounts in all their varying lengths, diverse contents and contrasting orientations. Rather, one specific account has been selected that addresses most of the relevant features.

We begin by reproducing the discussion of one 'case' between a social worker and her team leader.

Worker. You've heard the latest developments? Well, one month to the day of the supervison order she [daughter] went to Southtown shoplifting. Again! Got caught. Gave a false name — a friend of hers! (*laughs*) Well they found out. Anyway, she'll have to go before the magistrates up there. I shall be recommending a fine and continuation of the supervision but I haven't now. Jackie needs our help. But the trouble with the family is that you're lulled into a false sense of security, and then they blow.

Leader. Yes, this has been the pattern for years.

Worker. Yes, back when Glenda was working with them there'd be a crisis and then everything would be hunky dory.

Leader. Um, but they didn't accept her.

Worker. No, they're not very accepting. When things go wrong they scream for help. They've got this massive guilt thing which I believe is some sort of incest, which is why they avoid social services as much as possible. The family, er, the reason for the order is that it's imperative that a social worker goes in and has some sort of relationship with the girl. Er, I see the only basis of working with the family is working with the girl, getting her to trust us.

Leader. Right. It has to be on a regular basis not just responding to their crises and going out there.

Worker. Right. It has to be on a strict basis, er statutory.

Leader. Okay, so what are you going to do for Jackie?

Worker. Er preventing crisis and mediating with the family and hoping to get everyone to see how it is — er — you see you have a situation here where Jackie goes off to babysit for an older friend and stays with her boyfriend there. Parents can't control this. As soon as they try to stop her, up she goes and disappears. But as I said yesterday, perhaps it will phase out anyway — you know — if you make it a challenge it will go on. You see Jackie will only do what she's told not to do. If you tell her to do something she won't do it. But she's a reasonable girl who'll do a lot of things off her own bat. Like she'll do school work at home — but if someone suggested that, she wouldn't do it! So it's trying to introduce a softly softly approach into the family, so that the family see things in perspective and see the girl's pathology for what it is. She's got a lot of positives. She's a personable girl, pleasant, bright girl. One queer quality is an incredible neatness — her school work is absolutely immaculate. You can't tell the difference between one page and another. Every word the same!

Leader. Sort of obsessional?

Worker. Em, very tidy. Very tidy people. I don't know what she's got. She's certainly got it up there for the application of graphics — she's a bright girl. Although she's a problem in school behaviour-wise, she's likely to blow up. If she doesn't blow she takes quite a lot in. She does reasonably well in examinations, she's got many positives, she's not a negative girl altogether.

Leader. The criminal it does't fit in with this part of Jackie does it?

Worker. Well she's a well-known shoplifter — to the extent that a note comes up to the house saying 'Jackie can you pinch me a pair of trousers, will pay two pounds for them.' She's well known in her circle at school as the top shoplifter.

Leader. She's not far from becoming a labelled criminal?

Worker. She er yes. But her criminality is in (*pause*) er strange really, it's almost a mania. It has a quality about it that is almost psychologically driven. I don't know if that's the proper use of the term 'psychology' but — you know — the drive is there, er because of an abnormal psychology, there's something there all right.

Leader. Um how long has she been doing it?

Worker. Got caught for doing this year ago.

Leader. But not much recently?

Worker. She hasn't been *caught* so much! (*laughs*)

Leader. Yes there's something *there* in the family.

Worker. Um very much. Dad was an alcoholic ten years ago. Mother's a diabetic. You see the strange thing about it all is she has three other sisters. Mary the eldest is ESN, they've found a niche for her at [Special School], settled in quite well. The youngest had a school report which I didn't see but mother told me, and mother doesn't usually lie — she hides the truth but she doesn't actually lie — has A's in everything so she must be quite bright, and the third girl is quite bright. So you see there's lots of intelligence in the family which is quite a sort of solid working-class family. Mum's background is better than what she's got, but the kids are immaculate, lovely kids really (*pause*) er father, father's a weedy little creature, the original weed.

Leader. Natural father?

Worker. Natural father um. I know it's not relevant — he always wears black and white bri-nylon polo-neck jumpers which is a strange thing for a man (*pause*) and smart trousers, but he does nothing. He doesn't work — he's home to look after mum but he doesn't fiddle, like the bloke *could* earn on the side, but I'm sure the family are long term supben [supplementary benefit]. Er, you support things, the four kids and wife, well over the years things erode away you can't build things up when curtains get tatty, they don't get replaced, you need a new carpet you can't afford one, this sort of thing.

Leader. Have you looked into the financial side at all?

Worker. No, I'll have to do that. I would say that if there's anything to be got they would get it. He looks after the wife and I think gets all that's going.

Leader. Um, this is a pretty claustrophobic family?

Worker. This is what I've said all the time, four girls, this little man, they're all in the back room. It's not a large house — he's not a constructive man, he doesn't use his time as far as I can tell to do anything — like for instance the curtains have been down from the front rail and that's been down for eight weeks, well he has the screws or nails you know. The house is not untidy, the curtains are washed and ready to be put up but it's just not done and whenever I go there he's just sat watching TV. Er, strange negative man, hardly any male lead to his daughters whatsoever — pathetic male figure and if there's any suspicion of incest it would only add to it. She's unfortunate looking, pleasant personality and smiling but she's a small dumpy woman can't afford to dress and they don't go out anywhere — but she's a fat happy body. She's not deceitful but covers up what suits her and she criticises us like hell — not to my face — and she'll say 'I've been trying to get hold of you for ages' — the implication is you're never there when you're wanted.

Leader. I suppose in that situation little things can blow up?

Worker. Oh right! You see, they see me as someone to be put up with, poking my nose in — that comment comes from mother. But I've had to get in there. Glenda [previous worker] didn't. No disrespect to Glenda, she's a very direct social worker, calls a spade a spade and will actually say to the family you're doing this wrong or this wrong. With all due respect I wish I could work like that but I can't, this is the feeling I get from clients — she was very direct. Now she couldn't get anywhere with Jackie — that's not Glenda's fault, that's the way she works. But you see the school's the same they can't control her, but then they can't control half the kids we deal with. What I'm doing is continually chipping away at the family, beause the dynamics are not that bad — they're a criminal family, you know, in a criminal culture. They collude with Jackie's stealing but I wouldn't get my foot through the door if I accuse them of colluding with Jackie. You see there's the supervision order on Jackie, this gives me an in with the other children. Mrs [mother] I think is determined that the girls don't go the way of Jackie, she's given up with Jackie. Jackie will do what Jackie wants to do. I don't see the supervision as directive but supportive, Jackie can't be direct.

Leader. But you'll be seeing her on a regular basis?

Worker. Monthly. Well, I haven't worked this out yet. I must confess I haven't organised this yet but I feel it will need about monthly unless something happens, and working with her friend the babysitter as well, who's been involved with the shoplifting, and that's about it.

Leader. (*to researcher*) You can see the reasons for this supervision order it's quite a task here mainly one of accepting social work.

Worker. Yes, you have to do this on the basis this is quite a delinquent family, we're not going to change that fact of their life-style — it's cultural — I'm not going to change this you know — I don't intend to. The idea is to get Jackie through school into work and independent before there's a breakdown and she ends up on care, because in no way is Jackie residential material. Care won't help Jackie one bit because home is so strong and the links are strong, basically because of mother's strength, but she's been close to care.

Leader. Right then, you're on your way with this one, what's next . . .

Commentary

It is noticeable that the social worker's presentation of the 'case' is framed as a story right from the outset. She employs a common type of story preface — 'You've heard the latest . . .?' The narrative style of the case-talk is established as the social worker claims the right to tell a story. Interestingly, in terms of strict organisational or bureaucratic logic, she has no need to enter such a bid as there is no problem for her in claiming the floor for a storytelling. In fact, she is required to tell the supervisor about the latest developments in her cases. In this context, however, this opening is far from redundant or irrelevant. It has a very potent function in the discourse of 'case-talk'. By acting as a common type of story opening, and facilitating self-selection to recount a story, a preface of this sort establishes a sort of 'narrative contract' between the worker and the supervisor.

The story is introduced, then, precisely as that — a *story.* It is done in such a way as to foreshadow the development of a tale of problems and complications. A career of see-sawing stability and crisis is easily wrought from the case-narrative. It locates the clients in a typical seam of families dealt with by workers. From the outset, 'the latest' is portrayed as a further episode of concatenating problems. The most recent 'eruption' of shoplifting by Jackie is not related by the social worker to a specific cause. Rather, it will be treated as an *episode* in an unfolding saga. The precise timing of Jackie's shoplifting — 'one month to the day of the supervision order' — is not introduced, we suggest, as a 'diagnostic' category. It does not imply a correlation with precipitating factors or 'triggers' to renewed deviance. Rather, it has a rhetorical force. It creates the irony that one month *to the day* later she has got into trouble again. Implicitly, of course, this news creates further expectations about Jackie's behaviour and her frame of mind: the hearer may well find herself predicting that Jackie will turn out to be recklessly deviant, or some similar expectation.

Overall, it is to be noted how little explicit 'theorising' there is about this family and their problems. Certainly, there is very little recourse to technical vocabularies of social work. We shall argue that the social worker's presentation of the case relies much more heavily on the narrative force of her tale than on the overt deployment of expert knowledge. She is not devoid of expertise, of course. The way in which her account is framed and organised is itself a matter of occupational expertise, but that is qualitatively different from the use of explicit diagnostic categories.

It is significant how the term 'incest' is introduced early in the social worker's account. It hangs in the conversation without qualification, elaboration or clear attribution ('some sort of incest'). The term is not attached to any members of the family, nor to any behaviours. Here, as in other accounts of the sort recorded in the same setting, there are hints, clues, innuendoes and unverifiable guesses. Worker and supervisor share a common stock of occupational assumptions. As a matter of routine conversation and storytelling they move to and fro across the family history selecting what conveniently comes to mind, confident that the other (here the team leader) is able to gather the implicit meanings and draw appropriate inferences.

Likewise, the social worker has no need to explicate her aims for 'mediating', when called on to say what she is going to do for Jackie. She does not have to elaborate the way she will work with her client, nor the measures she will take to build up trust with the young girl. She may or may not have a detailed agenda in mind when she projects her course of action, but the worker and the team leader can proceed as if they shared an understanding of what is intended. The worker is able to state her aims in terms of 'mediating' with the family, preventing crises and hoping to get everyone to 'see how it is'. The worker does not specify what she means by this or how it will be achieved. Instead, she documents her intentions and abilities in the context of the drama and difficulties of family relations.

Here, as throughout the accounting, the team leader can probably recover relevance for the worker's attention to occupational norms and practices because the account itself 'proves' the worker has established a 'good' relationship, one that has unearthed the intimate and varied details of family life. The account will be occupationally appropriate and rhetorically satisfying in so far as it is furnished with local colour, characterisation and plot.

As in all accounts of this particular occupational genre, the family is the central motif. The worker constructs her narrative in such a way as to unpack aspects of the family and so reveal the 'problem', even while that problem's dimensions and aetiology remain implicit. Again, the problem is not specified in terms of a series of traits or propositions: witnessed or suspected faults, peccadillos and clues are selected and emptied out as conversational jigsaw pieces to be arranged and mulled over. The story is constructed by the worker as an act of *bricolage.* That is, bits and pieces of family life are picked out and reassembled into the narrative format of case-talk. 'The case', indeed, is an occasioned assembly of whatever fragments of evidence and evaluation the worker weaves together into a plausible story-line.

In this context it is worth exploring further how the social worker assembles the hints of deviance and pathology within the family saga. The hinted-at and implicit character of such 'problems' is reflected in the team-leader's acknowledgement that 'there's something *there* in the family'. The sketching in of the father is a case in point. The social worker builds a profile of oddness out of a series of stated or implied contrasts. Thus, he wears garments the worker finds inappropriate for a man (bri-nylon polo neck jumpers); he fails to exploit the possibility of 'fiddling'; he is 'little' and 'weedy'; he is not 'constructive' and has failed to put the curtains up again. Even the observation that he watches television during the daytime may, in this context, be heard as an imputation of 'unmanly' behaviour, since much of that consists of output such as soap operas aimed at a primarily female audience. Each of these fragments of character-sketch simultaneously implies some criterion for what is 'normal' and proposes grounds for finding the person so described as deviant from that norm. This discursive strategy is strongly reminiscent of what Smith describes in characterising 'contrast devices' (Smith 1978) in her dissection of a 'factual' account imputing mental illness. Here the social worker puts together 'evidence' for the father not being a 'proper' man, and links this with the suspicion of 'incest'. This, it will be recalled, had been introduced by the social worker earlier in her account, but left 'dangling'. Now it is reintroduced, again without elaboration, but deployed in conjunction with the other shreds of 'evidence' concerning the father's implied deviance.

What is at stake here is not whether the social worker is 'correct' in imputing some such character trait to the father. We are certainly not interested in deploring the activities of social workers (and similar professionals) in 'labelling' their clients. The interest lies in *how* the labelling gets done here. As we have been arguing throughout, the social worker accomplishes her 'diagnosis' by means of a narrative/descriptive mode of presentation. She does not refer explicitly to a set of criteria or collection of diagnostic categories grounded in a 'technical' vocabulary. She puts together a series of 'common-sense' characterizations which seem to allude to what any observer might see and infer from the life of the family.

The worker's portrayal of the family itself is composed of a concatenation of details. This cascade of observations indicates that the worker has made assiduous observations within the appropriate frame of 'family'. Her oral search through the family tacitly locates the daughter's conduct (shoplifting) as a problem to be grasped in the context of family roles and relationships.

The account reveals how workers in this social work office perceive their clientele through a kaleidoscope of occupational and personal views of proper domestic arrangements. We have seen how the father is particularised and reassembled in this vein. 'Mother' too fails to conform to the worker's expectations about appearance and moral rectitude of a female parent. But then too the parents are 'clients', those taken-for-granted problem people, potentially exploitative and dissembling. The mother, while not explicitly deemed 'deceitful', nevertheless is said to try to 'cover up' and thus inhibit the worker's investigations. Indeed, mother's attempt to influence the service and criticise the worker is an instance of her inappropriate behaviour, to be added to the pile of accumulating difficulties associated with the family.

Moreover, the descriptive detail with which the story of the household is furnished helps to establish the extent to which the worker 'knows' her clients and is 'on top of the case'. In addition to providing 'evidence' of the problems presented, the detail establishes the 'narrative contract' between the teller and her hearer. It portrays scenes and characters which can be recognised in ordinary, everyday terms — a backcloth against which problems can be formulated and discussed. A satisfactory 'story' normally depends upon a suitable density of description and detail. The narrative art of the competent social worker depends upon the ability to extemporise accounts which incorporate the 'right' sorts of background information in the right quantities, from which the 'right' inferences may be drawn: what counts as right does not depend upon an *a priori* set of criteria. These things are dependent on the context of the story itself and the occasion of its telling.

It is important to note that 'telling the case' provides scant detail of how the worker actually manages the encounter with clients. Descriptions of family life, however phrased, rarely include the worker's own behaviour and demeanour when in the presence of clients. To a considerable extent, this 'goes without saying'; it is assumed to be the sensitive presentation of a caring and capable professional. That this may not convince the consumer can be discerned in the observation that a previous worker (Glenda) was unsuccessful in gaining access to the family. This is no occasion for criticism by the present worker who emphatically justifies her predecessor's preferred mode of practice. Collegial competence remains intact, and any 'failure' is again cast within a family that would exclude a worker confronting them openly with her opinions and requirements. The worker refers to her own strategy as 'chipping away': the timetable and content of this future intervention apparently requires little elaboration on her part.

In the social work office, then, at least as evidenced in this case-study, everyday social work practice is seen, reported, understood and evaluated through spoken narratives. The workers provide stories of family life made up of incidents, observations, clues and curiosities. Parents, siblings, friends and relatives are decanted. The worker proceeds through family networks, relationships, biographies and behaviours. These are ransacked in order to find items that may have varying connection to 'problems' that are diffuse and largely undefined. Suspicions, intuitions and all manner of domestic manifestations are raised, connected by unstated assumptions about clients and their problems.

In the reported instance, the worker does not articulate her exact practices. It is sufficient to say only that one will continue to 'work with' parents and children. Of importance to the supervisor is not the worker's preferred way of working with clients, whatever that may be, but where she focuses her efforts and how she is motivated. The good worker applies herself to the family's private life. In doing so she can only explore the details of family life through a relationship that delivers up family intimacies. Such a relationship will only succeed, in social work's own terms, if it is 'caring'; and caring dedication is confirmed by an ability to persist in the exploration of problems — despite resistance.

Within the occupation, everyone knows that the job is replete with uncertainty. Problems resist identification, and efforts fail. Families move into crisis and there is never enough time to unearth the 'real' problems that lie beneath the crust of everyday family life. Yet the experienced worker, through soundings, brief forays and insightful observations of family relations, can construct a mosaic of suspicion that confirms the presence of 'problems' without specifying the precise cause or cure. This is sufficient to display appropriate practice. The construction of a 'case' is thus a *rhetorical* accomplishment. In an important sense, the 'case' does not exist independently of the stories a family gives rise to. And a case is not the inconsequential accumulation of inadequacies. A 'problem' or collection of problems is assembled and given consequence through the narrative ordering of 'case-talk'.

Overview

In this chapter we have documented our interest in occupational rhetoric, or 'ethnopoetics', through the detailed consideration of case-talk in one social-work supervisory encounter. Such occupational talk has particular implications for social work itself, and has more general implications as well.

Social work, like many people-processing 'professions', is an inherently uncertain enterprise. Lacking a sense of public esteem, faced by unpredictable demands and drawing on an unproven technology, the workers look towards themselves. They socially organise their world through a common-sense theory that emerges from experience and maps out the identities and relationships of a complex world of work. They make that work and themselves 'visible' through oral accounts structured by a complex weave of processes. The competent worker routinely accomplishes work through an awareness of the core assumptions of the work setting. He or she learns of the implausible search for unambiguously successful outcomes, the interpretative flexibility of clients' motives and identities, the moratorium on colleague criticism, and finally the worker's own ability to apply a skilful discretion in the way she presents herself to both colleagues and consumers.

Accounts are constructed and construed within this complex interplay of occupational assumptions. The assumptions themselves remain unspoken, while constantly informing the production and understanding of case-talk. In this respect, telling the case is itself a skilled practice accomplished by capable members. It is 'work' in a double sense. It is a complex construction in its own right; it also stands for work in relation to unobserved encounters.

Whatever actually happens between worker and client in the unobserved encounter, it is ultimately unknowable in the office setting. For example, the actual moment of client–worker interaction has no singular meaning, and is hostage to the varying understandings of the participants. Through the construction of case-talk accounts, that very singular occupational reality is constructed to make work a sensible and orderly event. To this end, the unobserved encounter finds meaning *in* the office setting, for it is here — through the talk — that work is 'witnessed' and assessed. In that sense, accounts *are* work. 'Good work' can only be seen through a 'good' account. In the social work office, such a satisfying account maintains the frame of 'family' and provides detailed pictures of domestic life. Satisfactory work requires an appropriate account, and a satisfactory account is itself an artful practice by a competent occupational member. Work can only be substantiated and tested in the oral displays provided by workers. Thus, whatever happens 'out there' in moments of intervention has but indirect bearing on the way work is symbolically constructed and socially organised.

While the details vary from occupation to occupation, our general observations are by no means confined to the arena of social work. The acquisition and display of competence in many occupational settings depend upon skills of oral presentation and narrative. As the practitioner recounts and 'presents' cases to colleagues, superiors or students, this is not merely an exercise in 'reportage'; the narrative skills brought to bear on the task are not merely elements of aesthetic embellishment. The rhetorical skills deployed by the professional worker in telling the case are constitutive of the worker's *expertise.*

Hitherto, scholarly attention to spoken interaction in people-processing and professional contexts has concentrated on the nature of interaction between worker and client: studies of the doctor–patient encounter provide the type-case of analyses of this sort, conducted from various theoretical and methodological standpoints. The ethnopoetics of professional workers in other contexts has received much less attention in the literature. Yet rhetorical and narrative skills of various kinds are of prime value in such occupations. Our understanding of spoken language needs to incorporate the ethnopoetics of occupational discourse; our understanding of work and occupations should likewise incorporate greater sensitivity to the range of spoken performances they involve.

References

Atkinson, J.M. (1984) *Our masters' voices.* London: Methuen

Atkinson, P.A. (1981) *The clinical experience.* Farnborough: Gower

Dingwall, R. (1976) 'Accomplishing profession'. *Sociological Review*, 24, pp. 331-49

—— (1977) '"Atrocity stories" and professional relationships'. *Sociology of Work and Occupations*, 4, 4, pp. 371-96

Goffman, E. (1981) *Forms of talk.* Oxford: Blackwell

Hammersley, M. (1984) 'Staffroom news'. In A. Hargreaves and P. Woods (eds) *Classrooms and staffrooms: the sociology of teachers and teaching.* Milton Keynes: Open University Press, pp. 203-14

Hargreaves, A. (1981) 'Contrastive rhetoric and extremist talk'. In L. Barton and S. Walker (eds) *Schools, teachers and teaching.* Lewes: Falmer, pp. 303-30

Hymes, D. (1977) 'Discovering oral performance and measured verse in American Indian narrative'. *New Literary History*, 8, pp. 431-57

—— (1978) 'The grounding of performance and text in a narrative view of life'. *Alcheringa: Ethnopoetics*, 4, 1, pp. 137-39

Labov, W. and Waletsky, J. (1966) 'Narrative analysis: oral versions of personal experience'. In J. Helm (ed.) *Essays on the verbal and visual arts.* Seattle: University of Washington Press, pp. 12-44

Manning P.K. (1971) 'Talking and becoming: a view of organizational socialization'. In J. Douglas (ed.) *Understanding everyday life.* London: Routledge & Kegan Paul, pp. 239-56

—— (1977) 'Rules, colleagues and justified actions'. In R. Blakenship (ed.) *Colleagues in organizations.* New York: John Wiley, pp. 263-89

Pinch, T. and Clark, C. (1986) '"Patter merchanting" and the strategic (re)production and local management of economic reasoning in the sales routines of market pitchers'. *Sociology*, 20, 2, pp. 169-91

Pithouse, A. (1984) 'Social work: the social organisation of an invisible trade'. Unpublished PhD thesis. University College Cardiff

—— (1985) 'Poor visibility: case talk and collegial assessment in a social work office'. *Work and Occupations*, 12, 1, pp. 77-89

Sherfey, Rev. J., Tilton, J. and George, K. (1977) 'Dressed in the armor of

God'. *Alcheringa: Ethnopoetics*, 3, 2, pp. 10-31

Smith, D. (1978) 'K is mentally ill: the anatomy of a factual account'. *Sociology* 12, 1, pp. 23-53

Sudnow, D. (1967) *Passing on: the social organisation of dying.* Englewood Cliffs, NJ: Prentice-Hall

Tedlock, D. (1972) *Finding the center: narrative poetry of the Zuni Indians.* New York: Dial

9

My Life in Your Hands: Processes of Self-disclosure in Intergenerational Talk

Justine Coupland, Nikolas Coupland, Howard Giles and John Wiemann

The elderly have been all but invisible in sociolinguistic research, even when sociolinguistics is broadly defined to encompass quantitative and qualitative language-based work across the disciplines of linguistics, social psychology, communication science and sociology.[1,2] Some recent studies (e.g. Giles and Ryan 1986; N. Coupland, J. Coupland, Giles and Henwood, in press) have pointed to the anomaly of this absence given that ageing is an increasingly salient issue — demographically, but in fact in every sociological respect — in Western society. This research has also begun to show the potential impact of sociolinguistic research on our understanding of social attitudes towards the elderly, intergenerational communication behaviours, the social and individual consequences of these, and indeed later life development as a whole.

The full range of these studies is in the early stages of development, and none more clearly so than the discourse analysis of talk between the generations — the micro-analysis of situated, particular encounters between young and old. Yet it is discoursal accounts that are arguably able to give the quickest return on the investment of academic resources, detailing the interactional experiences that are both the breeding ground of intergenerational perceptions, orientations and problems, and a forum for their enactment — the 'sharp end' of sociological, psychological and communicative theorising. Research efforts in this general area are beginning to accumulate. For instance, Boden and Bielby (1983, 1986) have explored past events as they constitute a conversational resource for elderly communicators; N. Coupland *et al.* (in press) present contrastive case-studies of intergenerational encounters and seek to model them through an extension of speech accommodation theory (cf. Giles 1984). Discourse analysis is increasingly recognised to have a part to play in the understanding of therapeutic procedures (cf. for example the well-known work of Labov and Fanshel 1977) and a recent inquiry by Hamilton (MS) has explored the discourse of elderly Alzheimer's patients and its implications in therapeutic contexts.

Perspectives on self-disclosure

The present chapter seeks to initiate a new line of discoursal inquiry into intergenerational talk, focusing on disclosure and disclosiveness. At the most general level, self-disclosure can claim a central place in a sociolinguistic account of ageing as part of an analysis of interactional 'information games', in the sense of Goffman 1959. If we construe social interaction as involving a 'potentially infinite cycle of concealment, discovery, false selection, and rediscovery' (p. 8) in participants' knowledge of each other's probable monitoring of both parties' behaviour, it is appropriate to consider why personal and sometimes intimate information is being disclosed, what socio-psychological functions are being fulfilled during disclosive sequences, and what evaluative and attributional processes are likely to be at work in particular social settings. While self-disclosure seems to fit Goffman's specification of 'expressions given' during interaction, it is profitable, therefore, to treat disclosure also as part of the general management of identity in talk and as the overt *and covert* presentation of self. Disclosure consequently needs to be interpreted as part of 'expressions given off' — Goffman's alternative category. A discourse analysis of the procedures of self-disclosure has the potential to show how the reporting of painful experiences may serve strategic purposes in elderly talk, is encoded and decoded against a variable appraisal of what is normative, and may on occasions lie at the root of problematical intergenerational interchange.

The foregoing should be read as a prospectus for a series of studies of elderly disclosure which depend critically upon the particular analyses to be presented in this chapter — analyses of the *implementation* of a specific sub-category of disclosure in a corpus of intergenerational talk. The particular focus of this chapter is the disclosure of personal 'painful' information. Our attention was drawn to this dimension of our data by first impressions of both the frequency and the intimacy of painful disclosures made; such behaviour is at least apparently counter-normative in the public context of video-taped interactions among strangers — issues we shall explore later in the chapter. The analysis we shall present of painful disclosure can be valuably cross-referenced with Jefferson's account (1980, 1984a, 1984b, 1985; Lee and Jefferson 1980) of 'troubles talk'. (But because the two frameworks have been developed in isolation, and with significantly different aims and assumptions, such cross-referencing as we can offer at this stage is given in an appendix to this chapter.) Our broader aim is to explore self-disclosure as a potentially significant mode of elderly talk. In the longer term, we would hope to draw inferences about disclosure as a locus for problematical intergenerational interaction, and even about elderly self-disclosure as the fulfilment of particular communicative functions and needs. On the other hand, until the *processes* by which disclosive sequences are managed interactionally can be made explicit, theoretical developments will be limited by inadequate accounts of what disclosure and disclosiveness *are*, and empirical studies of self-disclosure — in these data and other corpuses — cannot be rigorously pursued.

Self-disclosure is a concept which has been developed most in the social psychological literature (cf. for example Cozby 1973; Jourard 1964), where it is taken to refer generally to 'the voluntary and intentional revelation of personal information which cannot be obtained from other sources' (Pearce and Sharp 1973, quoted and endorsed in Berger and Bradac 1982, p. 85). While clearly disclosure, in our sense, is more restricted than this in that our data will focus uniquely on the disclosure of personal, painful experiences, we find there to be significant theoretical arguments for not offering a precise initial definition. Our analysis at this stage is exploratory and we would argue that what self-disclosure constitutes is not ultimately distinguishable from how disclosive sequences are brought about, managed and responded to. Some progress towards an adequate account can, however, be made before looking at data. Elementary semantics suggests that there are two aspects to a working definition of the phenomena we are considering — disclosure as *content* (i.e. information disclosed) and disclosure as *process* (the making known of such information). Both aspects are important to how we have proceeded this far. Our attention was drawn to disclosure in the data we are discussing by the simple fact that certain topics of talk arise where, by some accounts (cf. below) they should not, and pattern in quite striking ways (again, cf. below) across the demographic contexts of our study. Ultimately however, disclosure as process is the aspect most centrally relevant to our analysis, and the categories of content that we isolate as sub-types of 'painful disclosures' are merely a preliminary heuristic — a means of identifying a corpus for discoursal analysis.

The data

The data are approximately 100 disclosive sequences (within our topic-categories) from 40 video-taped interactions conducted in a video studio. Volunteer subjects, all females, were asked to 'get to know one another' and left alone for eight minutes knowing they were being video-recorded. Twenty of these pairs were intergenerational (young-old); 10 were peer-young (young participants are referenced as Y01–Y20) and 10 were peer-elderly (E01–E20). In this way, each subject was involved in two interactions, one within-generation, the other across-generation. The elderly women, aged 70–87, are all members of a Day Centre in Cardiff, Wales; most live alone and are widowed. They use the Day Centre as a social resource which can also offer certain particular services (such as hair-dressing, chiropody and a midday meal). As far as socio-economic status is concerned, and notwithstanding the intrinsic difficulty of assigning elderly females to conventional 'social class' categories, most are, at least historically, upper-working-class, having been married to, or themselves having been, for the most part, skilled manual workers. The young women, aged 30–40 and mostly lower-middle-/middle-class and married, were recruited through an advertisement in a local newspaper. Like their elderly co-participants, they were not given any detailed information on the specific aims of the study, apart from that they were to converse with other women of differing ages. In fact, the study as a whole was designed as an open-ended and exploratory investigation of talk within and across age-bands in a controlled and relatively formal context that would lend itself to multiple levels of sociolinguistic analysis.

In effect, this procedure sets up an exercise in information exchange, and levels and processes of self-disclosure need to be evaluated, by us and by participants, against that background assumption. While it will therefore be difficult to generalise convincingly from these data to generational tendencies in respect of self-disclosure in the full range of naturally-occurring situations, we at least have the opportunity of finding patterned differences in the interpretation of the 'get to know one another' brief in this context: for example, variation across expectations of having to seek, or on the other hand provide, personal information. At the same time, the brief does not of course stipulate that *painful* personal information should be either sought or given. And there are seemingly normative constraints on this sort of disclosure anyway, as we shall see. Independently of how generalisable they prove to be, the data should ultimately be of value for modelling potentially problematical passages of intergenerational talk (as we have suggested) as a development of existing accounts of interpersonal accommodation processes between the generations (Ryan, Giles, Bartolucci and Henwood 1986; N. Coupland *et al.* in press).

The particular topic sub-categories we have chosen to define the limits of this inquiry are not theoretically derived, but do exhaustively account for talk on notionally 'painful' topics in the data. The list includes five overlapping domains of painful experience:

Ill-health

Chronic or enduring ill-health is disclosed by elderly to young, elderly to elderly and in only one case by young to young (the same young interactant attempted a health-disclosure to her elderly partner but was prevented from doing so by her partner shifting topic).

(a) *Ongoing medical problems* such as emphysema, arthritis (including one young interactant), tinnitus, shingles, heart disease, ruptures, etc.
(b) *Hospital stays and operations* ranging from 'routine' operations like hip replacements to operations like mastectomy, anal polyps and colostomy. This sub-type includes disclosure of worry about future hospitalisation and recall of sufferings during previous hospital stays.
(c) *Sensory decrement*, including general problems with eyesight or hearing which, to an extent, are age-related and can restrict activities.

(d) *Accidents* such as serious falls, where they have short- or long-term consequences to health.

Where ill-health is disclosed as suffered by another (not the speaker herself), this is included in the analysis only if it is reasonable to assume that it is painful to the discloser herself and/or affects her life-circumstances (for example, if she has a constantly unwell husband).

Bereavement

Bereavement is disclosed by elderly to young, elderly to elderly and by one young interlocutor to a young partner and one (other) young interlocutor to an elderly partner. Bereavements disclosed are usually not recent and it is of course significant that all but two of the elderly women are widows. Apart from loss of husbands, loss of other family is disclosed: parents (by one elderly discloser and by one young discloser) and children. Several elderly women have lost middle-aged daughters, and some have lost babies as young women.

Immobility

This is disclosed by elderly to young and elderly to elderly. Disclosures of immobility (as one would expect) are often linked to disclosures of ill-health, and these often occur together textually. Immobility-disclosure usually takes the form of reporting inability to walk far enough to see friends or relatives, to shop or to arrive at the Day Centre without transport. The elderly also report being unable to do things they could once do (for example, housework and so on).

Disengagement and loneliness

Disengagement and loneliness are disclosed by elderly to young, elderly to elderly, and one young to elderly. The category subsumes reports of physical isolation and felt alienation both from others in society and from own previous social roles. Loneliness is often attributed to old friends losing touch, and families failing to visit as often as would be desired. Inability to fill time (left, for example, by freedom from housework and caring for husband and children) is usually accounted for by ill-health (e.g., E03 reports having had to give up piano-playing because of a stroke and E02 reports no longer being able to knit due to her deteriorating eyesight).

Others

Diverse difficult or painful life-events and acknowledged emotional responses to them comprise the final sub-type. For example, disclosure of own failed marriage (E11) or the failed marriage of the discloser's child where this has apparently in turn caused the discloser emotional pain and practical problems (there are two instances of a son moving back in with his mother bringing dependent children — E03 and E05). Others disclose on coping with rearing small children after losing a husband (E10 and E11) and one on nursing a dying friend with little outside assistance (E05).

We have, of course, no ultimate claim on the subjective 'painfulness' of these experiences, nor any direct access to subjects' own perceptions of painfulness.[3] In fact, whether these experiences are presented as painful or in a way that assumes they will be classified as painful by interlocutors is a feature in participants' discoursal negotiation of them. For this reason, and also because we have suggested that the discourse analysis is logically prior to any meaningful account of trends in the occurrence of self-disclosure in the video-taped data, it would be wrong to attach too much significance to the raw frequencies of disclosure events across the 40 encounters. On the other hand, and with these caveats, a gross frequency-count can at least provide a backdrop to the qualitative analysis this chapter offers.

Disclosing information in the above five topic-categories is predominantly a characteristic of the *elderly* women's speech. Of the 20 cross-generational encounters, such disclosures (usually more than one) are made in 18 by elderly interactants, and in only *one* of the 18 are there reciprocal disclosures (two) by the young interactant. There are no painful disclosures in one of the two remaining intergenerational interactions and only one brief disclosure by the young interactant in the other. Out of ten peer-young encounters, there are only five which include disclosures of painful experience. Of these five, in three there is only one discloser and in the fourth and fifth, a disclosure is 'topic-matched' by a partner (cf. below). Out of ten peer-elderly encounters, there are nine which include disclosure of painful experience by both partners, and in six of these, one of the partners makes more than one disclosure. There is some evidence, then, from the raw numbers of painful disclosures made both in the peer-elderly and peer-young encounters that the elderly do tend in this context to be more disclosive than the young (whether with their peers or with the young as their interlocutors). Moreover, there is a strong tendency in the data for elderly recipients of disclosures to make reciprocal disclosures in both peer and cross-generational encounters — a tendency not shown by the young recipients.

Any attempts to interpret such variability will also need to recognise the intrinsic significance of disclosure itself in our data-context, as we have said. General claims (which we review below) have been made about the operation of disclosure as a social process which amount to a set of culturally non-specific norms, assuming no significant cultural variation within Western Anglo society. Berger and Bradac (1982, p. 86) posit a set of regulative rules for disclosure which, in most significant respects, seem to be *contradicted* in our data. The three most pertinent prescriptions are:

'Do not disclose intimate information to new acquaintances';
'Do not disclose negatively-valenced information to new acquaintances'; and
'Do not disclose excessively'; (and the corollaries of all three).

Berger and Bradac do not specify any likely contextual constraints at this point beyond new acquaintance/intimate addressee. Despite the likelihood that some categories of personal information are being disclosed by participants in our data in fulfilment of the task-requirements, elderly disclosure of painful experience in the 40 interactions — which *is* clearly the revelation of 'intimate information' 'to new acquaintances', and 'negatively-valenced information', *and* arguably 'excessive' in some instances (by virtue of its elaboration, as we shall characterise it) — needs to be accounted for as supposedly *non*-normative. Various possibilities that we shall briefly consider at the end of this chapter are that Berger and Bradac's rules are biased towards norms for *young* interaction, and that the negative consequences which they suggest follow non-normative disclosing do not reflect the complexity of attributional and evaluative processes that can be operative in intergenerational talk.

Sequences of disclosure

From the video-tapes of the 40 interactions, all the sequences which include painful disclosures (in our defined sense) were transcribed using a modified version of the transcription conventions developed by Jefferson (cf. the 'Transcript notation' summary in Atkinson and Heritage 1984). The taxonomic overview this chapter presents outlines the range of alternative strategies which interactants (referred to as 'disclosers' of painful information and 'recipients' of disclosure) adopt at four different phases of disclosive sequences: pre-contexts (summarised in Figure 9.1a), disclosures (Figure 9.1b), recipient next-moves (Figure 9.1c) and closings (Figure 9.1d). The intention is to account exhaustively for all such alternatives realised in the data.[4] While we suspect that the various sub-categorisations have some applicability beyond our particular data (and cf. the brief discussion, in the Appendix to this chapter, of areas of overlap between our own taxonomy and Jefferson's account of 'talk about troubles'), it is important for us to emphasise that they are exhaustive *only* of the options realised in our current data-corpus and in respect of our defined categories of self-disclosure.

Beyond this, the strategies we identify are necessarily idealised to an extent in that it is sometimes impossible to assign any one utterance clearly and uniquely to a functionally labelled category. In fact, we would like to see this sort of uncertainty as potentially part of the dynamics of disclosure-management available to participants, for whom it may be valuable, as we shall try to argue (and cf. the more general discussion of the ambiguity of speech-markers by Brown and Fraser 1979), to obscure the 'actual' identity of moves they make at various points. Finally, although our four phases of analysis reflect, in a general way, the chronology of disclosive sequences, the progression of particular sequences will not always conform to this pattern. While all sequences of course have identifiable pre-contexts and particular forms or modes of disclosure (phases 1 and 2), recipients' next-moves (phase 3) may or may not themselves function as closings (our fourth phase) and may or may not lead to further disclosures being made by either party. Specifically then, in phase 3 we taxonomise formal alternatives within recipients' next-moves, while phase 4 taxonomises, on a functional basis, general strategies for achieving closing of sequences as a whole.

Figure 9.1a: A taxonomy of strategies in four phases of disclosive sequences: Pre-contexts

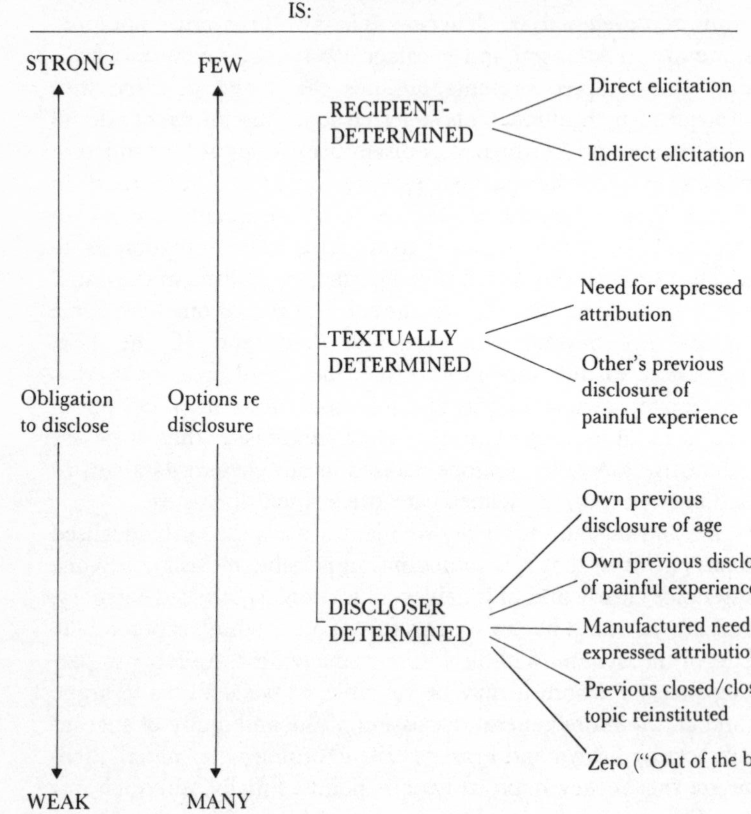

Pre-contexts

The pre-context to any disclosure of painful experience is, strictly, unlimited and should ideally subsume the whole of participants' relational histories and the history of the particular interaction in which they are engaged. Since at this point we are primarily interested in the interactional dynamics of disclosure, our sub-categorisation of pre-contexts relates specifically to the immediate contextualisation of disclosures and allows us to distinguish three broad means by which subsequent disclosures are triggered. The first of these means is labelled *recipient-determined* (in Figure 9.1a) and takes the form of elicitations by recipients (i.e. recipients of the future disclosure). The first sub-type, *direct elicitations*, involves opening moves from recipients, such as *are you keeping well?* (Y14 to E14), *do you sleep all right when you get to bed?* (Y06 to E06), *is your husband still alive?* (Y03 to E03 and Y10 to E09), *when were you widowed?* (Y12 to E12), and arguably *how are you?* (Y05 to E05). All these questions were asked by the young of the elderly and are assigned to the sub-category of *direct elicitations* as they directly invite and, to an extent, require disclosure of painful experience on specific topics. They reflect an apparent assumption by the young that they can elicit such disclosure from the elderly, or perhaps that such elicitation is accommodative or even normative. The specificity or 'closedness' of the question variably constrains the response-options available to the discloser. But we see direct elicitations as imposing some considerable degree of obligation upon the discloser to disclose painful experiences, assuming these are there to be disclosed.

A significant factor in our preparedness to label such utterances *direct elicitations* of disclosure is our own assumption that, in this context, even yes/no questions like *is your husband still alive?* will predictably elicit information within our painful experience category: in the case of this last example, *no I lost him two years ago love worse luck (.) the world isn't the same place without him* (E09 to Y10). Relatedly, it seems feasible to see utterances such as *how are you?* and *are you keeping well?* as likely elicitations of disclosure rather than as mere phatic openings (cf. Laver 1974) by virtue of some elderly's apparent propensity to define potentially phatic questions as contentful elicitations (N. Coupland *et al.* in press; cf. also Lee and Jefferson 1980, p. 13) and partly by virtue of their prosodic and non-verbal accompaniments: on occasions, an earnest facial expression, forward-leaning posture or word-stress clearly signal a non-phatic intent.

With the second sub-type, *indirect elicitations*, a recipient makes an opening move which does not specifically *invite* disclosure but certainly *enables* it (a weak form, then, of the first category). In this category, the recipient asks a question about the discloser's family or life-circumstances, and the response, which we judge to be not specifically foreseeable, is a painful disclosure. In the terminology of Searle (1969), disclosure is the perlocutionary sequel to these acts, even though they may not be disclosure-eliciting in their illocutionary force. For example: *where are your family living now? are they all fairly close to you or are you quite spread out*? (Y11 to E11); *have you got any family*? (Y13 to E13); *do you have any children*? (Y15 to E15); *what made you decide to go*? (move house) (Y18 to E18, and Y03 to E03). These questions are not inviting painful disclosure as such, but *may* indirectly impute frailty, incapacity or misfortune. The questioner here is less likely to expect painful disclosure than in the first sub-category, though she must acknowledge it as a possibility. The life-circumstances of the elderly in our population, and arguably the elderly in general, in fact establish a probability that there will be 'painful' events to report, in answer to questions about family and personal matters. Of course, it is a matter for conjecture whether the young in our sample perceive this as a probability, and there seem to be instances, in later phases of disclosive sequences, where the young ask questions not unlike the above as possible means of moving their interlocutors *out* of painful disclosures. The consequence, paradoxically enough, is that disclosure may in fact be sustained by these questions, and they are in fact one means by which disclosive chains (cf. below) are created.

Beyond the two sub-categories of recipient-determined disclosures, there are many disclosive sequences where the discloser herself, to a greater or lesser extent, establishes the pre-context for disclosure. There is, then, a *discloser-determined* category (towards the foot of Figure 9.1a) where there is relatively little interpersonal or textual obligation to disclose painful experiences and relatively many options available. But before discussing sub-types within this category, we need to explore an intermediate category (labelled *textually-determined* in the figure) in which disclosure appears contingent upon previous textual happenings, more obviously than being determined by either participant. It is as if the text's own development generates a need (though obviously a need experienced by interactants and to be satisfied by and in their talk) for painful experiences to be disclosed. On occasions, for example, a recipient (of the disclosure-to-be) makes an elicitation which has no apparent direct or indirect bearing upon painful experience. But an adequate and, we assume, truthful response which provides the information requested is not fully interpretable without an expressed attribution; and that attribution is a disclosure. In Extract 1, E02 (the elderly discloser-to-be) has just said that she is currently knitting squares to make a blanket. Presumably seeing this as a relatively simple knitting task, Y02 (line 1 and 2) asks if she has ever knitted before:

Extract 1 (from I02)

1 Y02 are you have you just star have
2 you ever kni knitted before?
3 E02 yes! I've made
[ ]
4 Y02 oh you used to knit did you?
5 E02 I've made myself cardigans and all=
6 Y02 =yes=
7 E02 =but my eyes are not so good see
8 Y02 so you want some something fairly simple is it?
[ ]
9 E02 I I got (.) I should have my (.)
10 rupture done and I won't go in
11 Y02 you've got a rupture in?
[ ]
12 E02 I'm too nervous behind the navel
13 Y02 ohh
[ ]
14 E02 and I'm too nervous to go in and have it done=
15 Y02 =are you?=
16 E02 =you follow me?=
17 Y02 =is it is it painful?
[ ]
18 E02 so I won't go in and have it done
19 Y02 no
20 E02 no it doesn't affect me I just get a my legs get a
21 bit tired
22 Y02 (nodding) oh I see=
23 E02 =and of course I I do have suffered I've had a couple
24 of blackouts (.) lately
[ ]
25 Y02 (nodding) oh yes=

E02 answers emphatically *yes*, going on to say that she has made *cardigans and all* — relatively complex knitting tasks. This response opens up an attributional void — *why* does she now knit squares? The void is filled by the disclosure that her *eyes are not so good.* In terms of obligations and options (the vertical scale in Figure 9.1a), we would see there being some significant obligation to sustain the logic of the text in this way, though there is a greater range of options here than in, for example, responding to direct elicitations of the sort discussed earlier. After all, the immediate requirements of textual coherence *have* been satisfied — an answer has been given — and it is of course *not* the case that all implicational, attributional and contextual queries are satisfied in conversation anyway. Disclosure can be avoided in these instances therefore by simple omission, while it can only be avoided in the context of direct eliciting by prevarication, falsification or tactical hedging.

An interlocutor's own previous disclosure is, we would argue, another type of textual determinant of disclosure, though different interpersonal goals are of course involved. Here we consider matched behaviours which appear to be central instances of speech accommodation whereby participants engage in similar sequential speech behaviours, generally to achieve communication efficiency or to promote speaker's social attractiveness (cf. standard accounts of accommodation processes, for example Giles and Powesland 1975).[5] In this way, a preliminary analysis of the sort of closely sequenced, mutual disclosure that we find in Extract 2 would suggest that we have matched, convergent disclosure, realising psychological convergence. Before the transcribed fragment of talk. E02 has already disclosed the death of her husband:

Extract 2 (from I04)

1 E01 my husband was with the Cardiff Corporation=
2 E02 =oh yes
[ ]
3 E01 and er(.) he'd only retired three weeks he had to retire
[ ]
4 E02 oh
5 E01 at sixty-five you see
[ ]
6 E02 my er husband went abroad and caught a germ abroad
[ ]
7 E01 and er and then
8 I er found him dead in bed (.) and he'd only retired three weeks

9 you see
10 E02 oh they don't have no retirement isn't it awful
[ ]
11 E01 and he was looking so forward
12 to his retirement
[ ]
13 E02 oh bless him
14 E01 yes=
15 E02 =what a shock for you
[ ]
16 E01 yes it was shock yes
17 E02 oh its marvellous you're like you are isn't it
18 E01 well (.) I'm eighty-six last may ((3 sylls)) (laughs)
[ ]
19 E02 oh god

In line 6, E02 is presumably initiating an account of the detailed circumstances of his death (he *caught a germ abroad*). The transcription shows that this is embedded within and therefore offered to match a disclosure by E01 (*he'd only retired three weeks* (line 3) . . . *I er found him dead in bed* (line 8)).

In terms of the revised sociolinguistic account of speech accommodation processes offered in N. Coupland *et al.* (in press), many other interpretative options are available. In particular, the matching of disclosures need not be seen as psychologically convergent if there are reasons to claim that participants are *not* attuning their discourse behaviours to each other's wishes and needs. In Extract 2, the significant criterion is whether E01 and E02 would evaluate their talk as attuned or complementary, or whether their disclosing is in a sense combative. The very fact of the two narratives overlapping, both formally (simultaneous speech) and functionally (interrupted narrative development), suggests that there is some competition to occupy the role of discloser. It may be that a more appropriate model of complementary talk at this point would find participants timing their contributions in a way that allowed narrative disclosures to develop and to be appropriately responded to (cf. below).[6] The immediate significance of examples of matched disclosure, however, is that disclosure itself is a significant pre-context for disclosure, whether convergent or combative. This observation is in fact one of the most frequently stated conclusions from social psychological studies, concluding that 'the most frequently shown determinant of disclosure is disclosure itself' (Won-Doornink 1985, p. 97; cf. also Ludwig, Franco and Malloy 1986).

The decision to match disclosure is of course under the control of the second discloser herself. Certainly, we need to see 'other's previous disclosure' establishing own-disclosive options and obligations by virtue of the discloser's perception of interactional propriety. This is a different social process from the previous sub-type (need for expressed attribution), where disclosure is required as a part of the general pressure upon any one interactant to maintain coherence in her own talk. Our ranking of these two sub-types is intended to imply that there might (*ceteris paribus*) be a greater degree of optionality in the accommodative case, although both sub-types can appropriately be labelled 'textually-determined' because they arise primarily from immediately previous textual happenings.

We are rather reticent to rank the five sub-types of the discloser-determined category in any precise order, because impressionistic ratings of degrees of obligation and ranges of options are too strongly influenced by particular contents and subtleties of context; other things are predictably *un*equal. We are also prepared to acknowledge that other criteria can equally well be addressed — e.g. socio- versus ego-centric and legitimate versus illegitimate — to validate somewhat different rankings of the strategies within Figure 9.1a. Our impressionistic ranking within the discloser-determined sub-category is based on what might be called markedness or unpredictability — given no obligation and with an equally wide range of options, the pre-contextual types at the bottom of the taxonomy are totally unpredictable and most clearly 'non-normative' in Berger and Bradac's (1982) terms. The sub-type listed last in Figure 9.1a relates to disclosing painful experiences at positions where there is almost totally unconstrained choice of topics and moves available, and seemingly no immediate obligation to disclose. These instances include one where virtually *no* pre-context either exists or is manufactured, and the disclosure is made 'out of the blue'. In Extract 3, where a lacuna develops, one interlocutor, from a potentially wide range of new topic options, chooses to disclose a painful experience to terminate the silence:

Extract 3 (from I20)

```
 1  E09  you from Cardiff?
 2  E10  pardon?
 3  E09  you from Cardiff?
 4  E10  yes I live in Llanedeyrn
 5  E09  oh yes nice there
 6  E10  yes
         [    ]
 7  E09  that's where we are now isn't it not far from there
 8  E10  no we're not
 9  E09  no (heh)
           [ ]
10  E10      ah (5.0)
11  E09  I get a bit tired walking now ((that)) er false legs er
                                                   [
12  E10                                            where
13  E10  have you been?
14  E09  I've got two false hips (.) so I get tired walking transplants
         [                     ]
15  E10  (astonished) you got what?
16  E09  yeah transplants
              [       ]
17  E10       good gracious me!
                          [  ]
18  E09                   yes marvellous isn't it
19  E10  oh dear
```

It is of course entirely possible to interpret silence as itself a pre-context to disclosure, and to argue that E09 is motivated by a desire to resolve an apparent breakdown in the conversational flow. Still, a wide range of other topics and strategies could have been selected to achieve co-operative talk (cf. Grice 1975).

Another discloser-determined pre-context, manufactured need for expressed attribution, also has an air of unpredictability although it is pre-contextualised with ongoing topics. Here, however, such topics are developed with unexpected shifts in levels of intimacy or affect. We find this in Extract 4, where the topic of lunch at the Day Centre, raised in line 1, is sustained to lines 9ff., where it is linked to the disclosure of colostomy and its consequences:

Extract 4 (from I03)

1 E01 every day (.) we have a nice meal (.) only sixty pence
[ ]
2 Y01 mm
3 E01 we pay (.) a cooked dinner=
[ ]
4 Y01 ((3 sylls))
5 Y01 =mm=
6 E01 =sweet and a cup of tea (.) but I nev don't have the sweet (.) I
7 only have um two cream crackers and a bit of cheese because it
8 suits me (1.0) (voice almost at a whisper, hand in front of mouth
9 I don't broadcast this but I've lived with a colostomy for
10 seventeen years you see (.) so
[ ]
11 Y01 mm
12 E01 I've got to be careful what I eat=
[ ]
13 Y01 yes
14 Y01 =yes=
15 E01 =well then they're (.) good in the centre they know that (.) and
16 they'll er (.) give me a little bit of fish if there's anything
17 with any onion in it
18 Y01 mm
[
19 E01 they're very good=
20 Y01 =mm mm
21 E01 so er (.) (lowering voice again) really and at the time I just
22 wanted to die
23 Y01 mm
[
24 E01 and er well I didn't know what they were talking about
25 Y01 mm
26 E01 but er so anyway I'm pretty good lucky ((I can't say
[ ]
27 Y01 mm
28 E01 anything could I good))
29 Y01 no

The colostomy is the expressed attribution for E02's not eating the sweet and is therefore clearly contingent. We do not mean to imply that the pre-contextual information (in this case the general discussion of the Day Centre lunch) is offered expressly to preface a planned disclosure, but that the discloser behaves *as if* the attribution is needed. In that sense, the need is manufactured by the discloser rather than textually generated. On the other hand, colostomy disclosure, markedly intimate, is likely to run counter to recipients' expectations of E01's topic development and needs to be framed with an appropriate disclaimer. The ironic *I don't broadcast this*, in a context where there are known overhearers, is a rare acknowledgement of the infringement of Berger and Bradac's norms, but at the same time highlights a preparedness knowingly to disregard them. Such a fragment suggests there is indeed a will to disclose and a general appreciation of interactional benefits accruing which offset recognised disadvantages. In fact, the general category of discloser-determined disclosures needs to be accounted for in those terms.

Where disclosures can be seen as coherent moves within a turn's textual development, relating with some degree of predictability to previous own moves, we can identify further sub-types of the discloser-determined category, slightly higher up (in Figure 9.1a) on the obligations and options scales. Sub-types of this sort include elements of disclosive chains where the fact of a discloser having disclosed on one topic establishes, albeit weakly, a relevance for a subsequent disclosure on a different topic by the same speaker. Extract 1 (above) shows E02 disclosing about her own failing eyesight at line 7 and Y02 pursuing this topic at line 8. E02's next disclosure about her rupture (lines 9ff.) constructs a coherence within the discourse which depends on the perception of 'ill-health' as a topic-bridge (our third sub-category, see Figure 9.1a).

Coherence can also operate or be imposed across non-adjacent moves, and a fourth sub-type of the discloser-determined category sees disclosers reinstituting a coherence between the topic of their disclosure and a closed or closing topic. In Extract 5, E05 and E06 appear to be closing a sequence on the topic of helping others. At line 12, E06 produces a summary or reformulation of E05's stated policy for helping others and E05's next move has the force of a generalised evaluation of her own just-endorsed position. To that extent, *that's the answer* predicts the closing of the 'helping others' topic. E05's reinstitution of the topic provides a context for the reporting of her nursing of a friend dying of cancer, in a way that is entirely topically coherent with the foregoing. However, the coherence has been re-established at E05's own instigation and the disclosure is afforded a relevance by discoursal choices the discloser herself has made:

Extract 5 (from I10)

```
 1 E05  =it's been my interest to (.) give collect and do (.) and
                                                         [    ]
 2 E06                                                     quite
 3 E05  even (.) take the shirt off my back if they wanted it=
                                                      [    ]
 4 E06                                                  yes
 5 E06  =I know=
 6 E05  =knowing they want something=
 7 E06  =yes=
 8 E05  =and that you're
 9 E06  yes=
10 E05  =ready to help them
                 [     ]
11 E06           lovely
12 E06  you have compassion
13 E05  that's the answer
14 E06  mm=
15 E05  =now I nursed a friend for f nine weeks day and
16      night with cancer=
17 E06  (sympathetically) =oh=
18 E05  =on my own=
19 E06  =yes=
20 E05  now and then visitors used to come for five minutes
21      ten minutes=
22 E06  =yes
23 E05  but I never changed my suit . . .
```

Talk about own age, the final sub-category we have located in the data, is another seemingly coherent pre-context for disclosure of painful experience. In Extract 6, E03 has disclosed her age at line 1 which seemingly elicits Y03's complimentary expression of surprise. The compliment is accepted but specifically (in fact specified non-verbally) in relation to E03's own facial appearance, with which she proceeds to contrast her mobility problems caused by thrombosis. Elderly reports of own-age appear generally to carry a potential as pre-contexts of painful disclosure in that chronological age can function as a baseline for the evaluation of own state of health. There is a trade-off between age and health which is given some overt recognition in E03's framing of her age report: *...you wouldn't believe it* (line 1). She is apparently well *for her age* or conversely can claim to appear younger than her age because she is apparently well:

Extract 6 (from I06)

```
 1  E03  you wouldn't believe it I'm eighty-seven
 2  Y03  wh eighty-seven good heavens you don't look eighty-seven
 3  E03  (gasps and laughs) well not up here (holds hand up to face)
                   [        ]  [                          ]
 4  Y03            (laughs)    I hope I look like you when I'm
 5  Y03  eighty-seven                                    [
 6  E03                                                  not up
 7       not up here (.) I'm not (holding hand up against face)
 8  Y03  ooh
 9  E03  (much more seriously) but it's this (lays hand on leg) I
          [  ]
10  Y03   aah
11  E03  ((2 sylls)) thrombosis ((1 syll))
                   [                          ]
12  Y03            so how did you get here today?
13  E03  (petulantly) oh! in the car that gentleman brought me
                                              [  ]
14  Y03                                        oh
15  Y03  well that's kind isn't it
                            [
16  E03                      yes wasn't it nice I thought it
17       was very nice                  [
18  Y03                                  yes (.) aah (.) so what
19       made you come today?
```

Modes of disclosure

The variant types of pre-contexts we find in our data have already led us to suggest that, as interactional events, disclosures may arise from quite different social motivations, may be marked or unmarked events in the unfolding of a conversational text, and therefore are likely to have quite different communicative and socio-psychological consequences. The justification for our taxonomising of pre-contexts at some length is therefore that the nature of a self-disclosure itself is in significant respects determined in relation to factors in its interactional history. On the other hand, disclosers may encode their disclosures (whatever their pre-contexts) in potentially significantly different ways, selecting options from several sub-systems that we set out in Figure 9.1b, under the general heading of 'modes of disclosure'.

Figure 9.1b: A taxonomy of strategies in four phases of disclosive sequences: Modes of disclosure

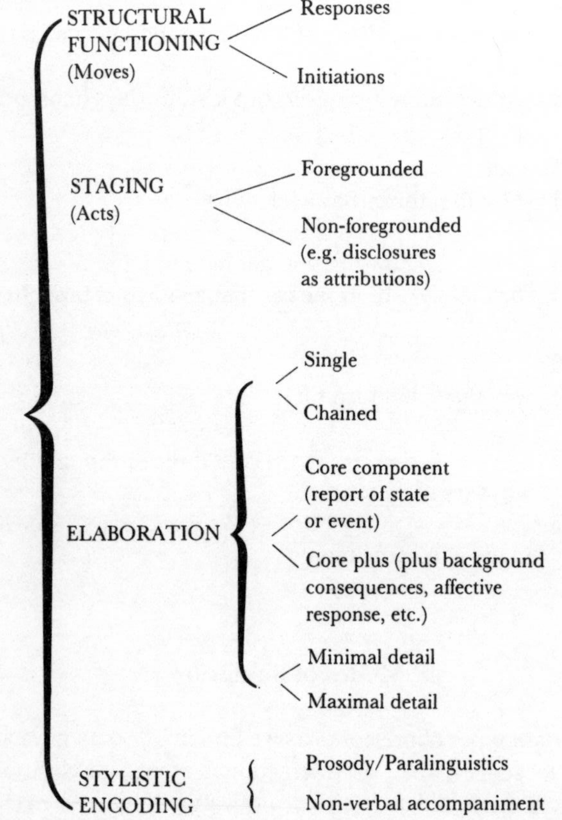

In terms of their function in the structure of an interaction, we have seen examples of disclosures which are *initiating* moves within conversational exchanges (in the general sense of Coulthard and Montgomery 1982, and Sinclair and Coulthard 1975) and others which are clearly *responses* to initiations by recipients; for example, *I should have my (.) rupture done and I won't go in* (E02 in Extract 1, lines 9–10) as initiation, and *but my eyes are not so good, see* (also E02 in the same extract, line 7) as part of a move responding to Y02's *oh you used to knit did you?* (line 4). Such a gross structural distinction merely re-states our earlier point that disclosures may differ in terms of options and obligations, since we can reasonably assume that responses are essentially predicted moves while initiations are essentially predicting moves (again cf. Coulthard and Montgomery 1982, p. 111).

A more sensitive analysis allows us to distinguish disclosures which, as individual communicative acts, are more or less textually foregrounded. Figure 9.1b presents this range of options under the heading of *staging*, a term we borrow from Brown and Yule's discussion of thematisation processes above the sentence level (Brown and Yule 1983, p. 134). Just as syntactic components within a sentence may be foregrounded or thematised, so communicative acts themselves are rendered more or less prominent by their relations to other acts. Again, our previous discussion of disclosures as (occasionally) expressed attributions has recognised the parenthetic nature of some disclosures (such as Extract 1, line 7, *but my eyes are not so good, see*). Within the staging alternatives, such instances can clearly be seen as non-foregrounded by comparison with focused accounts of painful states or events such as E03's disclosure of her thrombosis (Extract 6, between lines 6 and 11). A uniquely non-foregrounded disclosive act occurs in Extract 7 (lines 13 and 15) where E12 discloses her emphysema and osteoarthritis precisely as an attempt to support a claim that she is not *miserable and moaning* (line 7):

Extract 7 (from I21)

E12 you know (.) yes(.) mm (breathes) I think you see when you're
getting older at this age you (2.0) there's lots of things can make
us a bit miserable but (breathes) we have a look on the bright side
and
[ ]
Y12 (agreeing) oh yes mm

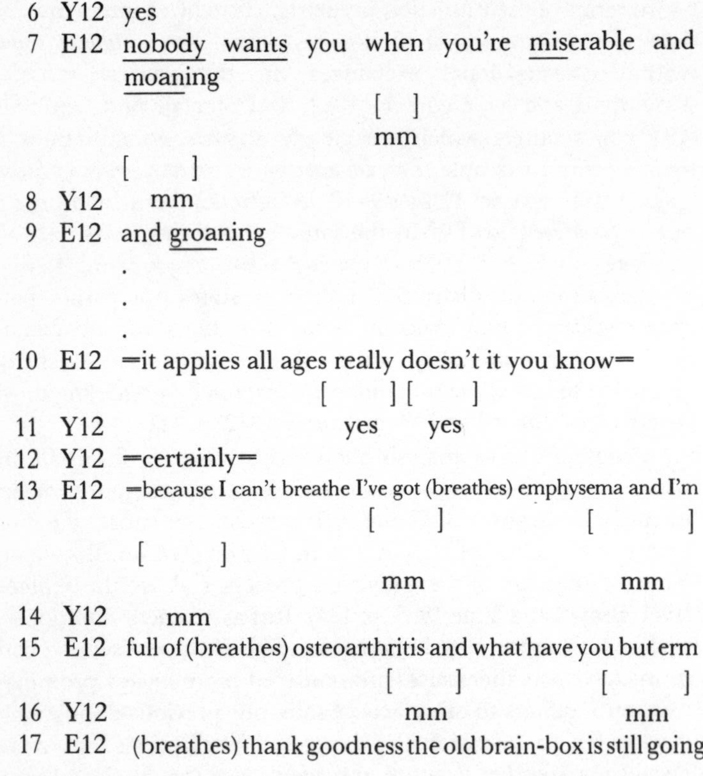

6 Y12 yes
7 E12 nobody wants you when you're miserable and moaning
[ ]
mm
[ ]
8 Y12 mm
9 E12 and groaning
.
.
.
10 E12 =it applies all ages really doesn't it you know=
[ ] [ ]
11 Y12 yes yes
12 Y12 =certainly=
13 E12 =because I can't breathe I've got (breathes) emphysema and I'm
[ ] [ ]
[ ]
mm mm
14 Y12 mm
15 E12 full of (breathes) osteoarthritis and what have you but erm
[ ] [ ]
16 Y12 mm mm
17 E12 (breathes) thank goodness the old brain-box is still going

The remaining sub-categorisations of disclosure-modes all have to do with the extent to which disclosures are elaborated in their telling. In the data, we find three co-occurring sets of alternatives in the elaboration system. These have to do with syntagmatic elaboration at progressively more delicate levels. Simply in terms of topics disclosed upon, we can distinguish single from chained disclosures. A speaker makes a single disclosure when she reveals information on *one* of the topic sub-types (listed above, pp. 205-7). Chained disclosures arise when previous own disclosure acts as a pre-context for disclosing on another topic; cf. again the chain of disclosures in Extract 1: sensory decrement (eyesight), ongoing medical problem (rupture) and an apparently unrelated further instance of the ill-health sub-type (blackouts). Within any disclosure, a speaker may restrict herself to what we wish to call a core component — the reporting or naming of the painful state or event and no more than this (e.g. again the references to emphysema and osteoarthritis in Extract 7). Alternatively, she may report some or a good deal of contextual information in addition, such as the outlining of consequences of colostomy (Extract 4, line 12, *I've got to be careful what I eat*) and affective response (lines 21 and 22 *and at the time I just wanted to die*). A final dimension of elaboration relates to the amount of detail a discloser provides *within* each component, core or otherwise. An instance of elaboration at this level, too long to reproduce at this point, occurs when E02, in the text which follows on from Extract 1, details the cause of her blackouts and the side-effects of the drugs prescribed, i.e. giddiness, inability to walk, and loose bowels.

Finally, it is of course the case that modes of disclosure can be sub-categorised by their stylistic encoding. At prosodic/paralinguistic and non-verbal levels, such variables as speech-rate and intensity, whispering and laughter, serious/smiling facial expression, posture and orientation will significantly colour the making of a disclosure and will probably also have variable interpersonal consequences. We might expect there to be a systematic correlation between stylistic choices made here and the intrinsic intimacy, recency, 'painfulness', or in some other sense the salience of the disclosure's context. However, modes of disclosing in our data are occasionally of interest in particular because of the *un*predictable, marked covariance of content and style. When E02 (in the elaborated sequence just discussed) is describing the most unpleasant side-effects she is suffering, she accompanies the account with expansive gestures, a generally animated non-verbal style, laughter, smiling and the prosodics of levity. To the extent that seeming incongruities of this sort regularly occur, they can be significant clues to the *presentational* function of disclosures. Possible interpretations here are that E02 is compensating stylistically for what she may perceive to be embarrassingly intimate self-disclosures; more interestingly, that she is 'smiling through' her adversity and seeking to *gain* face through giving face-*threatening* accounts in a controlled and cheerful manner. (Jefferson (1984b, p. 367) suggests laughter in troubles talk shows troubles-resistivity in the teller, showing that she is in a position to 'take it lightly'.) In any event, the *style* of a disclosure needs to be seen as a significant factor in facework (Goffman 1955) with its potential to offer a counterpoint to the dimensions of face carried in the content of disclosures.

Next-moves

Our motive for taxonomising recipient next-moves (in Figure 9.1c) is to generate discourse categories which will allow us to capture the *problematical* nature of at least some of the painful disclosures in our data. The categories will again be needed for later attempts (beyond the scope of this chapter) to model disclosure of this sort in terms of speech accommodation processes. But more particularly, we see recipient next-moves, and closing moves (phase 4 of our taxonomy) as integral elements of the structure of disclosive sequences. On the one hand, recipients' next-moves provide implicit or explicit commentaries upon the disclosures they follow, and help us assess their interactional significance. On the other hand, they play a central role in enabling or inhibiting further disclosive talk within the same or a new disclosive sequence. This latter function is in fact used to rank, again impressionistically, the taxonomic variants in Figure 9.1c.

We should note that, in respect of Figure 9.1b, we have been taxonomising what appear to be alternative strategies available to the *discloser*. With recipient next-moves, the perspective (mediated by our own interpretation, inevitably) shifts to the recipient, and strategic options available to *her*. To that extent, our 'encourage–discourage disclosure' scale is not intended to predict outcomes but rather what appear to be the interactional goals of the recipient herself.

Figure 9.1c distinguishes minimal moves from 'full' moves. Minimal moves are brief verbal or at least vocal utterances which may also occur as back-channel utterances overlapping disclosures themselves. The effective force of such moves is unclear from their transcribed forms, and heavily dependent upon non-verbal and prosodic/paralinguistic realisations. Some however, that we label *oh dear* responses, may be taken to encode sympathy, at least in their unmarked realisation, and can be distinguished from more affectively neutral responses (e.g. *mm*) and expressions primarily of surprise (e.g. *good heavens*!). Often, such utterances occur as next-moves by chance, perhaps having been encoded for the back-channel and happening not to overlap. Most commonly, they also head 'full' next-moves of the sort we shall consider. Their most significant function in interactive terms, however, is when they occur as isolates in place of full moves — as in Extract 8, where Y09's *oh yes yes*, *mm*, *oh well* and *um*, punctuated by pauses of increasing length, suggest she does

Figure 9.1c: A taxonomy of strategies in four phases of disclosive sequences: Recipient next-moves

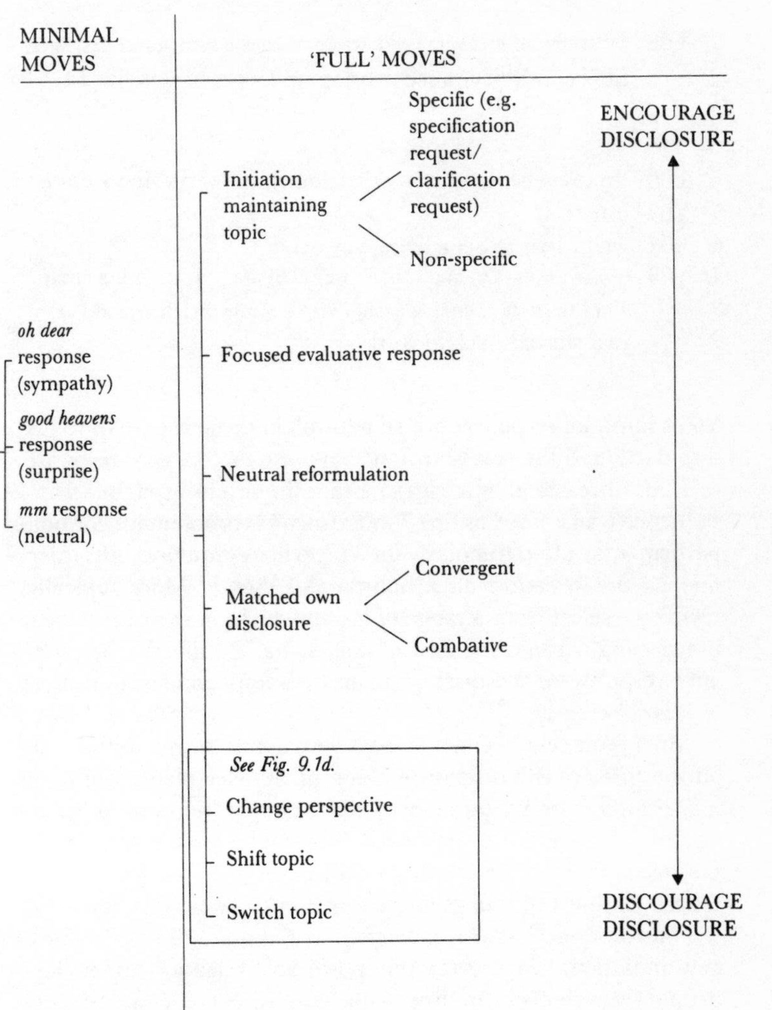

not readily find an appropriate 'full' next-move:

Extract 8 (from I18)

1 E08 =because when I was a widow you see after eleven years I had three
2 little children you see to bring up I worked very hard I
[ ]
3 Y09 mm
4 E08 done everything cook er parlourmad everything I done
5 Y09 mm hm
6 E08 well I had to get a living you see=
7 Y09 = oh yes yes (1.0) mm (2.0) oh well (3.0) um (.) I was going to say
8 I'm I've started working again I've got a little daughter and I've
9 just started back to work

Y09's minimal responses are all neutral, in the sense we have just discussed, and the closest instance in our data to a zero response. It is not unreasonable to suppose that the seven- or eight-second sequence transcribed as line 7 in Extract 8 is problematic for both participants, and particularly for Y09, who eventually shifts topic, making an initiation on a non-painful theme. More typically, recipients select from a range of moves which, in their most basic functioning, sustain the flow of talk, signal an affective or evaluative response to the disclosure, and develop conversation more or less coherently.

Most positively, recipients may, with a 'full' move, initiate talk on the topic of the disclosure being made. Recipients will often make topic-specific initiations, for example requesting specification of a condition described (e.g. *you've got a rupture in?* in Extract 1, line 11); requesting clarification (e.g. *you got what*? in Extract 3, line 15); and asking a discloser to evaluate a condition she has described (*is it is it painful*? in Extract 1, line 17). These new initiations impose (or reimpose) an obligation to disclose painful experiences, in line with our 'direct elicitation' subcategory of pre-contexts. An alternative is for a recipient to make a non-specific initiation, which again establishes (or re-establishes) a relevance for disclosive talk. In Extract 9, Y05's *were you*? offers a general possibility of further talk on E05's being a war-widow, information which she goes on to elicit more specifically (at line 5) when E05 does not take up the offer beyond a neutral *yes* (in line 4):

Extract 9 (from I09)

1 E05 I was a war-widow at the age of twenty-eight=
2 Y05 =were you?=
[ ]
3 E05 ((2syll))
4 E05 =yes
5 Y05 and you've been widowed since then you've never remarried=
[
6 E05 I've been widowed
7 E05 =never married no=
8 Y05 =how old were you when you left school?
9 E05 I was at school until I was sixteen I went to Canton
High School

Non-specific initiations of this sort can generally be distinguished from the minimal back-channel moves previously discussed, though classification here is dependent on subtleties of speech-timing (overlapped/non-overlapped speech) and prosody.

A broad category of moves labelled 'focused evaluative response' — always involving positive evaluations — expresses recipients' sympathetic/empathetic orientation to the states or events recounted, and by implication to the disclosing of them. For that reason, we tentatively rank this category again toward the 'encourage disclosure' pole. The responses are 'focused' since they evaluate the particular experiences related. In Extract 2, at line 15, E02 ventures that E01's husband's death was a *shock* for her; in Extract 10 (below), at line 11, Y11 notes that E11's bringing up five children alone *couldn't have been easy*:

Extract 10 (from I22)

1 E11 and when I got married
2 unfortunately my husband after I'd (.) had five children I
3 decided I'd had enough of him although (breathes) I didn't
4 want (1.0) I wanted my children to have a father
5 but er (.) I thought well he's no good to me he's
6 no good to the children because he was to used (.)
7 beat me around and so forth (breathes) so out he
[ ]
8 Y11 (sympathetically) oh dear

E11 went! (breathes) so I brought up the five of them on my
own
Y11 oh that couldn't have been easy
[ ]
E11 see
Y11 ((2sylls))
[ ]
E11 never knew where he was never had any (.)
(breathes) support from him 'til about three years ago (breathes)
and I wanted to go my daughter went off to Australia so
I wanted to go out to visit (breathes) but I had no pension
Y11 oh yes yes
E11 and er I wanted my daughter ((and)) well it must be sorted out
mum ((be)) you know I=
Y11 =yes
E11 which I did and to my surprise I had a little bit of money from . . .

As in both the quoted instances, moves in this category can often make an original contribution to the disclosed topic itself, as recipients evaluatively rework the account in terms of discloser's *own* hardships or painful experience, thereby to an extent sharing in the reconstruction of the painful states or events.

The previous two categories share the characteristic of, broadly, reinforcing disclosure. This means they are strategies which carry the possibility of escalating disclosive talk; one might say the 'risk' of doing this, to the extent that responding to painful self-disclosure is problematical, as our intuitions indeed suggest it may be. The most obvious problem at this juncture for recipients is that of response-finding, though the risk of escalation may also be a risk from the discloser's perspective, if reponses to an extent oblige her to engage in self-disclosive behaviours that she herself may find problematical. On the other hand (and again from both the participants' positions), as we shall see, several of the response-alternatives to be considered risk minimising disclosive accounts or signalling disinterest in the discloser's mode of talk. For these reasons, it would be surprising if recipients did not, on occasions, seek a form of 'safe ground' of neutral responses, apparently avoiding the interactional pitfalls of either extreme. In our data, however, few next-moves deserve to be labelled 'safe'. The category of 'neutral reformulation' (see Figure 9.1c) best fits this rubric, though even here we find attempts to reformulate aspects of disclosures which (the attempts) seem to be unsatisfactory in themselves.

In Extract 11, while E02 is disclosing on the side-effects of her course of treatment, Y02 produces a range of response-types, including moves (at lines 11 and 13-14) which do little beyond restating the discloser's own comments and decisions:

Extract 11 (from I02)

1 E02 ... I'm on (.) capsules (.) too much my blood's
2 too mu too thin=
3 Y02 =too too thin is it?
.
.
.
4 E02 I've left them I I shouldn't have left them off but I
5 have (.) left them off=
6 Y02 =mm=
7 E02 =for a week and I'm fine
8 Y02 yes
9 E02 well there's after-effects after them see
.
.
.
10 E02 ...I going to see him and tell him now =
11 Y02 =tell him that you're having side-effects
.
.
.
12 E02 so that's what I'm going to tell him when I see him
[ ]
13 Y02 oh it's just as
14 well isn't it to stop them and tell him

Such moves are clearly accommodative in signalling attention and understanding, and in being congruent responses to the problem — line 11, indeed, functions as an utterance-completor to E02's line 10 — though they fall short of positively eliciting further disclosure or making focused positive evaluations. The responses are therefore relatively neutral in respect of encouraging/discouraging disclosure (though again speech-rate, non-verbal accompaniment, etc. are highly relevant to the analysis) but they are accommodative as attuned discourse-management strategies (cf. N. Coupland *et al.* in press).

The remaining options available to recipients within this third phase of the analysis are covered elsewhere in our discussion. The possibility of a recipient matching a disclosure with one of her own — either convergently or combatively — we considered in the account of pre-contexts to disclosure. The three remaining options, changing perspective and shifting or switching topic, tend to both discourage more disclosure (as their prospective function) and (as their synchronic function) advance an ongoing disclosure towards its close. For this reason, these three options are appropriately discussed in our fourth phase — moves towards closing.

Moves towards closing

The closing of a disclosive sequence, like the closing of a conversation (according to the well-known account of Schegloff and Sacks 1973) is typically a complex interactional process which is to be *achieved* rather than merely happening. This perspective does not allow us to taxonomise closings themselves, but rather the moves that either or both participant(s) in our data employ as elements of their negotiation of closings. Taxonomised moves will frequently not actually achieve a close, and we often find multiple moves of the same or different sub-categories being produced by one or both participants. We interpret the structural and functional complexity we find in the phase again as evidence of the potentially problematical nature of disclosive sequences themselves, and of the heavy responsibility that the management of such sequences imposes upon participants.

Figure 9.1d lists moves realised by disclosers and recipients separately, and it is interesting to note the different ranges of strategies available to each. Also, we shall suggest that even those strategies which are identically labelled in the two columns can carry different precise interactional forces. Within both columns, we can distinguish between moves which refer back to painful information disclosed and seek to modify it by *changing perspective*, and moves which, on the other hand, develop conversation away from painful topics — *shifting or switching topic.* In the case of discloser-managed topic-shifts, a previous disclosure is by

Figure 9.1d: A taxonomy of strategies in four phases of disclosive sequences: Moves towards closing

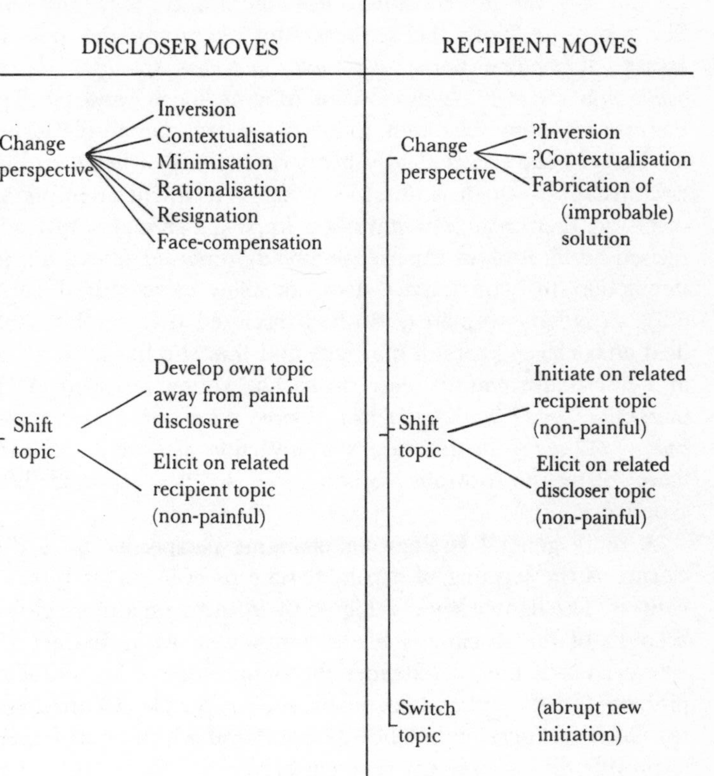

definition closed. Recipient-managed shifts or switches may or may not achieve a close.

Various sub-categories of disclosers' moves (those we label inversion, contextualisation, face-compensation and mimimisation) and all sub-categories of recipients' moves which change the perspective on a disclosure (inversion and contextualisation again, plus fabrication of an improbable solution) function to 'lighten' a disclosure, and to effect a change of key (in the sense of Hymes 1972). The inversion strategies are attempts to reinterpret disclosed information in a positive light, to look on the bright side, or make light of the trouble (cf. Jefferson 1984b).

In interaction 23 (the source of Extract 12, below), E11 has disclosed her loneliness which is caused by having moved to a flat at the top of a hill, inaccessible to her friends and old neighbours. She moves to close the sequence by describing the positive aspects of her new home, *it's healthy and there's plenty to see and you're near the shops.* A discloser is fully at liberty, and perhaps even under some obligation, to invert her own painful disclosure in this way since it is clearly her own analysis of her own life-circumstances which is at issue. When a recipient attempts an inversion, there is an inherent risk of imposing an inappropriately revised account of an experience already reported as painful. In interaction 18 (which space does not allow us to reproduce in full), an elderly woman (E10) had disclosed that her husband died after eleven years of marriage and that she has lived alone in a non-native country ever since. The young recipient (Y09) then offers *yes (1.0) ah well (.) still I mean it's nice that you're settled here (.) ((2 syll)).* In this case, the 'inversion' is barely apposite, there being no obvious 'bright side' to the reported life-experience.

A more general strategy for changing perspective on a disclosure is the locating of a painful state or event in its broader context. The lighter key is achieved by focusing on a more global account of the discloser's life-circumstances, as in Extract 12, where E12 (at line 6) redefines the significance of her mobility problem (lines 1 and 3). Like others, she has the Day Centre to go to, which can offer ambulance transport and which exists largely to provide the sociable environment her immobility would otherwise preclude:

Extract 12 (from I23)

```
1  E12  yes (breathes) well I can't walk far because (.) I'm full of
                                                  [     ]
2  E11                                              no
3  E12  arthritis (laughs)
             [      ]
4  E11       (laughs)
5  E12  but er (.) oh wh what else (.) can we expect something
6       that (.) we're lucky that we've got the day centre to go to
                      [   ]                              [        ]
7  E11                oh I                               oh yes (.) oh
8       I think they're marvellous places
```

On another occasion, in interaction 40, a young recipient (Y20) offers a virtually identical contextualisation move — at least in terms of its context — *so this is really good for you isn't it then to be able to go somewhere like this.* The move is made in response to a disclosure by an elderly interlocutor (E20) of having been widowed for 21 years. This contextualisation may well be generally appropriate — the Centre offers genuine social support for many who live alone — but it makes possibly unwarranted assumptions about the elderly interlocutor's particular circumstances and needs, and arguably patronises through assuming a knowledge of what is *good for* the discloser.

The third sub-category of recipient moves termed 'fabrication of improbable solution' shares (with inversion and contextualisation) the inherent problem of ignorance, a necessarily inferior awareness of the topic disclosed (cf. discussions by Burleson 1985; Lehman, Ellard and Wortman 1986). On one occasion, in interaction 10, E05 has been reporting the acrimonious break-up of her son's marriage, divorce and its painful consequences to all concerned. E06 responds *perhaps they'll go back together*, which is itself unlikely in terms of the account given and is in any case irrelevant to what has already passed — E05 has already commented that *the children . . . are very badly affected.* (Jefferson (1984b, p. 363), too, notes the propensity of recipients in her data to propound extravagantly optimistic reassurances.)

Disclosers have the further options of *face-compensation* and *minimisation*, still within the general set of strategies which 'lighten' disclosures to some extent. We find instances of disclosers compensating for the face-threatening (cf. Goffman 1955; Brown and Levinson 1978) disclosures they have just made by counterbalancing them with self-reports which build positive face. In interaction 2, E02 concludes a disclosure of her own immobility by saying *so I I find I can't do it so good*; her next turn is *so I but I do all my own work*, said assertively and cheerfully. The effect of the move is ultimately similar to that of the contextualisation strategies we considered earlier, though the immediate function of face-compensating moves is to contrast one particular report with another, rather than to set a painful experience in the context of its broader significance. With minimising strategies, disclosers seek quite simply to retract elements of their previous disclosure, to redefine their own painful experience as less painful than they earlier reported it. For instance, in interaction 15, a young interactant (Y07) has reported having just been told she has osteoarthritis in her hip. She is a sports teacher and county squash player, so that her sporting and career prospects are seriously in jeopardy. Yet, when her young interlocutor (Y08) suggests *it must have come as quite a shock*, Y07 says *yes (.) well no it'll go (.) apparently these things come ((and go))*. Of course, we have no access to how valid Y07 perceives this assessment of her own condition to be. Nevertheless, it contradicts her earlier account and, significantly for our current analysis, marks a transition from Y07's self-disclosure to her initiation of talk on a new (other-related) topic.

The two final perspective-changing strategies that disclosers adopt move to bound disclosures without alleviating their projected painfulness to any significant extent. A discloser may offer a rationalisation of how her painful circumstances have come to be, for example when E16 (in interaction 31) suggests that her grandchildren do not visit her because they are *interested in their jobs I suppose*. This is clearly a move to close, since E16 has shifted from revealing to accounting, and to accounting in a spirit of apparent acceptance. Her *I suppose* might suggest she doubts the validity of the account, however, and that is only the *interactional* difficulty (in this passage of talk) that is likely to be at all resolved. Exclusively in peer-elderly encounters, we find a move towards closing which is simply the expression of *resignation*. In the last quoted extract (12), E12's first move to close after her disclosure of being *full of arthritis* is *oh wh what else (.) can we expect*. As in our earlier discussion of talk about age as a relevant pre-context for painful disclosure, the fact of being elderly itself provides something of an account, and we've seen that accounting for disclosures can elsewhere also be a strategy for closing them. On the other hand, this last retrospective closing move stands out from all others in not clearly offering a means of 'recovering' from disclosure. And *recovery* seems a more appropriate concept here than 'repair', since the reported painful experiences, and indeed the interactional 'damage' that might be done in their reporting, can in no meaningful sense be made good.

As in previous phases of the analysis, we do not mean to imply that taxonomised strategies are mutually exclusive or cannot co-occur. In fact the 'change perspective' sub-types often preface the various means of topic-development listed in the lower two quadrants of Figure 1d. Given that there is a normative requirement for coherent topical development in conversation, it is not surprising that the strategies we find in our data generally involve progressive topic-shifts away from the reported painful experience. Once again, either participant can take the initiative for developing topic. A discloser may steer her own topic away from painful disclosure — as in Extract 10, where E11 develops her life-narrative, a compilation of reports of painful happenings, towards an account of good fortune (in the last line of the extract). While the young interlocutor, as we have seen, has provided responses to some of the disclosures made, responsibility for terminating the disclosive sequence as a whole is assumed by the discloser herself within the flow of the narrative. The effect here is to routinise painful disclosure in that no ultimate response from the recipient is required or even allowed:

Extract 13 (from I28)

1 E14 have you got any children?
2 Y14 yes
3 E14 oh you have=
4 Y14 =yes (.) four of them (laughs)
5 E14 (exclaims) four! oh dear you've done mind er (2.0) oh that's nice
6 I I think to have a family
7 Y14 mm
8 E14 we'd have had four if they'd lived but we er got two
and we lost two
9 Y14 (sympathetically) ohh (.) yes=
10 E14 =(louder) they're all in school are they?
11 Y14 um one is sixteen yes and thirteen and then I've got a nine year
12 old

And it is the same effect that E14 (in Extract 13, above) achieves over lines 8 and 10. The topic-shift is again coherent in that her question about Y14's children being in school (on line 10) develops from Y14's short reference (in line 8) to her own children. In the structure of the discourse, topic-shift is achieved this time by means of an elicitation on a related recipient-topic with no predictable painful associations. Once again, however, we see how a discloser can manage a disclosure in a way that requires minimal or no contribution towards closure from her recipient, however emotionally taxing the sequence may be in other respects.

When shifting to a non-painful topic is achieved by a recipient of disclosure, the same options exist of initiating (on a self-related topic) and eliciting (on a discloser-related topic). We find development by means of an initiation in Extract 8, line 7, where Y09 takes up E08's topic of working while bringing up children (lines 1, 2 and 4). Development by means of an elicitation can be seen in Extract 6, where Y03 (at line 12) advances E03's topic of her thrombosis of the leg through a question about how she travelled to the university. In both instances, recipients very resourcefully balance the closing of disclosive talk and the requirement to talk topically, though in *neither* case do participants' contributions appear fully attuned or complementary. Y09's initiation is topically contingent but grossly mis-matched in its emotional content. Y03's *so how did you get here today* may be heard to dismiss the essence of E03's disclosure — her thrombosis — in favour of the practical consequences it may or may not have had for her on this particular occasion. We are again drawn to see recipient moves towards closing as inherently problematical for one, or more likely both, parties to disclosive talk.

One fragment in our data challenges our earlier assumption of closure needing to be achieved interactionally:

Extract 14 (from I13)

```
 1  E07  because I'm not Welsh you see I was evac I was an evacuee (2.0) I
 2       was evacuated from London          [    ]
 3  E08                                      ahh
 4  E07  (1.0) and erm (1.5) I had twins well I lost one I lost a little boy
 5       (1.5) and I had the (.) daughter I I'm almost sure it was
 6       Llandough I went to but I'm not (1.0)
                           [  ]
 7  E08                    mm
 8  E07  not sure
         [      ]
 9  E08  if you pass my bag I could comb my hair
10  E07  mm?
11  E08  pass my bag I could comb my hair
         (2.5)
12  E07  you you want it?
```

In Extract 14 above, E07 has disclosed (at line 4) the death of her baby son. Neither she nor her elderly interlocutor produces any of the taxonomised moves towards closing, and the topic is switched abruptly by E08 at line 9. As an exhaustive account of strategies manifest in our data-corpus, our taxonomy needs to list this move-type, though it raises a host of questions about attentiveness, task-perception and norms of talk. A plausible analysis (though one of many) is that disclosive talk may become so routinised in the experience of some elderly people, and perhaps particularly those with restricted social contact (the Day Centre clients clearly fall within this category), as to make topic-switches like that of E08 far less markedly non-accommodative and dismissive than they would more usually appear. This analysis would be consistent with an observation we made above about the routinised encoding of some elderly disclosures.

Epilogue

Our analysis of disclosive sequences under the four headings above has been presented as an indispensable precursor to more fully interpretive and explanatory theoretical and empirical work in the area of intergenerational talk. Nevertheless, the analysis itself holds some broad implications for investigations of disclosure. Firstly, we are in a position to challenge and clarify non-interactional definitions of *self-disclosure itself.* We have seen that Berger and Bradac, for instance, endorse Pearce and Sharp's conceptualisation of self-disclosure as 'the voluntary and intentional revelation of personal information which cannot be obtained from other sources'. Our data show not only that many acts of self-disclosure are, directly or indirectly, elicited by interlocutor, but that many are also engendered by textual processes in their own right. There are clearly interactional settings where the supposed will to disclose (or *not* to do so) is overridden by interactional and textual pressures. Again, even within our broad category of discloser-determined disclosures, some speakers may (voluntarily) disclose seeming to have manufactured contexts for their disclosures, which can make them *seem other* than voluntary. In general, then, we prefer to see self-disclosure as a complex of discourse behaviours wherein the transmission of personal (and, in our case, intimate and painful) information is negotiated relative to considerations of interactional co-operation, interpersonal accommodation, textual coherence and self-presentational intent.

Secondly, our analysis has derived concepts which can be combined to offer a rich definition of *disclosiveness.* In the social-psychological literature, disclosiveness is typically seen as a personality trait (Kelley 1967; Berger and Bradac 1982, p. 86), though we would once again argue that the interactional manifestations of disclosiveness need to be central to its definition. From the initial numerical overview of disclosure in our data, we can hypothesise that certain groups of elderly conversationalists tend to be more disclosive than some young conversationalists. But empirical studies addressing such a claim could profitably define disclosiveness more sensitively than as the tendency to produce highly intimate information very frequently. Disclosive talk is better characterised as talk which (in addition) shows elaborated disclosures in our sense — disclosures which are chained, contextually developed, in considerable detail (cf. Figure 9.1b, above). Beyond these considerations, disclosiveness needs to be characterised in terms of the precise pre-contexts in which disclosures are made. By this account, a disclosive individual (or, more appropriate, an individual who may be deemed to be acting disclosively in a specified interaction) is one who discloses when there are few or no interactional obligations to disclose operative, and when multiple options are available. The extreme case of disclosive behaviour may therefore be *either* the making of 'out of the blue' disclosures, or the discloser's manufacturing of contexts where disclosures can be made. Further, disclosive behaviour may involve *not* enabling or allowing the recipient to make her *own* disclosures.[7] We shall need to consider whether and to what extent this interactional definition of disclosiveness allows us to relate findings from our own work with those in the existing (principally social-psychological) literature — for example that women in general self-disclose more than men, and particularly in same-sex dyads (Cline 1986); and that lonely people may 'over-compensate' in terms of self-disclosure (Solano, Batten and Parish 1982).

Correspondingly, our data suggest that processes of disclosure and disclosiveness cannot be dissociated from eliciting behaviours. If the elderly in our study behave disclosively, this is of course not unrelated to the possibility that the young, in intergenerational contexts, are behaving 'interrogatively'. Miller, Berg and Archer (1986) have in fact introduced the notion of 'openers' to identify that group of individuals who seem particularly skilled in enabling self-disclosure, inducing others to 'open up'. That the young females in our study may fit this categorisation is further supported by the observation (Petronio, Martin and Littlefield 1984) that young females in general have relatively harsh criteria for deciding when and how to self-disclose. Indeed, elderly disclosiveness may be appropriately interpreted as, in part, behaviour which accommodates young interlocutors' perceived propensity to interrogate. The younger women in our subject-group do indeed appear to adopt an 'interviewing' orientation, to dominate the topic- and turn-management of intergenerational talk, but to accede in terms of amounts of talk and personal information transferred. This chapter has had relatively little to say about modes of interrogation (and again cf. Berger and Bradac 1982, p. 81), though a systematic discourse analysis of problems of information-seeking in this and other conversational contexts will raise further significant empirical questions about the origins and broader functions of disclosive talk.

Our study has, finally, raised questions concerning the interactional (and therefore ultimately the interpersonal, intergroup and more broadly the social) consequences of disclosing personal painful experiences. Our interpretive analysis has assumed that responding to painful disclosures generally entails a responsibility for recipients, and can often be problematical. We have suggested that encoding these responses can be problematical because of competing, even contradictory goals and constraints. Responding to painful disclosures involves plausible uncertainties about what *is* accommodative talk at this point and invokes folk-theories about what is therapeutic (cf. Cohen, Sherrod and Clark 1986; Dunkel-Shetter and Wortman 1982) or beneficial behaviour. Figure 9.1c suggested that next-moves to disclosive acts may be inherently unsatisfactory, with recipients of painful disclosure forced into making one of a set of dispreferable moves: the aggressive or dismissive-seeming discouraging strategies of shifting or even switching topic; the potentially over-accommodative sympathy/empathy strategies; a bland and perhaps disinterested-seeming neutrality; and signalling interest and involvement (if this difficult strategy is manageable for recipients, if they have the relevant skills and experience) which risks sustaining and even escalating painful disclosure.

We can sense the problematical nature of disclosure, furthermore, in the patterning of closing strategies. When recipients do move to close (and even socially skilled, resourceful recipients like the young women in our subject population), there are sometimes discontinuities or implausibilities in their (presumed) attempts to console disclosers or lighten the conversational key. It is significant that disclosers themselves shoulder much of the responsibility for closing their own disclosures, inverting their painful reports to show the 'bright side', reappraising them from a broader perspective, toning down their reported painfulness, or developing new topics by some means. But there is *no* inevitable 'up-swing' here, and closings can often count in no sense as resolutions. Threats to a discloser's face therefore seem to be tolerated and left to lie ('resignation'), unless an attempt is made to compensate for a loss of face by promoting some other aspect of self-identity.

Our ultimate goal for work in this area is to offer a broader, explanatory account of why, and with what implications, the particular patterns and strategies of self-disclosure we have identified are variously employed by different generational groups and in interaction between them. This task will require detailed cross-referencing to several other lines of research in disciplines across and even beyond the language sciences — for example in the study of generational beliefs about and norms for talk (cf. Wiemann, Coupland, Giles *et al.*, forthcoming), situational construals and generational stereotyping. A host of particular research questions remains to be addressed to do with the interaction between these social processes before we can claim to understand the functioning of self-disclosure in talk within and across generational (and sub-generational or 'contextual', cf. Rubin 1986) groups. Nevertheless, we hope to have shown how an analysis of discourse has a central role to play in what must eventually be an interdisciplinary effort. Most humbly, a discourse analysis is an essential prerequisite to any explanatory theorising because of its potential to define the interactional phenomenon at issue — in this case the disclosure of painful experience. But its most significant contribution is in highlighting disclosure as a complex social process, which in fact resists any easy definition. While there are likely to be significant determinants of disclosive talk to be found in socio-historical and circumstantial dimensions of elderly people's lives, and while disclosure may satisfy some general emotion or therapeutic needs and realise general group-predispositions, we must recognise that disclosive talk still needs to be achieved interactionally. And contextual constraints and pressures are not merely the fine detail of socio-psychological processes, they are the means by which they are experienced, redefined and perpetuated. For this reason, explanatory theorising will need, at its centre, to model the management of painful disclosure in discourse, as the end-product of strategic interpersonal intentions against a backdrop of contextual possibilities.

Notes

1. This paper is based on research funded by the Economic and Social Research Council (ESRC, UK), reference number G00222002.

2. We are grateful to Karen Henwood, Karen Atkinson and Penny Rowlands for their involvement in gathering the data on which the chapter is based; also to UWIST Applied Psychology Department for the use of their video-recording facilities.

3. A follow-up phase of the study being reported did in fact elicit general subjective and evaluative information from the participants involved in the 40 interactions in one-to-one post-recording interviews. Data from these interviews is not systematically drawn on in this chapter, though they have informed our interpretation, particularly as regards subjects' perceptions of the problematical status of certain disclosive sequences.

4. Matters of coding reliability are not normally addressed in interpretive analysis of this sort, though we realise disciplines differ in the 'standards' of self-justification researchers are required to meet. In any case, we hope not to have overstressed points which hinge on delicate textual interpretations. We certainly recognise that analysts, and of course participants, may sometimes be unable to uniquely assign utterances to categories; this is likely to be particularly difficult in the case of adjacent sub-categories in our taxonomy. Nevertheless, all of our textual categorisations have emerged via a procedure of multiple independent coding and subsequent negotiation. By these means we hope to resist the charge of idiosyncracy.

5. Of course, the particular nature of a self-disclosive act is crucial to the predictability of its being matched accommodatively. Being the recipient of perceived 'over-disclosure' (Davis and Franzoi 1986) — and particularly *negative* forms of it (Taylor and Belgrave 1986) — has been shown to be likely to inhibit reciprocal behaviours.

6. The relationship between disclosure and accommodation is an important area of future theoretical development but beyond the immediate scope of this chapter. The distinction between convergent and combative disclosures is taken up in the discussion of next-moves.

7. A forthcoming paper deals with receptive/non-receptive listening by recipients, based on the same data.

Appendix

The issues we address in this chapter overlap with a line of Conversation Analysis research into 'troubles talk' — Jefferson 1980, 1984a, 1984b, 1985; Lee and Jefferson 1980. For purposes of comparison — to assess on the one hand the robustness, on the other hand the context-specificity of our own taxonomy, it will be valuable to summarise the basic schematisation of troubles talk (from Lee and Jefferson 1980, pp. 10-11). We present these authors' structural summary (their 'candidate sequence') under their own category-labels, adding some interpretive notes of our own, plus observations on overlaps/apparent inconsistencies with our own work. At the end of the appendix, we briefly discuss what appear to us to be the significant differences in focus between the two approaches, as possible explanations for variation.

The candidate troubles-telling sequence

A. Approach

1. Initiation:

(a) *inquiry* e.g. *how are you today*? Though the category overlaps with our 'direct elicitation', Lee and Jefferson's (J)'s data is talk between friends; hence, inquirers tend to know about ongoing troubles; if so, the issue of phaticity does not arise.

(b) *noticing* e.g. *do you have a sore throat*? The noticing of possible trouble, from paralinguistic features (hoarseness of voice; coughing). Our schema would recognise this origin of talk on ill-health under the general category of textual determination. But between strangers (our data), there is presumably uncertainty about vocal characteristics being attributable to ill-health or to setting (as permanent features of voice).

2. Trouble-premonitor:

(a) *downgraded conventional response to inquiry*, e.g. *oh not so bad*; *surviving I guess* The speaker is orienting his/her coparticipant to the presence/continuation of a trouble. This is a useful refinement of the structural account of disclosure-initiations, which might be added to our taxonomy of pre-contexts to disclosure. J's category shows a subtle means by which disclosers-to-be may 'determine', in our sense, the disclosive outcome. However, familiars will be more predictably able/prepared to pick up on such subtle cueing, and we worry about the reliability of non-participants' (analysts') perceptions of these speech functions in context.

(b) *improvement marker*, e.g. *better*; *much better* Again, not relevant to participants without a relational history. This category, as J's data show, will sometimes preface troubles-talk, though we doubt it predicts it. Throughout, our own analysis tries to stress possible causal associations between pre-contexts and disclosive 'outcomes'; J's seems to favour structural observation.

(c) *lead-up*, e.g. *he went for his X-rays on Friday*; *the next time you see me I'm gonna be looking like hell you know why* This is said to be used in response to inquiry, but especially where talk about a trouble is being initiated by the teller. It indicates the presence of something 'untoward' and/or begins to tell the nature of the trouble. The category, like (a) above, can refine our analysis of the onset of disclosure, though it would fall within our phase 2 account of 'disclosures' (themselves, not their pre-contexts).

3. Premonitor response:

e.g. *mm*; *yeah*; *yes* — a 'continuer' produced by recipients in order to show they are ready and expect to receive further talk. Just as our own analysis has not identified 'premonitors', so we have not distinguished a 'premonitor response' category. In our account, these utterances are considered minimal back-channel moves by recipients during disclosures.

B. Arrival

1. Announcement:

e.g. *we got burgled yesterday*; *her mother is terminal*; *I had to have my toe-nail taken off* The equivalent of our core disclosure. It is interesting that J takes announcements of troubles *not* to be integral elements of their 'delivery' (the next major category). This suggests that, among familiars, to report painful experiences in summary form may be taken to be structurally incomplete; hence, another precursor to fuller telling. Such expectations are not clearly apparent in our own data-context, where 'announcements' may be the whole painful report, particularly in non-foregrounded disclosures —

hence we see them as core elements, not in any sense precursory. This importantly suggests that functiuonal categories and category-systems are (and ought to be) altogether context-dependent.

2. Announcement response:

e.g. *oh really*; *you did*? — which elicits further talk on the trouble but does not necessarily 'align' the recipient with teller; and e.g. *nah no*; *oh shit*! which 'commits' recipient to the troubles-telling. Since for us these are responses to disclosures, they would feature as either neutral, sympathetic or empathetic minimal next-moves, the precise categorisation depending heavily on prosodic enactment — cf. our stylistic encoding dimension (which J does not report, except in marking emphasis in the transcribed examples).

C. Delivery

1. Exposition:

(includes descriptions of 'symptoms', 'events', etc.): This broad category is differentiated in our account under the various dimensions of elaboration — single versus chained; core versus core plus; minimal versus maximal detail.

2. Affiliation:

e.g. *Jesus!*; *he's crazy!*; *oh baby!*: Context again explains the non-occurrence of such emotional responses in our data. We suggest this general category of recipient-utterances is distributed across back-channelling and focused evaluative ('full') responses, depending on precise timing and details of encoding.

3. Affiliation response:

e.g. *it just hurt so bad Helen I was crying* — emotionally heightened talk from the troubles-teller, giving descriptions of events, ailments, affective reaction to troubles. J notes that C2 followed by C3 is not found in British data; even where C2 is found, C3 does not follow. C3 does not feature in our data either; necessarily, because we don't get emotional C2s.

D. Work-up

Consists of a range of activities including diagnoses, prognoses, reports of relevant other experiences, remedies, etc. The work-up positions the trouble by reference to more general circumstances so that talk starts out focused on the trouble but does not end up that way. Closure is becoming relevant, but not imminent. The work-up is achieved by teller *and/or* recipient, with no acknowledgement that quite different interactional motives, forces and consequences may be involved across these two conditions. To the extent that the unifying property of the work-up (to us, an otherwise amorphous category) is 'invoking the relevance of a move towards closure' (Lee and Jefferson 1980, p. 35), it seems difficult to differentiate the category — at least in functional terms — from E below. We suggest that a structurally-based analysis like that of J may require the identification of multiple categories, while our more functional approach is happier to assign sequenced utterances to the same category when they are perceived to carry the same interactional force, albeit at different textual points.

E. Close implicature

1. Optimistic projection:

e.g. *it'll iron itself out; I'm gonna be alright the doctor says I'm doing fine* Examples (in the Lee and Jefferson discussion) in this category are all in the speech of tellers; to that extent, our nearest category is minimisation as a discloser's move towards closing. Elderly disclosers in our data are probably less likely to be in a position to project optimistically, of course, in cases of severe health problems, sensory decrement, etc. However, recipients do, as we say, fabricate improbable solutions to (elderly) disclosers' problems; cf. too Jefferson 1984b, p. 363. The infelicitously labelled further possibility of 'substitute optimistic projection' (e.g. *whatever's to be's to be that's all*) is what we call resignation (by disclosers).

2. Invocation of the *status quo*:

e.g. *oh God we had the police round all night it was hectic so I hardly got any work done* This re-engages the trouble with ordinary everyday activities, as shared by the two participants. In our data-context, of course, there is no such sharing, and *status quo* for them can only be defined as 'non-painful' talk. Once again, J's account does not distinguish participants' roles in achieving this. Hence, in our taxonomy, we identify a variety of perspective-changing and topic-shifting strategies variously used by disclosers and recipients.

3. Making light of the trouble:

e.g. *well you probably got at least a week . . . a week before you die*
Again, either participant is said to make light of troubles, and generally involving laughter. Laughter does not occur in our data in connection with disclosure, though we do note instances where disclosers use a 'light' key in the course of disclosing. Certainly, recipients in our data do not make light of troubles, beyond their attempts to invert and contextualise painful disclosures.

F. Exit

1. Boundarying off:

(a) *Conversation closure* — in the context of telephone calls, hanging up. Troubles-telling frequently occurs as topic of last exchanges of conversations in J's data. Quoted instances show confusing overlap with later sub-categories; hanging up does not appear to be structurally prior to, or an alternative to, say, 'reference to getting together' (cf. below).

(b) *Conversation restart* — a switch of topic (our sub-category) is brought about (clearly within the same conversation, in the more usual sense, though embarking on a quite new transactional field) by either participant.

(c) *Introduction of pending biographicals* — a topic-switch to an especially warranted new topic of prior concern to both. In relation to what we term both switches and shifts, it is important to note the quite different underlying assumptions operative in the two data-contexts. Participants in J's data have a shared background of interpersonal knowledge which can render what for our participants would be major switches in topics more like shifts — to different but already consolidated areas of common experience. The solidary effect of the topic-changes J identifies in this category cannot therefore be achieved in our data, where participants can only manipulate interpersonal distance symbolically, through degrees of discoursal accommodation.

(d) *Reference to getting together*, e.g. *can you come out for a drink tonight?*; *maybe next weekend if you and Freddy want to come up*
This established conversation closing strategy has a particular appositeness in the context of post-troubles-telling, showing affiliation. Since it is true (cf. above) that troubles-

> telling tends to be conversational-final, it seems difficult to identify reference to getting together as part of the management of troubles-sequence-closing, rather than conversation-closing as a whole.
>
> 2. Step-wise transition into other topics (cf. Jefferson 1984a):
> This detailed schematisation is a particularly valuable elaboration of what our taxonomy simply labels as topic-shifts and assigns to either participant. The model of progressive, interactive achievement of topic-transition is certainly likely to be a better reflection of the textual subtleties of moving out of painful self-disclosure, though we would still want to interpret the significance of each participant's efforts towards achieving closure.

Overall, then, several of the categories in Lee and Jefferson's and our own framework are motivated in direct response to the different interactional settings of talk — public vs. private; involving strangers vs. familiars. The relational histories of J's co-participants are a background against which new troubles (or new aspects of old troubles) are intrinsically salient, and a highly predictable topic for talk. The structural development of troubles-telling can directly reflect this: as when 'noticed' paralinguistic cues can trigger elicitations of painful reports, or when troubles are 'announced' prior to being detailed. Our own starting-point has been the assumption that, in our context, *any* recounting of or even reference to own painful experiences is interactionally 'charged' and salient — it is disclosive, a term not obviously appropriate to J's troubles-telling. The troubles-telling phone-calls are more up-dates than self-disclosures, and less presentationally focused, hardly relevant to the projection and perception of social categories.

Beyond this, J's analytic focus is principally the structural mechanics of talk, as the shared construction of social events. Troubles-talk is discussed in terms of 'a progession through a template ordering' which 'constitutes an elegant and effective machinery by which the polar and competing relevancies of attention to business as usual and attention to the troubles can be managed' (Lee and Jefferson 1980, p. 71). On the other hand, we have developed our taxonomy as a preliminary effort toward understanding interpersonal and intergroup processes, which requires us *above all* to attend to precisely *what* contributions to ordering are made *when, by whom*, even *why*, and *with what consequences.* (We do not claim to have made significant progress to many of these objectives as yet.)

From the outset, we have conceptualised the disclosure of painful experiences as a locus for problematical interchange — within and across the generations. This focus is almost altogether lacking from J's discussion, not least because of the established relationships in which troubles-telling is exemplified. The troubles themselves are occasionally severe, including reports of terminal illness and hospital operations, as they are in our own data. But recipients in our context are exposed, unwittingly, to self-disclosures, and however resourceful they may be interactionally, they do not have the resource of relational back-up. Again, however, there is a difference of intention, even beyond the contextual disparities. When J does recognise interactional 'problems' occurring, it is interpreted in relation to sequence, not to participants. For example, extracts which show a recipient being 'troubles-resistive' (seeking to avoid being told a trouble) are discussed in terms of the interactants' being 'improperly aligned' which will result in the segment being 'topically and sequentially deranged' (p. 75). Disruption of the candidate sequence is a major consideration in the 1980 report, but its relation to *experienced* disruption (does the candidate sequence have any psychological validity as participants' preferred model of how troubles-telling will or even should best proceed?) is not at all clear. Lee and Jefferson in fact acknowledge that their ordering is 'not an index of problems in the running off of the sequence'. They do say it represents 'how the sequence ought to run' (p. 71), but is this as a descriptive generalisation or a felt preference, whereby actors 'suffer' if the sequence is not fulfilled?

It is not that our taxonomy achieves this, but that we hope it may have some limited advantages over Lee and Jefferson's sequence in modelling interactional alternatives that can, as we intend, be taken into more explicitly evaluative empirical studies of responses to and effects of the disclosure of painful experiences.

References

Atkinson, J.M. and Heritage, J. (eds) (1984) *Structures of social action: studies in conversation analysis.* Cambridge: Cambridge University Press

Berger, C.R. and Bradac, J.J. (1982) *Language and social knowledge: uncer-*

tainty in interpersonal relations. London: Edward Arnold

Boden, D. and Bielby, D. (1983) 'The past as resource: a conversational analysis of elderly talk'. *Human Development*, 26, pp. 308-19

——— (1986) 'The way it was: topical organisation in elderly conversation'. *Language and Communication*, 6, pp. 73-89

Brown, P. and Fraser, C. (1979) 'Speech as a marker of situation'. In K.R. Scherer and H. Giles (eds) *Social markers in speech.* Cambridge: Cambridge University Press

Brown, P. and Levinson, S. (1978) 'Universals in language usage: politeness phenomena'. In E.N. Goody (ed.) *Questions and politeness.* Cambridge Papers in Social Anthropology (8). Cambridge: Cambridge University Press, pp. 56-289

Brown, G. and Yule, G. (1983) *Discourse analysis.* Cambridge: Cambridge University Press

Burleson, B.R. (1985) 'The production of comforting messages: social-cognitive foundations'. *Journal of Language and Social Psychology*, 4, pp. 253-73

Cline, R. (1986) 'The effects of biological sex and psychological gender on reported and behavioural intimacy and control of self-disclosure'. *Communication Quarterly*, 34, pp. 41-54

Cohen, S., Sherrod, D.R. and Clark, M.S. (1986) 'Social skills and the stress-protective role of social support'. *Journal of Personality and Social Psychology*, 50, pp. 963-73

Coulthard, M. and Montgomery, M. (eds) (1982) *Studies in discourse analysis.* London: Routledge & Kegan Paul

Coupland, N., Coupland, J., Giles, H. and Henwood, K. (in press) 'Accommodating the elderly: invoking and extending a theory'. *Language in Society*

Cozby, P.C. (1973) 'Self-disclosure: a literature review'. *Psychological Bulletin*, 79, pp. 73-91

Davis, M.H. and Franzio, S.L. (1986) 'Adolescent loneliness, self-disclosure and private self-consciousness: a longitudinal investigation'. *Journal of Personality and Social Psychology*, 57, pp. 595-608

Dunkel-Shetter, C. and Wortman, C.B. (1982) 'The interpersonal dynamics of cancer: problems in social relationships and their impact on the patient'. In H.S. Friedman and M.R. DiMatteo (eds) *Interpersonal issues in health care.* New York: Academic Press

Giles, H. (ed.) (1984) *The dynamics of speech accommodation. International Journal of the Sociology of Language*, 46. Amsterdam: Mouton

Giles, H. and Powesland, P.F. (1975) *Speech style and social evaluation.* London: Academic Press

Giles, H. and Ryan, E. (eds) (1986) *Language, communication and the elderly.* Special issue of *Language and Communication*, 6, 1

Goffman, E. (1955) 'On face-work: an analysis of ritual elements in social interaction'. Reprinted in J. Laver and S. Hutcheson (eds) (1972) *Communication in face to face interaction.* Harmondsworth: Penguin, pp. 319-46

——— (1959) *The presentation of self in everyday life.* New York: Garden City

Grice, H.P. (1975) 'Logic and conversation'. In P. Cole and J. Morgan (eds) *Syntax and semantics vol. 3. Speech acts.* London: Academic Press, pp. 41-58

Hamilton, H. (MS) 'Problems in accommodating the other: the case of Alzheimer's Disease'. Paper presented at the Minnesota Linguistics Conference on Linguistic Accommodation and Style Shifting, September 1986

Hymes, D. (1972) 'Models of the interaction of language and social life.' In J.J. Gumperz and D. Hymes (eds) *Directions in sociolinguistics: the ethnography of communication.* New York: Holt, Rinehart & Winston

Jefferson, G. (1980) 'On "trouble-premonitory" response to inquiry'. *Sociological Inquiry*, 50, pp. 153-5

——— (1984a) 'On "stepwise transition" from talk about a "trouble" to inappropriately next-positioned matters'. In J. Atkinson and J. Heritage (eds) *Structures of social action.* Cambridge: Cambridge University Press, pp. 191-222

——— (1984b) 'On the organisation of laughter in talk about troubles'. In J. Atkinson and J. Heritage (eds) *Structures of social action.* Cambridge: Cambridge University Press, pp. 346-69

——— (1985) 'On the interactional unpackaging of a gloss'. *Language and Society*, 14, pp. 435-66

Jourard, S.M. (1964) *The transparent self.* New York: Van Nostrand

Kelley, H.H. (1967) 'Attribution theory in social psychology'. In D. Levine (ed.) *Nebraska symposium on motivation.* Lincoln, Nebraska: University of Nebraska Press

Labov, W. and Fanshel, D. (1977) *Therapeutic discourse.* London: Academic Press

Laver, J. (1974) 'Communicative function of phatic communion'. *Work in Progress 7.* Department of Linguistics, University of Edinburgh

Lee, J.R. and Jefferson, G. (1980) 'On the sequential organization of troubles-talk in ordinary conversation'. Unpublished report to the Economic and Social Research Council

Lehman, D.R., Ellard, J.H. and Wortman, C.B. (1986) 'Social support for the bereaved: recipients' and providers' perspectives on what is helpful'. *Journal of Consulting and Clinical Psychology*, 54, pp. 438-46

Ludwig, D., Franco, J.N. and Malloy, J.E. (1986) 'Effects of reciprocity and self-monitoring on self-disclosure with a new acquaintance'. *Journal of Personality and Social Psychology*, 50, 6, pp. 1077-82

Miller, LC., Berg, J.H. and Archer, R.L. (1983) 'Openers: individuals who elicit intimate self-disclosure'. *Journal of Personality and Social Psychology*, 44, pp. 1234-44

Pearce, W.B. and Sharp, S.M. (1973) 'Self-disclosing communication'. *Journal of Communication*, 23, pp. 409-25

Petronio, S., Martin, J. and Littlefield, R. (1984) 'Prerequisite conditions for self-disclosing: a gender issue'. *Communication Monographs*, 51, pp. 268-73

Rubin, A.M. (1986) 'Television, aging and information seeking'. *Language and Communication*, 34, pp. 67-77

Ryan, E.B., Giles, H., Bartolucci, G. and Henwood, K. (1986) 'Psycholinguistic and social psychological components of communication by and with the elderly'. *Language and Communication*, 6, pp. 1-24

Schegloff, E.G. and Sacks, H. (1973) 'Opening up closings'. *Semiotica*, 8(4), pp. 289-327

Searle, J. (1969) *Speech acts.* Cambridge: Cambridge University Press

Sinclair, J. McH. and Coulthard, M. (1975) *Towards an analysis of discourse.* Oxford: Oxford University Press

Solano, C.H., Batten, P.G. and Parish, E.A. (1982) 'Loneliness and patterns of self-disclosure'. *Journal of Personality and Social Psychology*, 43, pp. 524-31

Taylor, D.A., and Belgrave, F.Z. (1986) 'The aspects of perceived intimacy and valence on self-disclosure reciprocity'. *Personality and Social Psychology Bulletin*, 12, pp. 247-55

Wiemann, J., Coupland, N., Giles, H. *et al.* (forthcoming) 'Beliefs about talk: intergenerational perspectives'

Won-Doornik, M.J. (1985) 'Self-disclosure and reciprocity in conversation: a cross-national study'. *Social Psychology Quarterly*, 48(2), pp. 97-107

10

Discourse on Language and Ethnicity

Glyn Williams

Introduction

The conceptual meaning of discourse varies greatly within the social sciences, each meaning being located in different theoretical problematics. At times it is used to discuss the dynamics and analysis of speech situations (Gumperz 1982). On the other hand it is used to relate speech to subjectivity (Benveniste 1974). It is also used within a conflict epistemology to refer to the ideological nature of language (Pecheux 1975). Others would deny any epistemological referent and claim that there is no knowledge outside of discourse (Achard, Gruenais and Jaulin 1984). While it is not my intention to refer to theoretical issues in this chapter, such an appraisal having been undertaken elsewhere (Achard, MS), it is necessary briefly to consider the relationship between theory and method.

It is often claimed that there is no unity in the methodological aspect of discourse analysis. Such a claim would appear to disregard the relationship between theory and method that is so evident in much of social science. As such it is blind to the relationship between the philosophical assumptions associated with theory and the objective of any methodological enterprise. Within theories which are tied to epistemology there is a clear dichotomy involving consensus and conflict orientation. Thus it is often claimed that the discourse analysis of Zelig Harris (1952) represents a consensus orientation while that of Michel Pecheux (1975), for example, is unashamedly conflict orientated (Torode 1985, pp. 12-13). Their theoretical positions are reflected in their methodologies. For those who deny the relevance of epistemology there remains one crucial problem. There is a tendency to draw upon linguistics in order to analyse discourse. Yet if there is no knowledge outside of language, then the end result is that epistemology is drawn upon in order to analyse within a context which denies epistemology. These are some of the issues which students of discourse analysis will have to confront.

Deconstruction (Leitch 1983) involves the close reading of a text so that conceptual distinctions within it and on which the text relies may be shown to be employed in an inconsistent and paradoxical way, to the extent that the text fails by its own criteria. Yet it is more than the mere display of inconsistencies, it involves the reflexive application of the text to itself. Specific techniques of analysis which can be useful in this respect involve relating concepts to their textual relationships in different sections of the text and also relating concepts to their substituents. Once concepts have been isolated and placed in context it becomes possible to refer to a general problematic or philosophical context for the text as a whole. It should also be possible to relate any contradiction which derives from the inconsistent use of concepts to the epistemological contradiction associated with mixing concepts drawn from different problematics. In unravelling the problematic of a discourse we are also capable of determining what can and cannot be said from the place of that particular discourse.

Perhaps the initial starting-point of any such analysis involves what Foucault (1972) referred to as the right to speak. This involves ascertaining the status of a discourse in terms of the enonciateur. Thus a medical discourse expressed by a surgeon is legitimised to a far greater extent than the same discourse expressed by a practitioner of folk medicine. This legitimisation derives not merely from the individual but from the entire institutional assemblage associated with discourse and which constitutes the place, in terms of power, from which that discourse emanates. It is also important in this respect to ascertain the nature of the audience which the discourse is aimed at. It should be clear therefore that not all discourses within any discursive formation carry the same status. In most cases, the discourse which carries the most status is the official discourse. The status of a discourse does not derive merely from its institutional context but also from the nature of its relationship to earlier discursive forms. The predominance of the official discourse, however, does not mean that it has free reign; it must conform to ritual as discursive practice. It must also relate to other discourses within the discursive formation, since wherever there is power there must be resistance, and the context of any inter-discourse is established by the relationship between discourses rather than by the pure relationship of power. One discourse must bear relevance to its counterpart.

These kinds of issues were expressed in the early work of Michael Foucault who was most responsible for the position which claims that there is no knowledge outside of discourse, thereby dismissing any epistemological context for discourse. In his later work the emphasis shifted from a discussion of the production of discourse to the production of meaning, a line pursued by his followers who would claim that a meaning followed discourse. One consequence of this development is that the emphasis shifts from theoretical to methodological issues. Unfortunately much of the methodology involves the use of an epistemological science, linguistics. Thus a theory which denies epistemology draws upon a methodology grounded in epistemology in order to pursue its objective. The actual analytical methodologies vary considerably. What they all share is the emphasis that, unlike the logico-Formalist tendency of linguistics with its subjectivist notion of individual creativity as the necessary precondition of language, the assumption of individual creativity is inadequate with reference to semantics. Although variations in the phonological and syntactic elements of a language, whether or not they correspond to specific socio-historical conditions, can be easily integrated with a general theory of language, this is not the case with semantics. This is because the relationship between the signification of an utterance and the socio-historical condition of that utterance's production is constitutive of signification. Evidently this reference to semantics is the basis for the relationship between philosophy and linguistic science rather than being part of linguistics.

The data context

The text which is the subject of analysis in this chapter consists of a Report (1985) written by the chairman of a Tribunal established by the Race Relations Board to investigate accusations against Gwynedd (North Wales) County Council that two women were discriminated against in being refused employment on the grounds that they were unable to speak Welsh. The protagonists in the case were represented by legal counsel and the case was conducted as if it were a customary court of law. In the Tribunal, the case against Gwynedd County Council was proven. The Council in turn appealed to a higher court and the decision was reversed.

Tribunals exist to provide an apparently autonomous form of dispute-settlement by adjudicative devices in governmental or governmentally approved programmes. Their aim is 'to apply, impartially and even-handedly, rules which have been made by departments and approved by Parliament' (Birkenshaw 1985, p.27). There is strict control over the appointment of Tribunal chairpersons and members who are usually appointed by the Lord Chancellor or by the Minister presiding over the department which is involved. Chairpersons tend to be lawyers and the members tend to have had some experience in and a specialist knowledge of the field of activity the Tribunal is concerned with. In the case in question we must refer to the Commission for Racial Equality since proceedings in respect of discriminatory practice can only be brought by this body. Britain's first Race Relations Act was passed in 1965 and was followed by another Act three years later. The 1976 Race Relations Act replaced the other two. This Act established the Commission for Racial Equality and gave it powers to monitor, investigate and enforce the Act. The terms under which this is possible include wide powers to obtain any necessary information. Any named persons must be given an opportunity to make oral and written representations and a Report, with or without recommendations, may be issued.

In the remainder of this chapter I propose to focus upon methodological issues through the analysis of a single text. This invariably raises several problems, not least of which is that any text contains its own coherence as an entire document. If we are to respect this form of coherence, then we are strictly speaking obliged to analyse the entire text, a process which will produce an analysis which is far beyond the customary length of a chapter in a book such as this. The text which I propose to analyse — the Report of the Tribunal — naturally has such a coherence. Furthermore, it is clear that within this report there are three primary forms of discourse: (i) the legal discourse of the Race Relations Act; (ii) the pseudo-legal discourse of the Report as presented by the chairman of the Tribunal; and (iii) the written evidence submitted by one person who gave evidence to the Tribunal and which is presented verbatim in the Report. In order to come to terms with the text it is necessary to analyse all three discursive forms. Thus what I propose to do is to retain the 'story' that constitutes the text, but not to conduct an exhaustive analysis of each piece of text that is considered — rather to demonstrate what each form of analysis seeks to achieve. What I hope will become evident is that key concepts such as 'language', 'community', 'ethnicity', 'race' and 'Welsh' are not closed, objective entities. Rather, they are the subject of negotiation. As such it will be clear that they only assume meaning within discourse even though they may appear to feature in 'commonsense' knowledge. Thus such signifiers represent an indefinite set of notions with very different signification according to the discursive formation in which they exist. Furthermore, it is always a matter of struggle, over which no group can claim a privileged view, to situate them within the symbolic where they can gain a 'proper designation'.

Rationale of the debate

The rationale for the hearing is presented in a letter written by the Chairman of the Commission to Dafydd Elis Thomas, MP. Two paragraphs of this document are of particular interest in setting the scene for the Report. These will be treated separately.

> The Commission's position on community languages is clear. We strongly support their maintenance and recognise the nature of the relationship between language, culture and the whole complex of historical and other factors which affect a community's sense of identity.

Beyond establishing a position on 'community languages', the paragraph presents the Commission's definition of them. With reference to languages as a plurality, what is marked here is 'community'. There is, thereby, the possibility that there is a non-marked converse, i.e. non-community language(s). This would refer to a language or languages which align with the converse of community or at least with some entity which does not proffer the elements of community. We are told something of this essence of community in the second sentence: it is an entity which has a 'sense of identity', that is, it has a subjective, psychological quality. This identity, and consequently community (for the possibility of community without identity is precluded), is 'affected' by the relationship between 'language, culture and the whole complex of historical and other factors'. Even though 'other factors' is open-ended we do find that a sense of identity associated with community is linked to language, culture and history. Yet this is not a reference to any language or to language in the abstract since the reference to community at the end of the sentence relates to the prior use of language. Thus it is community language that is referred to, which begs further questions about a different form of language not related to community. The existence of such an element, unmarked here, would mean that it may well not relate to 'culture', history and other factors'. Another question is raised about community. Is it possible to treat 'community' and its 'sense of identity' as separate; i.e. can you have a community without a 'sense of identity'? It would seem that it is impossible to have a 'sense of identity' based upon language, history, etc. without community since these are qualities of community — community language, community history, etc. Thus the answer to the question is no. Some further light is thrown on the issue in the Welsh version of the latter which, presumably, was a translation. It states (trans.) 'the community's feeling of its particular features'. This sounds particularly cumbersome in English but it does suggest that the identity that is referred to is an identity in terms of the community's unique features.

The opposition community/non-community deserves further attention and to be located historically. From the end of the eighteenth century there has been a tendency to refer to community as an inherent part of the state. This is clearly quite different from the feudal or anarchist discourse where the community and the state are seen either as one and the same or as mutually antagonistic. Society was envisaged as consisting of a primordiality which generated a cohesion which was the basis of order. However, progress demanded that this condition be undermined and replaced by a social form devoid of order. This left a vacuum with reference to the production of order, a vacuum that was filled by the state. Progress was not only desirable but also inevitable; thus evolution paid the cost of the loss of community, tradition, etc. and they were replaced by the state as the ultimate source of all authority and order. It was this discourse which was the basis of individual liberalism and the associated discussion on the rights of man and ultimately on the relationship between law, the individual and the state. Thus the state and community were seen as inherently related since both became the source of order. Mutual antagonism between them was precluded. What is missing in the above statement is the converse of the primordial form which is presented in terms of community. Interestingly enough, the same is true of the discussion of ethnicity later on in the document to the extent that the two concepts, ethnicity and community, overlap discursively. It is of course there in the form of silence which can be reconstructed through difference.

Since the converse of 'community' is not marked in the above paragraph, we can do nothing more than infer that it represents the state. If so, and let us for the moment maintain that it is, it would mean that the language of the state is not in question. Also the difference, state/community, would mean that the qualities of the state are not those of the community, that is, the state is above 'history, culture and other factors' unless the state is seen to be the sum of all the communities within its territory. If this is the case, then it begs the question of whether a language can simultaneously be both a state language and a community language and if so how? Clearly the answer would be yes, since if we consider the British state its language is clearly English and since most of the population consists of monoglot English speakers the exclusion of English from being a community language would exclude most of the population from membership of community. Achard (1980) has indicted the nature of language within this discourse. The language of the state is held to be the language of reason and the unmarked non-state language is thus held to be somehow outside of reason — this involves the dichotomy rational/emotional and is evident in the difference in French between *langue* and *patois.* What I am suggesting, and it is no more than a suggestion, is that what we witness in the preceding statement is the opposition between the language of the state as the language of reason, and community languages as the languages of emotion which relate to the generation of the emotional condition of identity. Thus the opposition does not preclude referring to English as either the language of the state or as a community language, as an emotive language and as the language of reason. Welsh, on the other hand, would merely be a community language, somehow outside of reason. Furthermore, this opposition raises the issue of the status of language with reference to the state/community distinction. I shall return to this issue later.

The second paragraph of the letter I would like to refer to states:

> The Commission has a general concern about language requirements which I must mention to you. We have had a number of examples, all relating to the English language, where employers have asked for levels of written or oral English which have not been related to the needs of the job in question. These have been found to be discriminatory. So we are anxious that employers generally do not use language, unintentionally or otherwise, as a means of shutting out anyone who could in practice, manage the job to which the requirement has been related.

While the opening statement (7–8) refers to language requirements rather than language *per se*, the second sentence (8–12) explicitly refers to a specific language — English. There does not seem to be any contextual reason why there should be any reference to English. The specification of English here could be seen as denying any suggestion that the Tribunal was an attack on the Welsh language specifically, thereby shifting the emphasis to employment practices *vis-à-vis* language. It also sheds light upon the previous paragraph which refers to the Commission's position on 'community languages', in that there is an implication that if it has acted with reference to the English language then English can to that extent be seen as a community language.

Another point relates to the relationship between language and employment. The language requirements involve both written and oral modes of English, and since these features do not relate to the 'needs of the job' they must relate to 'shutting out'. However it is clear that some other criterion relating to the job has precedence as a measure of ability. Thus the issue is not that of whether or not someone should or should not be 'shut out', but of how this is to be done. It is not a question of an open labour market; some limitations, unrelated to language, do exert closure. Such a notion is, of course, part of the idea of professionalisation which claims that certain occupations require certain skills and that the possession of these skills marks the boundary of the profession. Closure is exerted on the labour market by membership of the profession. The acceptance of this principle is pitted against the concept of individuals competing in an open labour market. Thus while the Commission acts to ensure access, this is qualified by the recognition that there is competition for work.

My objective in discussing this letter in some detail is to place the report of the Tribunal in the context of the Commission's priorities and remit. It allows us to begin to recognise how a Commission of *Racial* Equality is interested in language. Its main concern involves establishing, and safeguarding, the principle of free access to employment unhindered by attributes which can be considered to be 'racial', providing that the candidate is capable of managing that job. Any process which violates this principle is regarded as being 'discriminatory'. Language can be one such process which discriminates. This is perfectly consistent with a capitalist economic system based upon an open labour market differentiated along lines of ability alone. As such it sustains an associated class system in terms of ability and qualification rather than relations to the means of production; that is, it is integrated into a liberal philosophy of employment which emphasises the technical division of labour. The contradiction between the principle of an open labour market where the individual job-seeker competes and the closure exerted by differentiation on the grounds of technical competence disappears. Yet language is not treated as a matter of technical competence. It is this tension which emerges in the following discussion of the report itself.

The Tribunal Report

Ethnicity

It is the legal discourse of the 1976 Race Relations Act which sets the frame within which any subsequent argument must lie. Before proceeding to the Chairman's interpretation of this act, it is useful to consider the legal discourse of the Act itself (18–35); and how this demands interpretation while also constraining the nature of that interpretation:

. . .on racial grounds he treats that other less favourably than he treats or would treat other persons; or
ii) he applies to that other a requirement or condition which he applies or would apply equally to persons not of the same racial group as that other but
a) which is such that the proportion of persons of the same racial group as that other who can comply with it is considerably smaller than the proportion of persons not of that racial group who can comply with it, and
b) which he cannot show to be justifiable irrespective of the colour, race, nationality, or ethnic or national origins of the person to whom it is applied, and
c) which is to the detriment of that other because he cannot comply with it.

Several things predominate in any legal discourse (Burton and Carlen 1979). The following are relevant to the section of the 1976 Act quoted in the Report and which becomes the basis of the Chairman's interpretation. Firstly there is the transactive which is employed because of the need to demonstrate the respective rights of protagonists. Secondly, there is the hope of employing forms which refute any sense of ambiguity. Thus, with reference to ambiguity the manner in which 'cannot' is employed above is instructive (30). 'Can' often tends to be problematic because it can refer either to the ability and the will to do something or to the ability and some external factors which relate to doing something. Such ambiguity can be precluded by context. What we witness is the tension between modal auxiliaries which reflects the tendency for modality to establish the degree of authority of an utterance on the one hand, and the systematic ambiguity with reference to the nature of authority. The same is true of tense, with modal auxiliaries being vague with reference to temporality — they tend to refer to the present but they can also be interpreted as a general law which applies now, in the past, and in the future. In order to resolve this tension, heavy use is made of transactives which distinguish absolutely between causer and affected.

Another feature of legal discourse is the tendency towards complexity which serves to legitimise law but is also the consequence of the search for clarity with reference to transactivity. The section of the Race Relations Act quoted in the report is full of transactives such as 'he treats that other' or 'he applies to that other'; the syntactic form gives a schematic representation of casual relationships. It is also full of qualifications which seek to delete any ambiguity — 'which is such that'. This results in a complexity which is reflected in the nature of the transactive relationships or the relationship between agent and affected. Therefore it is rare within such discourse to encounter deletion of either agent or affected. The preponderence of the passive form serves to create an impression of objectivity through impersonalisation when this is required — where such passives occur in association with agent deletion the agent is usually easily recoverable, e.g. 'which he cannot show to be justifiable'. Clearly ambiguity does not disappear and relationships brought out in the legal text are never clear. Interpretation is therefore inevitable, even if such interpretation insists upon its objective nature.

On a more substantive level there are some other interesting points. Firstly it is clear, as one would expect of a legal system which is premised upon the philosophical discourse of individual liberalism, that the law refers to the individual as a member of a racial group. Secondly, since the discussion is about individuals as members of groups, there will be no reference to the relationship between groups in terms of minority/majority or dominant. This contrasts with much of the social science discourse on race and ethnicity where such a relationship is discussed within the context of power. None the less, as we shall see, there is a reference in the report to numerism and an implicit reference to minority/majority groups in terms of numerism.

Beyond this, there is a preoccupation with the nature of the groups in question and the Act offers the following guidelines in this respect:

> . . .racial grounds means any of the following grounds, namely colour, race, nationality or ethnic or national origins. Racial group means a group of persons defined by reference to colour, race, nationality, or ethnic or national origins, and references to a person's racial group refer to any racial group into which he falls. The fact that a racial group comprises two or

> more distinct racial groups does not prevent it from constituting a particular racial group for the purpose of this Act.

Within this attempt at definition there are two issues to which the Tribunal had to give careful consideration: the nature of Welsh ethnicity and its relationship to language. It is these two issues which I would like to consider next. There are several points which emerge in the Act itself. In section b) (32) and again in the qualifying section there is a reference to 'origins': 'nationality or ethnic or national origins'. The role of 'or' differs. In the first case it is a conjunction which presents an alternative while in the second case it serves to link both 'ethnic' and 'national' to 'origin'. Thus 'origin' applies merely to the last two qualities. Secondly the categories are not meant to be mutually exclusive but, it would seem, they are meant to be all-inclusive. It would appear that, at least in so far as ethnicity and nationality are concerned, that a matter of ascription rather than prescription is involved here.

The counsel for the defence states:

> For a group to constitute an ethnic group in the sense of the 1976 Act, it must, in my opinion, regard itself, and be regarded by others, as a distinct community by virtue of certain characteristics.

He acknowledges the priority of the Act: 'in the sense of the 1976 Act', and its role in constraining the establishment of meaning with reference to the key concepts. Within this limitation he sees the main issue as that of interpretation which is a matter of subjective assessment. However, since it also involves what the group itself and 'others' feel, there is a double subjectivity involving 'what I think about what others think'. He proceeds to outline how he thinks the issue can be resolved:

> Some of these characteristics are essential; others are not essential but one or more of them will commonly be found and will help to distinguish the group from the surrounding community.

Several questions arise here. There is a distinction between 'group' and 'surrounding community'. It is not clear whether the two are seen as qualitatively different, in the sense that the 'surrounding community' is not ethnic or whether it is seen as 'other ethnics'. However what is clear is that the totality that is referred to pertains to 'community' — that is, the absence of community is not possible within the totality. Thus if we return to the state/community opposition, this would suggest that the state consists of a sum of communities which means that the state and the community cannot be in opposition.

The defence then proceeds to outline what it feels to be the essential characteristics of ethnicity:

> The conditions which appear to me to be essential are these: 1) a long shared history, of which the group is conscious as distinguishing it from other groups, and the memory of which it keeps alive; 2) a cultural tradition of its own, including family and social customs and manners, often but not necessarily associated with religious observance.

This refers to a collective consciousness involving an element of primordiality. While there is no indication about the process of reproduction of history and tradition it is obviously achieved to the exclusion of the 'surrounding community' since it is what distinguishes the 'group' from it. Thus this process must exclude the state's reproductive function which is universal. The second part refers to culture, a concept capable of numerous meanings. It is linked to tradition, to an exclusive tradition. In this case it would seem that culture refers to the transmission of behavioural norms different from those of the 'surrounding community'. These are the essential characteristics but there are others:

> In addition to these two essential characteristics the following characteristics are, in my opinion, relevant: 3) either a common geographical origin or descent from a small number of common ancestors; 4) a common language, not necessarily peculiar to the group, 5) a common literature common to the group, 6) a common religion different from that of

neighbouring groups or from the general community surrounding it, 7) being a minority or being oppressed by a dominant group within a larger community, for example a conquered people (say, the inhabitants of England shortly after the Norman conquest) and their conquerors might both be ethnic groups.

Let us treat each of these 'characteristics' in turn. Characteristic 3 refers to a 'common geographical origin' which seems to involve an autochthonous group, a group with territorial affinity, while the reference to 'descent' involves a kinship criterion. These two are presented as alternatives by the conjunctive 'or'. The fourth and fifth characteristics raise the questions of whether a language group can be treated as different from an ethnic group and if the non-literate members of an ethnic group are to be treated as a sub-group of the ethnic group. These are issues we shall return to when the focus of the debate turns to language. Although religion was not drawn upon in the ensuing debate, the section which refers to the sixth characteristic does refer to both 'neighbouring groups' and 'the general community surrounding it'. Again it raises the question of whether the group is different from the community and of whether the 'general community' is more than 'neighbouring groups' or whether these two entities are synonymous. The final characteristic again raises the issue of the relationship between minority, numerism and power. It is evident that here 'minority' refers to numerism since it is opposed to 'oppressed or a dominant group' — the power referent. The inclusion of the noun 'people' rather than 'group' is also interesting since it suggests that the English constitute a 'people' rather than a group or groups. On the other hand the final sentence makes it clear that the two terms are interchangeable or synonymous.

These characteristics were not drawn upon at random but were enacted by an eminent judge, Lord Fraser. It is interesting that it was the work of a legal person rather than a social scientist that was called upon to establish the nature of an ethnic group. Of course either side involved in the Tribunal could have used the services of expert witnesses with reference to this or any other issue if they so wished. Indeed, as we shall see, one member of the Tribunal was elected for his expertise with reference to matters of ethnicity. The defence chose not to resort to such an expertise and, in so doing, deferred to the legal definition, a definition which placed severe constraints on the discussion of the relationship between language and ethnicity.

Two further paragraphs refer to Lord Fraser's attempt to come to terms with the nature of ethnicity:

> ... a group is identifiable in terms of its ethnic
> origins if it is a segment of the population
> distinguished from others by a sufficient
> combination of shared customs, beliefs, traditions
> and characteristics derived from a common or
> presumed common past, even if not drawn from what
> in biological terms is a common racial stock.
> It is that combination which gives them
> an historically determined social identity in their
> own eyes and in the eyes of those outside the
> group, they have a distinct identity based not
> simply on a group cohesion and solidarity but also
> on their belief as to their historical antecedents.

It is evident that a distinction is drawn between ethnicity and race. Also it would seem that the racial group is part of something while also being different from the 'others' which, together with it, constitute that something. What marks this difference are the shared traits involving customs/beliefs/traditions/characteristics which have a historical referent. It seems that the entirety consists of the sum of ethnic groups and that at some time in the past these groups were separate, whereas they are now drawn together into some form of unity. The process whereby this historic change has taken place is not specified. The ethnic group is cohesive and solidaristic, something which, in relation to social identity, is separate from 'belief in historical antecedent'. Thus social identity can derive from a sense of cohesion and solidarity or from beliefs. Yet it would seem that both are in a sense 'beliefs' but that one is derived from the collective memory and the other from the present. Again we do not know what, in the present, generates this cohesion and solidarity. It is this social identity which seems to constitute ethnicity which at the same time is the shared customs, beliefs, traditions and characteristics. The whole argument seems to be tautological.

These were the conditions which the Tribunal, including the defence and the prosecution, accepted as the criterion by which ethnicity or ethnic group was to be determined. It would appear that an attempt has been made to produce a definition which implicates everyone in ethnicity. The consequence of this discursive use of ethnicity is that it contrasts with the original reference to the concept, in which the ethnic group need not be a subordinate part of a larger political society but may be the dominant element within a state or may cross state boundaries. It is, of course, not surprising that the legal discourse which is associated with the state adopts this meaning, since it speaks from the place of the state rather than that of the ethnic group (unless both are coterminous). Also the tendency to apply the concept ethnic group to numerous types of group obscures vital distinctions between various forms of identity. It would seem that in the preceding legal discourse there is an attempt to accommodate both forms of meaning which begs the question not only of contradiction but of priority in meaning.

When we turn to a more careful consideration of what the legal discourse refers to as 'shared customs, beliefs and traditions' which generate a psychological condition, it is evident that there is the danger of mistaking the tangible manifestations of the ethnic group for its psychological essence. It is of course possible that the group could lose all of the tangible manifestations while retaining its sense of self-identity or uniqueness. Thus the tangible characteristics are significant only to the degree to which they contribute to the notion or sense of the group's self-identity or uniqueness. It would seem from the translation of the letter that was referred to at the beginning that the Commission believes that such identity is not possible without the tangible characteristics since the identity is of these characteristics.

Alluding to the guidelines in the above legal discourse, the defence offers that there is such a thing as a Welsh ethnic group in that:

> . . . the Welsh people had a long and shared history of which the Welsh people was conscious as distinguishing it from other groups and the memory of which it kept live. He did not concede however, that, although it had a cultural tradition of its own, that culture involved language. He reminded us, as is a known fact, that the great majority of Welsh people do not speak the language and for that reason alone,

> if none other, the language could not be part of the cultural tradition of the Welsh people.

Again 'people' is made synonymous with 'group' and it is the group which keeps the history alive. The bone of contention becomes whether or not Welsh can be accepted as part of the 'cultural tradition' of the 'Welsh people'. We shall return to this issue in a moment.

Before proceeding any further I would like to consider the composition of the Tribunal; the reason for doing so will become evident in due course. The chairman of the Tribunal states:

> I indicated at the outset that the Tribunal comprised Mr. Evans, a Welsh speaking Welshman, and Mr. Hawkins, nominated for his race relations experience. I am a non-Welsh speaking Welshman.

The order is interesting. Priority of position is given to the 'Welsh speaking Welshman', the one who is most clearly the equivalent of the prosecuted. Presumably the etiquette of authorship insists on the third position (108). It is also interesting that Mr Hawkins is 'nominated', a condition not employed with reference to the other two. Thus we do not know whether or not the cumbersome concepts 'Welsh speaking Welshman' and 'non-Welsh speaking Welshman' were of relevance in nomination in the same sense as 'race relations experience'. These two concepts are not common usage in English where it is more customary to refer to 'Welsh speakers' and 'non-Welsh speakers'. But they are common in the Welsh language where the distinction between *Cymru* (Wales) and *Cymraeg* (the Welsh language) makes the concepts *Cymro Cymraeg* and *Cymro di-Gymraeg* (where 'di' equates to 'without') alliterative and thereby less cumbersome. The noun/verb/complement sequence suggests that the main concern here is with attribution and classification. The negative particle of the last sentence is 'taken into' the form of the word which then becomes a single word — non-Welsh. This tendency to make the negation a single unit results in the negation becoming a positive element, or at least that it loses its specifically negative force. The transformation in which 'a Welshman who does not speak Welsh' becomes 'a non-Welsh speaking Welshman', means that the verb becomes a participle, an activity becomes an object, the specific becomes general. It also means that it is no longer marked for tense which serves to avoid some of the classificatory acts which are obliged with verbs. The new nominals reappear throughout the remainder of the text which can mean that the perceptual and cognitive inventory of the language and therefore of the language user has been altered.

What is clear is that we have two different kinds of Welshman and that the existence of two different types of Welshman is taken for granted and unquestioned. On the other hand the odd-man-out is not counterposed with 'Welsh man', that is, he is not presented as an English or any other type of man, but rather, as an expert, which would suggest that the expertise of the other two lies in their different forms of Welshness rather than in their knowledge of race relations. The distinction between the two kinds of Welshman suggests that language rather than ethnic group is an important criterion in the 'nomination'. There is a suggestion that there is another distinction here — that between the subjective insider, 'the Welshman', and the objective outsider, 'the specialist'. This is partly clarified in section 8 of the text where it is claimed:

109 We had, to some extent, to rely upon our
110 knowledge and understanding and experience of
111 Wales and Welsh matters.

I have already referred to the fact that, within the legalistic terms of reference, ethnicity is a subjective matter. What is important here is that if the two Welshmen feel themselves to be Welsh, as is clearly the case from the above statement, then there must exist a Welsh ethnic group which consists of Welsh speakers and non-Welsh speakers — the matter is prejudged. Yet the discourse has a different effect. Since the affected is deleted in the above statement (109–11), interest shifts from the actors and the causers of the process to the process itself, thereby making it appear to be an objective act.

Given that the existence of a Welsh ethnic group has been accepted within the terms of reference of the Act, and that this group may consist of two sub-groups, one puzzling fact remains. With reference to the two women who brought the case, the Report states:

112 Both were born outside Wales but both have now

> lived in Wales for some time and Miss Doyle's
> education was at a school in Anglesey.

It also states:

> The allegations in this case are that there has
> been discrimination against a non-Welsh speaking
> sub-group by the Welsh speaking sub-group.

What has puzzled many observers is that someone who was not born in Wales can still be regarded as part of the Welsh ethnic group. This view clearly defines 'ethnic group' much more narrowly (Welsh ethnic = Welsh born) than the definition encompassed in the Act's usage. It would seem that those characteristics which refer to primordial and autochthonous membership are not involved, which means that the claim for membership is based upon self-identity *vis-à-vis* cultural tradition, etc. Yet since, as we have discussed above, the state school system is not part of the transmission of this awareness — since it would be universal rather than particularistic — it is difficult to see exactly how mere residence in Wales would allow for the change of ethnicity from one to another, unless of course one can simultaneously belong to more than one ethnic group, a position which raises other problems. This is further complicated by the initial claim on the part of the prosecution that:

> . . .we were involved with 3 racial groups —
> 1) English and all others not Welsh; 2)
> Welsh but not Welsh speaking and 3) Mother
> tongue Welsh.

Yet the first category was non-marked throughout the discussion, in which case its appearance in this statement is puzzling. Here 'English' is redundant but marked. It begs the question of the implications of a case in which discrimination might be on the part of the Welsh against the English. Within the terms of this particular case this is certainly feasible but politically much more explosive than that involving two sub-groups of a single ethnic group. Yet it would seem that this was the original intention:

> It seemed apparent from reading the ITIs of both applicants that they were basing their claim upon discrimination against them as Welsh people. Mr Nicholls [their counsel], on the 14 May, made it clear that he was relying on the fact, as one limb of his claim, that both applicants were not of the Welsh ethnic group.

It was only following the debate which preceded establishing the Welsh people as an ethnic group that this was amended.

The ability of an *individual* to change ethnic *group* as easily as is suggested would appear to make any reference to an ethnic group little more than meaningless. It also suggests that multiple ethnicity is possible. This of course is consistent with both individual liberalism and with the situation in Britain where the distinction between state and nation tends to be clouded. It means that anyone who lives in Wales who wishes to feel Welsh is designated as a member of the Welsh ethnic group. On the other hand if a person, or indeed the same person on a different day, chooses to feel something other than Welsh then he or she is no longer ethnically Welsh.

It should now be clear that the attempt to discuss the case within the context of an acceptable definition of ethnicity has been restricted by the nature of the legal precedent which has been established with reference to this concept. This legal discussion of ethnicity departs from much of what has been written in the social sciences about ethnicity. As such it accommodates a consensus approach to inter-group relationships which emphasises the individual rather than the group. The main thrust of this conception is subjective self-identity which underlies the need for members of the Tribunal to understand the nature of the Welsh self-identity. Yet the Tribunal seeks to present a legalistic image of a detached objectivity and it is this which is evident in the specific form of discourse, characteristic of legal discourse in general. However, the legal precedent is merely a guideline and in its attempt to accommodate every case while also making ethnicity relevant to every individual's identity it constitutes a level of generalisation vastly different from that of the case in hand. Consequently while this precedent sets the frame for the debate it also means that there is considerable room for the negotiation of meaning.

Language

I would now like to turn to the issue of language as it relates to ethnicity in the Tribunal. It is the relationship of language and ethnicity that is after all in question. Since ethnicity involved a sense of identity which, in part at least, was held to derive from cultural tradition, the role of language in that tradition was central to the debate:

> 129 He [counsel for the defence] did not concede,
> 130 however, that, although it [Wales] had a
> 131 cultural tradition of its own, that cultural
> 132 tradition involved language. He reminded us,
> 133 as is a known fact, that the great majority of
> 134 Welsh people do not speak the language and for
> 135 that reason alone, if none other, the language
> 136 could not be part of a cultural tradition of
> 137 the Welsh people.

There seems to be an agreement here that Wales has a unique culture, that is, a culture different from the wider entity, since it is 'its own'. However, one side claims that this unique quality does not involve language. The second sentence (132–7) appears to have an emotive connotation for the enonciateur. The verb 'reminded' and the phrase 'as is a known fact' convey a sense of irritation as if the listener was being talked down to. There is no referent to the phrase, it is not marked, which therefore implies that it can be taken for granted that everyone knows, or should know, this fact. Furthermore there is an emphasis here in that the adjective 'great' is redundant. Also the reference is to 'speak' the language rather than to an alternative such as 'know' or 'use'; it refers to oral function and the willingness to employ an ability. Indeed it can be said that we do not know how many people 'speak' Welsh since the census information pertains to the number who profess an ability in the language rather than its use.

The chairman of the Tribunal states:

> 138 We cannot accept that submission. Whilst we accept
> 139 that the vast majority of the Welsh people do not
> 140 speak the Welsh language, the Welsh language is as
> 141 much a part of the cultural tradition of Wales to

142 them as it is to the Welsh speaking person. To the
143 non-Welsh speaking Welsh person Welsh songs and
144 music are as much part of their tradition as it is
145 to the Welsh speaking person.

The authority of the Tribunal is very much in evidence here. The collective 'we' is used, and the authority 'accepts' while the defence 'submits'. What is interesting in the above statement is that, as we have seen, the cultural tradition is passed from one generation to another, which raises the question of how it is possible to transmit that which is not known. Clearly this can be resolved by claiming that it is the group rather than the individual which transmits, which means that there can be no Welsh group of this nature without Welsh speakers. Secondly there must be a difference between the 'do not speak' of the text and 'knowing' which would imply that the reference is to knowing about the language as opposed to speaking it. Thus the referent would be the 'memory kept alive' of the previous statements. The category 'non-Welsh speaking Welsh person' again attracts attention. It is not any person, nor indeed any 'Welsh person' that is referred to, but a Welsh person who does not speak Welsh. It raises by implication the issue of the 'Welsh speaking non-Welsh person' *vis-à-vis* language and identity. Yet if cultural transmission is a necessary feature of being Welsh, and if both Welsh speakers and non-Welsh speakers are Welsh, then language plays no part in its transmission unless it is transmitted through the common language — English. If this were the case then the Welsh language would have little bearing, if any, on Welsh ethnicity. What is implied is a reluctance to see cultural difference as being related to language. Indeed language is seen as equivalent in importance to music and songs. It draws one back to what was said about the language of reason and the language of emotion, with Welsh being presented within the emotional in the same sense as music. That it is a Welsh song is clear but we are not told what makes it Welsh. It could be that the language of the song is Welsh — since song refers to the linguistic feature of music — but since Welsh culture does not require the Welsh language this is not necessarily the case. This is also reflected in part of the evidence which referred to a statement by Lord Elton in the House of Lords:

146 ... I am sure that the Noble Lords opposite

would not for a moment therefore wish to appoint people who are efficient or competent simply because they are fluent in the musical tongue of their fathers.

While there seems to be a play on 'The Land of My Fathers' (the national anthem) here the important point is that language is seen as a 'musical tongue'; the emphasis again is on speech and not language, and it is a musical speech, that is, it has an emotional and not a rational connotation.

However, referring back to the prior statement, it would seem that language is not seen to be a medium for the transmission of culture, it *is* culture. It is seen as culture in the sense referred to in the Act — as part of the customs and manner or tradition of a people. It becomes clear that, once it has been established that a Welsh people exist, if some of the cultural traits pertain only to some members of that group, it becomes the basis for subdividing that group. All of these traits are treated as if they carried equivalent importance.

The discourse of the chairman is interesting in a stylistic sense. It reiterates what has been said above about the nature of the legal discourse. The agentless passive form is typical of academic or scientific discourse. It creates an impression of objectivity through impersonality and the distancing of the enonciateur. The temporal structure of the passive is also interesting and relevant. 'Is a known fact' (133) has two temporal moments and modalities: there is the 's' marker which indicates the certainty about validity which the enonciateur has at the moment of speaking; on the other hand 'known' carries the 'en' marker which indicates anterior time. That is, there is a process concerning the fact that precedes the present subjective certainty, and the past object of certainty, with the latter being absorbed into the former. The past is incorporated into the confident nature of the subjective present. As a consequence we are not expected to question what is known any further, nor either to qualify it. There is a broader enunciative position with reference to the reader who must not locate him/herself outside of the non-Welsh speaker domain if s/he is to entertain the text's assumptions.

Whenever a concept is employed with two different meanings it is probable that these uses derive from different theoretical positions or problematics. Since each theoretical position is premised upon different philosophies of knowledge it highlights the basis of the conflict between the protagonists. It is this that becomes evident in the following discussion of the evidence offered by the defence where, in contrast to the conception presented by the chairman of the Tribunal, language is seen as the basis of communication:

151 Miss Hughes told us that she regarded Welsh
152 speaking as a very necessary qualification for
153 all of the jobs. She said that even a domestic/
154 kitchen assistant needed to be able to speak
155 Welsh to maintain the accepted atmosphere within
156 a residential home when the majority of the
157 residents' first language was Welsh.

There are patronising statements here, but more important for the question in hand is the claim that there exists an 'atmosphere' which relies upon Welsh for its 'maintenance', which implies that this atmosphere derives, in part at least, from the language. Also:

158 We were told that the elderly in residential homes
159 and the clients in the social work scene might, in
160 moments of trauma or stress, need to speak in their
161 native tongue ... the majority of people had Welsh as
162 their first or native language.

The issue tends to be played down in that there is reference to the fact that there 'might' be a 'momentary' need for the language, suggesting that in all other contexts some other language would suffice. This is quite a different emphasis on the extent of language use from that in the preceding statement (146–50). I will return to the issue of 'first or native language'.

There are more relevant points in these two statements. In the former statement the emphasis is on personalisation. The enonciateur is referred to as 'Miss Hughes' (51) and as 'she' — twice (151, 153). The first statement could have been expressed as 'Miss Hughes said that Welsh is a very necesary qualification ...' But 'told' and 'regarded' introduce an ambiguity; the personalisation serves to create a subjective mode. In the second part of the first of the two statements (153–7) the sting is taken out of the affected (residents) by the insertion of two agents between the enonciateur and the affected and by the qualifying 'majority' and 'even'. Consequently considerable doubt is associated with the entire testimony of this witness as reported by the chairman.

In the second of the two statements (153–7) agent and subject are deleted. This means that the cause associated with the claim is also deleted while the process is portrayed as a finished rather than an ongoing process. Attribution rather than cause is emphasised. The deletion of agency makes 'we' appear to be the agent. It is unclear whether this 'we' refers to the corporate 'we' of the Commission or the Tribunal, or whether it is the collective 'we' of those involved in the hearing. If it refers to the corporate 'we' there is the danger that it can alienate, since if the reader is excluded from the discourse she/he may well transform the 'we' into 'they'. It is also suspect in that the relevant individuals cannot be identified. It appears that there is an attempt here to separate the evidence from the individual presenting it and thereby making this a general rather than an idiosyncratic statement. This form of abstraction means that any refuting of the claim made in the statement bears no relationship to the author of that statement.

This theme of language as the basis of communication is further emphasised in the evidence of one of the witnesses for the defence. It is here also that we encounter a different discursive form:

163 The use of the Welsh language in Gwynedd is not
164 artificial. Those who speak the language do not
165 do so as a gesture of respect to the past nor is
166 it a conscious political gesture. It amounts,
167 rather, to the natural exercise of a mother tongue
168 in a community which still contains a sufficient
169 number of Welsh speakers to make its use public
170 and social and not merely private and individual.
171 Thus it is, for the majority of its speakers, the
172 language in which they conduct their daily lives
173 and through which they most naturally express
174 themselves.

This evidence was presented by an 'expert' although the chairman appears to treat this role with some scepticism. We are told both what Welsh is and what it is not. In stating that it is not artificial (164), there is a negation of any link to the past and to the political, both referents of 'artificial'. Neither is it private and individual. Rather it is the converse of these in being 'real'. Thus we encounter the opposites political/natural, private/public and individual/social. Within the statement there appears to be an attempt to play down the political nature of language as well as an attempt to separate it from 'tradition'. There is here, as indeed in most of the statements about Welsh, a comparison with English as a non-marked entity. It is an attempt to place Welsh on a footing comparable with English rather than as its converse in functional terms. Welsh has more than an atavistic, primordial role. In referring to the relationship speaker/language, the evidence is presented as a generalisation on behalf of all speakers — it must therefore be the evidence of what is regarded as 'an expert'. Yet some of the terms of reference are confusing: in what sense can a language be artificial, to what does the 'natural exercise' of a language refer, how can a language be 'private and individual'? Despite this confusion it is clear that what is being conveyed is the view of Welsh as the basis for communication within a preferred context. That is, there is again a silent reference to another language which is not marked. What has to be assumed is that the speakers of Welsh are bi- or multi-lingual, but it is implied that the relationship between the languages is not that of equality: Welsh is 'natural' while the other language(s) must therefore be somehow non-natural. We have already confronted this in the earlier statement which refers to Welsh as a first language, asserting some form of priority in language relationship.

The tendency for the 'expert' witness to play down the political nature of the language group relationship relative to Welsh and English is repeated albeit with the emphasis reversed:

> Nevertheless, the figures of decline show that natural usage is declining. One need not read any conspiracy or deliberate ill-will into the nature of the threat.

What is implied is that some, unstated, non-political, non-malicious, non-voluntaristic process is responsible for the 'decline'. This is shown by 'figures'; that is, it is related to an empirical, and thereby objective, discourse which again reinforces the distancing from political causality and reference. This 's' form within an agentless passive expresses a certainty about its validity as a statement. However, although this would suggest that the process is somehow natural, the use of the noun 'threat' (178) and the verb 'decline' (176) implies that it is not a desirable process. Yet the end-result of this process is the creation of even more 'non-Welsh speaking Welsh persons'. This is, of course, obscured by the tendency to reify language and thereby to ignore the fact that it is not a language that declines but the number of people who express an ability to be able to speak it. If this is a non-political process then it becomes difficult to call upon power as something which is unequally distributed *vis-à-vis* language groups, and therefore to address language 'erosion' in power terms. The alternative is to resort to a consensus argument involving an appeal to democracy and numerism while viewing language change as a natural, if undesirable, process.

179 The brute facts of the situation are threatening
180 since the majority language in Gwynedd is the
181 minority language in Wales, let alone the rest
182 of the United Kingdom. The boundaries of the
183 County are not closed and the wider influences
184 which pervade are not Welsh.

Thus the adjectives 'minority' and 'majority' refer to numerism and not to power. An appeal is made to the will of the majority and the principle of numerical democracy. In order for this appeal to succeed, the marked entity must constitute the boundary which includes the relevant majority — this marked entity is the County of Gwynedd. It is counterposed with the other marked entity of the same category — 'the United Kingdom'. This is the only occasion in the entire document when anything outside of Wales is marked, making the issue appear to be one involving only Welsh people. The reference to Welsh as the majority language in Gwynedd clearly disregards the claim that all Welsh speakers also speak English in that accepting this claim would make Welsh speakers a minority. Thus what is polarised here is the same two entities as those referred to above — Welsh speakers and non-Welsh speakers.

The preceding statement also begins to identify the process of language erosion. The author speaks from a particular place in that the change in the fortunes of Welsh is 'threatening' and is evident not from mere facts but from 'brute facts'. The author speaks from the place of the concerned Welsh speaker who is obliged to confront the objectivity of 'facts'. We are told that it is 'wider influences' which are somehow responsible. These influences constitute more than language and therefore they are 'wider' and not 'Welsh'. Again the converse is unmarked and we are not told what the non-Welsh refers to. If it refers to any entity which is not Welsh in terms of language then it would include the category 'non-Welsh speaking Welsh people' which the Tribunal has maintained is Welsh. We are also told that these influences operate because of the openness of the County's boundaries. The linking of the openness to the County seem to suggest that it is the willingness of the County to retain an open boundary that somehow allows, and even invites, this condition to exist. Clearly since the County is in no position to close its boundaries this amounts to an admission of powerlessness, or an imputed will to be influenced. None the less it also conveys an impression of benevolence which acts against the interest of the benevolent. It is a consequence of rejecting any discussion of language group relations in terms of power. This is elaborated:

> Thus there is a paradox, the majority language within Gwynedd is, within any wider British context, a minority language, and the minority language within Gwynedd is, within any wider British context, the majority language. Thus the language of the local majority, as the linguistic statistics in the County show, is subject to the process of erosion.

The repetition of phrases and concepts suggests that this section of the evidence has been carefully thought out and that the oppositions are purposeful. The main oppositions, not all of which are marked, are: wider/local, Gwynedd/Britain, majority/minority, erosion/persistence. Since the wider context is British, the opposition here does not refer to different features of Wales such as Gwynedd/Wales, nor to Wales/Britain but to Gwynedd in its relationship to Britain. Of the three alternatives suggested here it is the least contentious politically since it involves a county within the British administration system rather than any contestation on the basis of 'nation' or of the relationship between parts of Wales which is, in any case, a highly contentious concept. Yet Gwynedd and Britain are also substitutions for local and wider. However, in the second sentence the marked entity, the County, is closed, which means that the reference to 'local' here is not opposed to 'wider' but to a non-marked, perhaps a non-local minority? The erosion occurs because the language of the wider British context is not the language of Gwynedd — which would seem to imply that if the language of Gwynedd is not English then it must be Welsh. Of course, this is qualified by reference to numerism, but if we assume that the reference to numerism is a form of justification associated with numerical democracy, then this holds. However, this statement exists within a context — it is there in order to justify the language policy of the County. The implications are that such a language policy is not rooted in a sense of natural justice based on the equality of language, or cultural or linguistic relativism, but will only be of relevance where the majority of the population speak the language in question. Thus this statement achieves two things simultaneously: it explains the process of language erosion and it justifies the existence of a language policy. If there is a link between these two then policy exists in response to the process of language erosion, and since the cause of this erosion is 'the wider influences that pervade', then this policy must be against some external, wider influence. Yet the entire discourse, as we have seen, is couched in consensus, conciliatory terms.

However, there is more than a desire to safeguard the numerical status of Welsh in the policy:

> Local Authorities exist to represent local interests and to provide services to the community. In its role as the provider of services Local Government must be responsive to the needs and character of its community.

The first sentence purports to be factual. It is not expected that it be contested. Yet there is no reason why it should not be. For example, Local Authorities can be seen as existing to serve the interests of central goverment which may be in opposition to local interest. That is, the concept of Local Government again assumes a very specific problematic context. Yet what is clear is that it constitutes a premise upon which the second sentence is constructed and in this sense disagreement would have wide repercussions. While the interests are local they are plural, but since previous statements have established that local is a substitute for Welsh then it raises the question of whether these interests can be anything other than Welsh interests. While the interests are plural the community is singular. While community is a noun, i.e. an entity, it is ambiguous as to its reference to singularity/plurality: there is only one within each Local Authority. If it is singular then the difference, or even conflict of interests is subverted by the drawing together into community, or Welsh community. The adjective 'responsive' suggests that the initiative comes from the object which in this case is the community. However, it is the needs and the character of the community that it must be responsive to and this leaves open the question of initiative. Yet the interests of the subject — Local Government — are subservient to those of the community. This creates the impression that, with reference to service provision, which includes language, the Local Government is passive. It also means that if 'needs' and 'character' are variables then each Local Government is unique and not subject to blanket situations. Part of the uniqueness lies in the concept of community which is linked to the Local Authority by the pronoun 'its'.

The link between language and Local Authority services is now made more explicit:

> Since a great many of the services provided, such as education and social welfare, depend upon communication between the provider of a service and its recipient it would be unreasonable and unacceptable to impose a particular language as the medium of that communication, the more so if the language chosen were not the first language of the majority of the population. The convenience of the providers of a service, and the interests which they may have, cannot be the determining factor in services which are meant to serve a community. Not only would such a policy be unacceptable in principle it would also be unsatisfactory in practice.

The first section of the statement is a clear indication of the need for bilingualism in services since if services depend upon communication, and if one language or another is not imposed, then it would seem that whoever is providing the service must be able to accommodate both languages. Communication in this sense, since it involves the provider and the recipient, involves interaction. In the second sentence the service is to the community and to the individual, yet the emphasis seems to be on individual interests in terms of client interests seen as individual interests. If all clients speak English, the only way in which this position can be justified is by not making the two languages equal, hence the reference to first language and, by implication, second language. No reference is made either to language or to language groups but it is clear from the reference to 'first language' and 'majority of the population' that this marked population involves bilinguals. The discourse speaks from that position although it would appear to speak from the place or interests (not the same thing) of any client. The adjectives 'unacceptable' and 'unsatisfactory' do not have any referents. It must be 'unacceptable' to someone, but the fact that it is qualified by 'in principle' suggests that it is an abstract unacceptability that is meant — one that implies an abstract, pragmatically ethical, position. In direct contrast, 'unsatisfactory' refers to practice, which means that there must be an object: since it is the interests of the client that are paramount, s/he would seem to be the relevant object, although it may also include the provider. Further light is thrown on this issue:

> I am impressed by the number of professional people in the caring professions who seek to learn Welsh because they are hampered in their professional practice by their inability to communicate in the first language of their clients.

That he is 'impressed' not only implies a form of praise but also that the act is out of the ordinary. The reference is very specific, the subject is a professional who practices within a caring context. It implies that professionals take their work seriously because they are concerned. That they 'seek to learn' means that it is a voluntary act but could also imply that they seek but don't succeed! The fact that such professionals are 'hampered' underlines the point that it is the client who should have priority; i.e. professionals are in a condition of subservience to the interests of the client because they do not possess an attribute which the client does. The verb 'hampered' suggests being obstructed, which would imply that it is the subject which is hampered and not the client. That is, they are the active party who seek to resolve problems rather than the client drawing upon the professional to resolve the problem. The nouns ‘people’, ‘caring’ and ‘practice’ are all qualified by ‘professional’; the effect is to elevate these agents to a position of respect and seriousness different from the ordinary person who practices care.

What is remarkable about the discourse of this particular enonciateur is the number of passives and deletions of the affected that are included. One of the consequences of passives is that power relationships are mystified, and it is a particularly effective way of diffusing a potentially explosive situation. Both the agent and the affected are frequently deleted (e.g. 163–4) which places the emphasis entirely on process. Furthermore, the actor is no longer attached directly to the verb but is now linked by ‘which’. As a consequence the link between actor and process is weakened; that is, the causal condition is syntactically weaker. The actor is diffuse and the cause of ‘influences’ becomes vague. This tendency is heightened by the introduction of the verb ‘to be’ which leads to the aspect being continuous. There is also a suggestion in the change from the transactive to the attributive that the main concern of this statement is attribution rather than causality.

Having considered the evidence of the defence on language in detail, and especially that of the ‘expert’, who was a key witness, I would now like to consider the position of the chairman of the Tribunal, and the prosecution. There is here an air of ambiguity with reference to the relationship between Welsh and English. The chairman states:

> It is appropriate to say that when I refer to ‘Welsh speaking’ that means bilingual because all who speak Welsh also speak English.

Here he is creating a situation of equality relative to ‘speaking’ the respective languages. On the other hand, in referring to the two women who brought the case he appears to accept a condition of different ability with reference to language:

> Neither can speak Welsh, although, like a lot of Welsh people, they understand a certain amount of Welsh and can speak a few phrases of the language.

There is a clear contradiction between the first reference to the ability to 'speak Welsh' and the second: 'can speak a few phrases of the language'. A distinction is also drawn between 'understanding' a language and 'speaking' a language. Understanding and speaking 'a few phrases' is allocated a different weighting from 'speaking the language'. It would seem that even though they have different conceptions of language with reference to this issue the two sides are saying the same thing, albeit with reference to different actors and different languages.

The negation in the first phrase is interesting. As stated previously 'can' is inevitably ambiguous, referring either to an ability and a will, or to an ability and an external factor. We get the impression that 'can' (222) relates to the former, but when we learn that there is some semblance of ability, this is brought into question. However, since agency is deleted, it is impossible to claim that the latter is the case. The modal auxiliary also makes temporality vague, the entire situation becomes ambiguous. This is important because of the apparent claim that both 'do' and 'do not' proffer an ability in Welsh. Furthermore, the preponderance of plural forms in the statement makes things appear complex and diffused with the result that there is no focus in the statement. The entire process is mystified. The conjunction 'although' serves to transform the negative of the first part of the statement into a positive of some sort, with the result that the focus of the statement shifts to the positive — inability becomes a positive attribute. The starting-point of the process in the initial phrase is the ability to speak Welsh. 'Can' weakens its force, throwing it into the future as something possible or permissible. The most obvious substitute for 'can' is 'do not' but, although this form has been used previously (139), 'can' is the less definitively negative of the two. Even the appearance of 'neither' clearly indicates that it is negative. The absence of a specific agent in this first phrase means that this cannot be positive action. Furthermore, the noun–verb–noun structure is not transactive, thereby seeming to simplify the process.

The evidence of the 'expert' made reference to Welsh as a 'mother tongue' (167). The chairman, in his comment on the prosecution's initial claim that one of the racial groups is 'mother tongue Welsh' (cf. 120–1) states:

226 We agreed with the first two categories but not
227 with the last. No reference was made in the

228 evidence to 'mother tongue' Welsh. We feel that
229 the third category ought to be Welsh speaking
230 Welsh people.

'Mother tongue' is customarily held to refer to the language of a nation. This would introduce the concept of nation as distinct from ethnic group, although the former is accommodated within the latter in the Act. It would mean that if Wales was accepted as a nation, reference to Welsh as a mother tongue would establish Welsh as the language of the nation or as the national language. This would have profound implications not only for any discussion of the relationship between Welsh and English within Wales but also for the argument presented by the Tribunal. It would mean that the position of the two women who brought the case relative to the mother tongue and the nation and their claim to be part of a Welsh ethnic group would be, to say the least, ambiguous.

The tendency to polarise the two language groups is evident in the statement by the counsel for the prosecution:

231 ... whatever else Mr. Nicholas Edwards was saying,
232 he ultimately was saying that there was a place
233 for both English and the Welsh speaking people in
234 Wales.

Since all Welsh speakers are held to be also English speakers, the appropriate distinction would appear to be 'Welsh speakers' and 'non-Welsh speakers'. Yet the use of the preposition 'the' before 'Welsh speaking people' gives the impression that the two groups in the statement are mutually exclusive while also making the second category appear to stand out as problematic in some way or another. It is also interesting that the reference is to 'in Wales' rather than 'of Wales'. That is, the territory of Wales is marked which suggests that any right that pertains to Welsh speaking applies only to the territory of Wales. On the other hand, the two groups which are referred to are not marked by the same principle; indeed, they could be drawn from anywhere.

This textual reference differs markedly from that discussed above with reference to language in that the element or process is missing, as also is the relationship between language and society. There is a tendency to ignore the issue of the respective relationship between the two languages with reference to individual speakers. This derives partly from the tendency to ignore reference to English which remains unmarked throughout most of the relevant textual reference. Where there is a reference to both languages, the emphasis is on a relationship of apparent equality, this being essential if the claim is that monoglot English speakers are being 'shut out', and means that Welsh speakers cannot be 'shut out' since they are bilingual.

Conclusion

It should be clear from the preceding discussion that the debate encompassed within the Tribunal hearing was framed by the contents of the 1976 Race Relations Act. It was this discourse which set the limits upon what could and could not be said in the debate. However, since this Act sought to implicate the entire citizenry in language, ethnicity and community, its terms of reference are extremely broad, encompassing numerous different cases. Part of the exercise undertaken by the Tribunal involved establishing which case was most relevant to the issue in hand. As a consequence,the debate hinged upon the determination of a specific case, and the concepts of language, ethnicity and community were crucial for such a determination. Consequently the nature of these concepts was open to negotiation. Yet this process of negotiation was not conducted in an arbitrary manner but was subject to the procedural and discursive canons of legal practice. It is this, as much as anything, that is responsible for the discursive styles which have been analysed above. These styles relate to the place from which the enonciateur speaks.

This was most evident with reference to the discursive style of the various participants. The author of the report as chairman of the Tribunal exercises his right to pass comment on the various statements in making his own views akin to factual 'truth'. This derives from the authority vested in the judicial place. It refers to what Foucault discusses in the following quotation:

> Who among the totality of speaking individuals is accorded the right to use this sort of language? Who is qualified to do so? Who derives from it his own special quality, his prestige, and from who in return does he receive if not the assurance, at least the presumption, that what he says is true? (1972, p. 50).

The chairman is justice and since justice derives from truth then the chairman must assure himself that, despite the space accorded negotiation, he had encountered the truth. Something similar is associated with the discourse of the 'expert'. While not being able to allocate to himself the same authority of place within the judicial as the representative of the judiciary, he has the role of 'expert' bestowed on him. In so doing, he appears as the presenter of a special form of 'truth', rather than as a mere witness who presents facts which are to be queried. Furthermore this 'expert' truth is allocated additional status through being presented in written form. As an 'expert', the witness must distance himself from polemic in order to substantiate his expertise through objectivity. This objectivity is cushioned by an air of concern which conditions any hint of subjectivity that is inevitable from his representing one of the protagonists in the hearing.

While recognising that the style of discourse has a bearing on how meaning is established in discourse, it is useful to consider the content of discourse separately. Evidently, the concepts 'language', 'ethnicity' and 'community' are the central components of the discourses in question as they relate to the issues of Welshness and racial discrimination. It is also clear that these concepts assume different meanings within the respective discourses.

At times the meanings of these three concepts are explicit whereas at other times they can only be revealed through the principle of difference which clarifies the meaning by semantically establishing the converse. By pursuing the meanings assigned to the concepts we uncover two crude models of Welsh language and ethnicity. On the one hand we have the conception of language as a traditional cultural trait which serves as the basis of an emotive identity uniting people into an ethnic community. On the other hand we have the conception of language as the basis of reason and, as such, it is of relevance for communication between rational social actors within a modern, open society, premised upon economic rationality. This is not to imply that these discourses are clear-cut, for they are constructed out of different, often unrelated, statements. Indeed, there are numerous instances of an enonciateur drawing upon fragments of both. Indeed, given that the discourses are conditioned by the assumptions implicit in the Race Relations Act any attempt to develop an argument which shifts away from these implicit assumptions, while simultaneously being conditioned by them, will inevitably lead to the contradiction which derives from employing concepts drawn from different problematics. Thus in accepting the legal framework as the basis of a working definition of ethnicity, the defence was drawn into a problematic premised upon a limited space for ethnic/language groups within society. It accepted an understanding of ethnicity which emphasised the individual rather than the group. Yet its position on language expressed the converse in claiming that language had a function beyond that of being an expression of identity, in stating that language was the basis of communication and was, therefore, a collective feature.

This polarisation should be familiar to social scientists and social philosophers. It involves the discussion of a social totality — the state — in terms of its constituent parts — communities. The community is the source of identity and as such carries an emotive connotation which contrasts with the rational nature of the state which serves the interests of individual community members. This community identity is serviced by a link with the past through tradition, in contrast with the state which is 'of now' — it is modernisation. The primordiality of the community contributes to the sense of social order with the state existing to preserve that order where the community fails or where, for some reason, it does not exist. The state is the ultimate source of social order. As such it claims to dispense a uniform justice for all individual members of the state. It also ensures a common understanding through communication in a common language, and the absence of that language among the citizenry is seen to be the converse of the democratic principle which involves equal access to the state and its institutions through access to the language of reason. Thus an inability in this language of reason is equivalent to remaining outside of reason and consequently outside of modernity. Language is the source of collective integration. It is a discourse which derives from the historical conjuncture at the end of the eighteenth century when the new states based upon the principle of democracy were being formed. It is the discourse of that and subsequent epochs which much of what we now know as 'social science' derives from. In more recent times, it is most evident in the theories of ethnicity which derive from the USA and more specifically the melting pot and assimilation/acculturation theories premised upon the immigration experience of the USA.

This discourse lays claim to the existence of a single nation or state within which the individual is allowed to preserve his/her ethnic features as traditions, that is within domestic and community life. On the other hand this concession should not discriminate against any other individual. The principle of non-discrimination takes higher priority than ethnic rights. This view makes the Welsh a single cultural group among many within a national society defined by the common language, English. This model of cultural pluralism insists that apart from the cultural features, including, and perhaps primarily, language, the Welsh are no different from the English since all cultural communities are equal. In claiming that the Welsh language is a cultural trait and no more, it would seem that the chairman and his co-panelists remain closest to this discourse. The defence, on the other hand, while subscribing to the view of ethnicity expressed herein, seeks to deviate from the conception of language by claiming that Welsh should have a role similar to that of the language of the state. In so doing it is confronted with a contradiction which it does not appear to comprehend.

In totality, it seems that the report which has been considered is situated at the place of the anglophone speaker (a non-marked position) relating to the rights of the Welsh speaker (marked position) within Gwynedd (marked position) and with other parts of Britain and the English language being treated as unproblematic. That is, although the Tribunal purported to be about the rights of non-Welsh speakers it said more about the rights, or lack of rights, of Welsh speakers as Welsh speakers. Clearly there is a tension here and it is impossible to discuss one without, at the same time, discussing the other. That is, social positions are defined as a discourse relationship. This is not the product of the individual protagonists as authors of their own discourse but rather it is the product of a long history which constitutes a specific way of relating a series of social places. It involves the history of the official discourse on the relationship between Welsh and English.

References

Achard, P. (1980) 'History and the politics of language in France: a review essay'. *History Workshop*, 10, pp. 175-83

—— (MS) 'Sociolinguistique et analyse de discours: peut-on parler d'une école française?'

Achard, P., Gruenais, M. P. and Jaulin, D. (1984) *Histoire et Linguistique.* Paris: Maison des Sciences de l'Homme

Benveniste, J. (1974) *Problèmes de linguistique générale.* Paris: Gallimard
Birkinshaw, P. (1985) *Grievances, remedies and the state.* London: Sweet & Maxwell
Burton, F. and Carlen, P. (1979) *Official discourse.* London: Routledge & Kegan Paul
Foucault, M. (1972) *The archaeology of knowledge and the discourse on language.* New York: Pantheon
Gumperz, J.J. (1982) *Discourse strategies.* Cambridge: Cambridge University Press
Harris, Z. (1952) 'Discourse analysis'. *Language,* 28, 1, pp. 1-30
Leitch, V.B. (1983) *Deconstructive criticism.* London: Hutchinson
Pecheux, M. (1975) *La Vérité de Palice.* Paris: Maspero
Report of the Industrial Tribunals of Jones and Doyle vs. Gwynedd County Council held at Colwyn Bay, May–July 1985
Torode, B. (1985) 'Discourse analysis between Harris and Pecheux'. In T. Hak, J. Haafkens and G. Nijkof (eds) *Working paper on discourse and conversational analysis.* Rotterdam: Konteksten, pp. 7-19
Williams, G. (1987) *The sociology of Welsh.* The Hague: Mouton

11

The Rhetoric of Deterrence[1]

Christopher Norris and Ian Whitehouse

There is, we shall claim, a very precise sense in which those who argue the case for nuclear deterrence don't know what they are talking about. That is to say, there is no *concept* of 'deterrence' — no rational ground or coherent justification — which could possibly support their arguments. (For further discussion of these issues, see Norris 1986a, 1986b, 1987; Chilton 1985; Blake and Pole 1983, 1984). What we find in its place is a language of entirely suasive, rhetorical or — in speech-act terms — performative character which achieves its purpose by evading the requirements of rational discourse. That this language has so largely prevailed upon public opinion and become the major currency of 'informed' nuclear debate is in no sense a measure of its hard-headed realism or its grasp of current politico-strategic aims. Those aims are themselves incoherent to the extent that they are based on confusions intrinsic to the so-called 'logic' of deterrence.

Now it may be that the orders of fiction and reality have become so mixed up in this unnerving situation that it is virtually impossible to separate the one from the other. There might come a stage of extreme (perhaps terminal) unreason where the rhetoric of deterrence had so far distorted our perceptions and determined what should *count* as 'realist' thinking that there simply wouldn't exist any working basis for enlightened critique. No doubt this stage has already been reached by those relatively few (politicians, military strategists, star-wars researchers and the like) whose executive power and resources are dependent on maintaining such a widespread falsified consensus. They inhabit a world of proliferating paranoid discourse where the mere possibility of reasoned dissent — of grasping the motives that sustain such a rhetoric — is increasingly rendered unthinkable.

It is the function of much that passes for public debate of these issues (especially in the popular media) to pre-empt the very terms of such debate by identifying 'realism' with a continued belief in the concepts and logic of deterrence. On a pessimistic view this process has now gone so far that there is scarcely any prospect of reasoning the electorate (or a sufficiently large part of it) into a real understanding of nuclear issues. Language itself seems to promote the cause of unreason, since there is a common-sense willingness to believe that where a *word* exists — a word like 'deterrence' — it must correspond to some intelligible *concept*, and must therefore be based on good solid grounds which others (the experts) are of course better placed to understand. So anyone who questions the logic of deterrence will appear to be either ignoring the facts (human nature, aggression, the Soviet menace) or worse still colluding with 'the enemy' at home or abroad. Realism in these matters can thus be defined as a readiness to accept that paranoid logic wherever it may lead, and to view the world on terms laid down by a rhetoric of nuclear unreason. At the limit, this presages an Orwellian situation where any kind of deviant (critical) thinking must be judged either a case for psychiatric treatment or a species of punishable thoughtcrime.

But already, nearer home, there are signs of a different, less overt but perhaps more effective arrangement for the suppression of dissident ideas. The perfection of a totalitarian system lies not in its power to inflict punishments on a stubbornly resisting minority but in the means it possesses to marginalise that minority to the point where their ideas become simply inconceivable to the right-thinking mass of citizens. Among the first candidates for this treatment is the view that Eastern European regimes have no monopoly on thought-control; indeed, that the management of public opinion through sophisticated, non-violent forms of ideological coercion is a much more effective technique to this end than anything practised outside the 'free world' of Western liberal democracy. But of course this must sound decidedly paranoid to anyone convinced of the truthfulness or realism of free-world rhetoric. From their point of view any attempt to complicate the bipolar scheme of values (East/West, oppression/freedom, war plans/legitimate self-defence) can only be the product of ignorance, malice or connivance with the 'enemy within'. There is simply no need for all the clumsy, self-defeating apparatus of overt suppression if people can be brought to identify their interests entirely with the standard, commonsense perception of what those interests must be. It would then stand to reason that anyone disposed to question the logic of deterrence (or the various strategic considerations brought up in its support) would place themselves quite simply beyond the pale of rational argument.

Francis Barker has recently made this point with regard to Milton and his great campaign against the threat of renewed state censorship under Cromwell's regime (see Barker 1984). In *Areopagitica*, we see very clearly how an argument *against* the imposition of external checks and controls can go along with an argument that obliges the individual subject to exercise his or her own powers of internalised self-discipline. Thus Milton bases his claims on the fact that the English people have achieved their revolution and shown themselves capable of assuming that burden of freedom and responsibility which other nations have yet to attain. It is a retrograde step and a failure to acknowledge this decisive historical change when the censors seek a return to their old (now redundant) powers and prerogatives. Thus the 'great art of government', according to Milton, lies in discerning 'in what the law is to bid restraint and punishment, and in what persuasion only is to work' (Milton 1931, pp. 318-9; quoted by Barker, p. 47). Otherwise there would exist no means of distinguishing the *genuine* virtues (self-discipline, sobriety, individual conscience) from the passive obedience enforced by the dictates of arbitrary sovereign rule. 'Under pittance, and prescription, and compulsion, what were virtue but a name, what praise could then be due to well-doing, what grammercy to be sober, just or continent?' (Milton p. 319; Barker p. 47). The old system of external constraints backed up by exemplary punishments gives way to an internalised courtroom-scene where the subject is cast simultaneously in the roles of defendant, prosecuting counsel, judge and jury. Such (Barker argues) is the moment of transition from a feudal to a bourgeois order of moral and political representation. It is a passage marked by the withdrawal of power in its more spectacular or public forms, but also by a massive intensification of the pressures exerted on each individual conscience. 'The state succeeds in penetrating to the very heart of the subject, or more accurately, in pre-constituting that subject as one which is internally disciplined, censored, and thus an effective support of the emergent pattern of domination' (p. 47). So Milton's clarion call to freedom can also be interpreted as something altogether more ambivalent: a signal episode in the march toward ever more complex and tightly self-regulating forms of social control.

One could easily transpose the terms of Barker's analysis to the present-day ideological conjuncture that sets up a straightforward binary opposition between Western liberal democracy and Soviet totalitarian politics. It would then be a matter of showing how this contrast depends on values and assumptions deeply inscribed in the rhetoric of cold-war ideology, especially the kind of 'free-world' rhetoric that suppresses all knowledge of its own historical determinants. The Soviet instance could then be seen as a belated showing of that older, more overtly repressive order which operates through forms of highly visible sanction and constraint. But it would also serve (as the old monarchical regime served Milton) as an ideological foil for disguising the hidden powers of coercion vested in different, more sophisticated forms of ideological control. Thus the freedom of conscience that Milton demands is a freedom earned through the proven capacity of Englishmen to arrive at moral and religious truths which are none the less divinely sanctioned and a part of God's providential plan. It is in the name of this national birthright that Milton (like the present-day ideologues) can construct a world divided into two great opposing camps. On the one hand are those, God's elect, who have shown their fitness for wise self-government by achieving revolution and the subsequent freedom from arbitrary rule. On the other are the nations still groaning under various despotic regimes and as yet incapable of managing such freedom or the heavy responsibilities which of course go along with it. We can recognise here the same basic form of ideological mystification which finds a reverse image of Western democracy in Soviet totalitarian politics. And on Barker's analysis this could only be viewed as an extension of that powerful though diffuse apparatus of state control which interpellates the subject apparently on terms of his or her own free choosing, but in fact through a whole complex system of unrecognised coercive restraints.

In his closing pages, Barker has some cryptic reflections on the upshot of this process in the latter-day drive toward nuclear annihilation. 'This death-wish', he writes, 'of which nuclear weapons are now the instrument and the manifestation, is in a strong form intrinsic to the modern discursive regime' (p. 111). The technology of power first deployed through forms of extended ideological control is now materialised in man's capacity to destroy the world through means of his own ingenious devising.

> A nuclear dénouement — apocalypse and, in the sense of the consummation of knowledge, anagnorisis — would secure the no more than felicitous conclusion in an instance of punctuality which bourgeois discourse is committed to seeking both as the imaginary, consolidating end, and also the unacknowledged drive, of its self-generation. (Barker, p. 111)

This sentence requires a good deal of conceptual unpacking, but the general sense can be stated plainly enough. It is reason itself, or 'bourgeois' reason — the epistemic will-to-power through knowledge and truth — which here stands indicted as the ultimate cause of looming nuclear catastrophe. In this respect Barker follows Foucault (and ultimately Nietzsche) in rejecting the distinction between 'knowledge' and 'power' which has characterised the outlook of enlightened thinkers at least since Kant. (See especially Foucault 1980 and 1985.) That is to say, he adopts the Foucauldian view that our standard, bourgeois-liberal ideas of progress and enlightenment are in fact just a cover, a legitimising myth, for the purpose of extending social control through new and more sophisticated means of surveillance.

This argument is developed in Foucault's writings on the history of changing attitudes to madness, criminality and sexual mores. In each case he finds a proliferating discourse of 'power/knowledge' that seeks to *analyse* and *classify* these phenomena (especially in their 'deviant' forms) and hence render them amenable to the purposes of administrative reason. So the fact that we nowadays talk such a lot about sex — that the subject is apparently 'out in the open' after centuries of obsessive privacy and repression — is for Foucault not in the least a hopeful sign. Rather, it is the upshot of a process that began with Christian techniques of surveillance (the catechism and confessional), and which now continues in secular form through such instruments as psychoanalysis and modern sexology (see Foucault 1978). Far from representing a new-found freedom — a lifting of the old repressive interdict — these practices afford a kind of dream-machine for the exercise of power over henceforth self-regulating subjects. And this because power is no longer located in a visible, external source of compulsion whose authority (like that of the absolute monarch) would always be open to challenge. The difference in these modern technologies of power is that the subject is induced to identify his or her interests so completely with the ruling discourse that no such resistance is thinkable. Hence Foucault's reference to Christian confessional techniques as a model instance of this new configuration in the instrumentality of power/knowledge. It is the same mode of argument that leads Francis Barker to the point of equating nuclear apocalypse with this inbuilt 'enlightenment' desire for knowledge and truth. For such must be its aim, Barker writes: 'to find in a general catastrophe, the devices of which bourgeois science in a direct line of descent from Descartes has provided, the end of all desire, of every discourse and narration' (p. 111).

But then one has to ask: what could be the role of critical theory (or indeed any kind of oppositional thinking) in a discourse which starts out by utterly renouncing all claim to distinguish knowledge from the effects of power/knowledge? Certainly it would leave no room for deconstructing such pseudo-concepts as 'deterrence', or for showing how they rest on certain more or less systematic techniques of rhetorical confusion which may yet be accessible to reasoned analysis. Foucault's project entails what amounts to a wholesale rejection of the values and assumptions of enlightened critique. Like Nietzsche, he treats all truth-claims as partaking of a generalised will-to-power which effectively levels or annihilates such claims. This results in his distinctly Hobbesian vision of society as a struggle of conflicting interests where power alone — the power to impose some particular, self-authorising viewpoint — determines the nature of truth. He takes no account of those differences in the civil and socio-political sphere which distinguish the forms of liberal democracy from other, more crudely repressive regimes. Thus (as Michael Walzer remarks in a recent essay (1986)), he tends to regard all modern societies as variants on the Gulag model, their differences amounting to nothing more than a choice of superficial rhetorics. This follows directly from Foucault's stance of extreme epistemological scepticism, his belief that any claims on behalf of reason or enlightenment can only be further moves in the struggle to legitimise certain sectarian interests. He can therefore review the entire modern history of social and political institutions and find nothing but repeated evidence that truth = knowledge = power.

This marks the clear limit of Foucault's usefulness for the purposes of nuclear criticism. One can readily admit that here, more than anywhere, the discourse of reason has been overwhelmed by the interests of a power-seeking rhetoric whose symptoms are the manifold irrational aporias of current strategic doublethink. One may even come to believe (in dark moments) that reason is not only powerless in this present situation but somehow directly responsible for it; that the nuclear threat is indeed (as Barker suggests) the upshot of a long historical process in which reason — instrumental or technocratic reason — has extended its dominion over nature and its powers of tyrannical social control. It would then seem hopelessly beside the point to criticise the rhetoric of nuclear debate from a standpoint of confidently 'rational' understanding. Such critique would fall into the same self-deluding trap that reason has constructed for itself down through the history of Western 'enlightened' thought. It would reproduce the structures of exploitative power/knowledge which (according to Foucault) define the very nature of this epistemic will-to-truth. In which case there could be no distinguishing between the *authentic* kind of reason that consults human interests (like the interest of collective survival) and the kind that overrides such concerns in the drive toward a maximum efficacy of social or military–strategic control. Both would come down to a species of rhetoric, to be judged solely in 'performative' terms, that is to say, by its power of suasive command or its straightforward instrumental capacity to get things done. Any attempt to distinguish between the two kinds of reason — as for instance on Kantian ethical grounds, by appealing to a genuine (enlightened) community of shared interests — could only appear as yet one more example of instrumental knowledge deludedly concealing its own will-to-power behind a rhetoric of noble concern.

Such is indeed the position arrived at, not only by Foucault but by those (like Jean-François Lyotard) who proclaim the advent of a 'postmodern' era beyond the old regime of determinable truth and falsehood. For Lyotard, all truth-claims are henceforth to be treated as rhetorical or narrative ploys, moves in a game whose rules are made up (so to speak) as the game goes along, and which cannot be reduced to any kind of rational or 'meta-narrative' statement (see Lyotard 1984). Knowledges are legitimised not by the appeal to some ultimate, transcendent principle of reason but only in so far as they demonstrate their power to influence ideas and events. The truth-value of statements can no longer be judged according to standards of right reason or argumentative validity. Truth is a matter of 'performative' effects, of the way that certain utterances work to bring about the discursive conditions under which they count as true. Operational efficacy is henceforth the only criterion by which to decide upon a statement's veridical worth. Any other ground of appeal — any argument resting on logic, reason or conceptual justification — is for Lyotard quite simply untenable, since we have now moved into a postmodern epoch where the old modes of legitimising argument have ceased to persuade or convince. Moreover, such appeals should be treated with suspicion, since they always seek to have the last word, to foreclose or distort the ongoing dialogue of language-games which typifies the postmodern epoch. Thus the break with theoretical (or 'meta-narrative') modes of explanation is for Lyotard a consummation devoutly to be wished. That we can now dispense with those delusive totalising claims — whether Kantian, Hegelian, Marxist or whatever — is a sign of our at last having emerged into a pluralist culture of freely competing discourses where the will-to-truth no longer exerts its compulsive hold.

Lyotard's arguments are open to criticism on several counts. Firstly, they ignore the extent to which dominant interests can always successfully exploit a situation where sheer persuasive power — like that of the mass-media — very largely conditions what people think and do. It is naïve in the extreme to suppose (as Lyotard apparently does) that access to new technology, through personal computers and so forth, will tend to equalise everyone's share in the free-market exchange of knowledge and information. In fact — as all the evidence so far suggests — the tendency is rather to create vast networks of passive dependence upon systems that are so designed as to be quite incapable of acting back on the centres of control through the kind of reciprocal, open-ended dialogue that Lyotard hopefully imagines. It is the same false optimism that argues from the rise of the popular press and mass-media to the advent of a genuine participant democracy. What such arguments ignore is that structural divorce between the interests that effectively control those media and the attitude of passive acquiescence engendered in consumers with no alternative source of information. Thus people can always be persuaded to take up subject-positions wholly against their own best interests or powers of rational grasp. On a whole range of issues — unemployment, nuclear policy, welfare provision and so forth — their thinking is dictated by a 'common-sense' rhetoric which works to exclude or to marginalise any kind of effective oppositional stance. Hence the large-scale support for policies which can benefit only a tiny proportion of the electorate — those with the wealth and power to secure such consensus — and which otherwise present a uniform prospect of increasing deprivation and social injustice.

Lyotard is fitfully aware of all this, remarking at one point that the postmodern outlook is characteristic of late consumer capitalism, and that present conditions are such as to promote 'a massive subordination of cognitive statements to the finality of the best possible performance' (Lyotard 1984, p. 45). In which case his reading of the signs should surely function as a grim diagnosis and not as any kind of celebratory or affirmative discourse. Yet elsewhere — and more typically — Lyotard describes postmodernism as if it were not only a present reality but also a wholly *desirable* release from the false constraints of that old 'metanarrative' regime. His arguments in this sense enact their own point, staking whatever truth they possess on the 'performative' capacity to change our ways of thought and block any access to alternative (epistemological) grounds of enquiry. And if this involves, as one of us has argued elsewhere (Norris 1986b) a determinate misreading of specific passages in Aristotle, Kant and other thinkers, Lyotard can always declare such objections entirely beside the point. For the notion of right reading only makes sense on the terms laid down for intellectual enquiry by that same (now obsolete) tradition. It is ruled out of court by Lyotard's insistence that truth is — or henceforth ought to be — defined as what is good, effective or convincing in the way of practical belief. Any queries raised as to Lyotard's competence in terms of theoretical argument will thus be taken as a clear sign that the objector has not caught up with the current postmodernist rules of the game.

What such arguments amount to is a vote of no confidence in reason itself, or in the power of thought to distinguish truth from the plausible appearances of true-seeming rhetoric. And this brings us back to the question of nuclear criticism. For here, more than anywhere, thinking is affected by rhetorical gambits and strategies which pass themselves off as hard-headed practical wisdom but which in fact possess not the least semblance of logical accountability. In one sense this provides a very striking endorsement of Lyotard's case: an example of how language-games (the rhetoric of deterrence or the current state of nuclear bluff) can reach the point of virtually dictating our real-life acts and perceptions. What is 'real' in this context has little to do with the rational weighing-up of strategic interests or the accurate assessment of war-fighting strengths and capacities. As Jacques Derrida remarks: 'if there are wars and a nuclear threat, it is because "deterrence" has neither original meaning nor measure ... its "logic" is the logic of deviation and transgression, it is rhetorical–strategic escalation or it is nothing at all' (1984, p. 29).

Those who argue the case for deterrence are resting their defence on a double and contradictory set of assumptions. On the one hand they justify the possession of nuclear weapons on the grounds that they have actually preserved the peace by convincing potential aggressors that any threatening moves on their part will be met with massive retaliation. (In much the same way a heavy smoker might argue that cigarettes prevented lung cancer, since *he'd* been addicted to tobacco for the past 40 years and hadn't yet contracted the disease.) On the other hand they declare that deterrence itself offers sufficient guarantee that merely *possessing* such weapons is a very different thing from having active or practical plans for their use. And yet of course, by the logic of the first argument, their possession can only exert such deterrent effect if it is understood on each side that the other is genuinely prepared to use them under certain circumstances. The whole complex chain of decision and command rests on an inbuilt assumption that war plans exist and can always, at the moment of 'unthinkable' crisis, be put to the test of armed confrontation and nuclear exchange. Without this performative aspect — the issuing of threats that must lack all force if not taken seriously — deterrence would be just an empty notion and both lines of argument devoid of sense. Such are the aporias of nuclear discourse, as Derrida reads them: given over to an escalating play of threats and counter-threats whose outcome is beyond any practical or logical reckoning.

This is why 'deterrence' is not so much a *concept* as a word whose currency and influence derive from its power to perpetuate the arms-race precisely in so far as it lacks stable, 'original' sense. The paradoxes of deterrence — its resistance to any kind of reasoned conceptual justification — don't in the least count against it on strategic or rhetorical grounds. For the whole effect of such pseudo-concepts is to raise the nuclear stakes to a point where no form of rational calculation any longer applies. And so it has come about, Derrida writes, that 'all of them [the scientists, politicians, military thinkers] are in the position of inventing, inaugurating, improvising procedures and giving orders where no model ... can help them at all' (Derrida 1984, p. 22). So great is the range of rhetorical gambits — bluffs and counter-bluffs, simulated responses, imaginary scenarios of all kinds — that reason is powerless to determine the consequences of any new move in the game. Facing up to this unnerving predicament involves a recognition that nuclear 'reality' is an eminently *textual* domain; that, as Derrida says, 'we [i.e. critical theorists and students of discourse] can consider ourselves competent here because the sophistication of the nuclear strategy can never do without a sophistry of belief and the rhetorical simulation of a text' (p. 24). Nuclear criticism will therefore take account of all those conflicting modalities of language that go to create such an utter confusion of strategic means and ends. This account must include 'the relations between knowing and acting, between constative speech-acts and performative speech-acts, between the invention that finds what was already there and the one that produces new mechanisms or new spaces' (ibid.).

There might appear to be no great difference, in practical terms, between this programme and Lyotard's outlook of thorough-going 'postmodern' pragmatism. Derrida likewise argues that we are living through an epoch of drastic changes in the relation between power, knowledge and the forms of legitimising social control. There has come about a widespread shift from 'constative' to 'performative' modes of understanding, or (what amounts to the same thing) from authority vested in the principle of reason to power that takes effect through rhetorical or suasive means. And nowhere is this more evident, he thinks, than in the field of nuclear debate. This forces an urgent reappraisal of the assumptions that have governed rational enquiry from Plato to Kant and his successors; most centrally, the idea that opinion (*doxa*) can be criticised from the standpoint of a knowledge (*episteme*) impervious to the effects of mere rhetorical suasion. It is impossible to maintain this distinction, Derrida argues, in the face of a nuclear predicament which far exceeds all the knowledges available to 'experts' in this or that technical field. Thus:

> the dividing line between *doxa* and *episteme* starts to blur as soon as there is no longer any such thing as an absolutely legitimizable competence for a phenomenon which is no longer strictly techno-scientific but techno-militaro-politico-diplomatic through and through, and which brings into

> play the *doxa* or incompetence even in its calculations. (Derrida 1984, p. 26)

In their stress on the performative aspects of nuclear discourse — on everything that eludes the grasp of theoretical or 'constative' reason — such statements would appear to place Derrida squarely in the postmodern-pragmatist camp.

But this is to misread Derrida's text in much the same angled or partial way that Lyotard misreads Enlightenment thinkers like Kant. It ignores his reiterated argument that these are pathological disorders of an epoch where knowledge is indeed reduced to a reflex of manipulative power-seeking interests, and where a certain narrowed and perverted form of means–end rationality has usurped the role of genuine critical reason. It may be (and Derrida suggests as much) that theory itself is to some degree complicit with these latter-day forms of technological will-to-power; that it is no longer possible honestly to believe, like Kant, in philosophy as a pure, disinterested search for the principles of knowledge and truth. To this extent Derrida takes up the critique of instrumental reason carried on by Adorno, Horkheimer, Habermas and the proponents of Frankfurt Critical Theory. (See especially Adorno and Horkheimer 1972; Habermas 1972.) But he also, like them, preserves a keen sense of the need to mount a cogently argued *critique* of these irrationalist tendencies at the heart of what currently passes for common-sense wisdom. That is to say, Derrida implicitly rejects the kind of unresisting generalised endorsement that Lyotard extends to the so-called 'postmodern condition'. For otherwise there can be no place for nuclear criticism, or for any kind of reasoned discourse on the pseudo-concept of 'deterrence' and its allied rhetorical terms.

This necessity of preserving crucial distinctions leads us on to the question of what differentiates the Western and the Soviet instances of nuclear rhetoric. As we argued above, one effect of simply equating 'knowledge' and 'power' in Foucault's wholesale, indiscriminate fashion is to blur those differences of a socio-political order which any informed analysis will need to take into account. The same applies to Lyotard's habit of reducing all truth-claims to a levelling regime of performative efficacy or (more simply) what's good in the way of belief. This would leave the analyst wholly unequipped to remark those differences of strategy and style which exist between the US and the Soviet stance on matters of nuclear policy. In what follows, we take two typical pronouncements (from speeches by Andropov and Reagan) and attempt to draw some lessons for the practice of nuclear criticism. Reagan's is indeed a prime example of 'post-modern' discourse: sublimely unconcerned with consistency or logic, exploiting every kind of handy rhetorical device, its language a collage of intertextual echoes and allusions that seek to secure assent at a level of preconscious identification where reason has no part to play. The Soviet 'line' is contrastingly tough-minded and practical, its rhetoric that of a steady refusal to set aside grim realities in the quest for mere fantasy solutions. To the hopelessly naïve American talk of 'flexible response' and a limited (survivable) nuclear war it opposes a stark insistence that any first use on the American side will be met (as strategic reality dictates) by an all-out Soviet response.

In this context of last-ditch exterminist logic it is perhaps absurd to claim that the latter represents a more 'rational' or consequent position. But one can point out the very real difference between a strategy that seeks to come to terms with this prospect of remainderless catastrophe and one which shelters from such knowledge in a fantasy world of its own rhetorical creating. And one could doubtless go some way toward explaining this difference in historical and socio-political terms. Soviet perceptions are still bound up with what Lyotard would call a 'modernist' paradigm, a rational appraisal of strategic means and ends, even where this leads to the enforced contemplation of absolute, terminal disaster. Like so much in the massively accelerated history of Soviet development, this emphasis on forward planning and assessment is more nearly related to an earlier stage of Western capitalist growth. On the American side, postmodernism figures as the outcome of forces which work to disintegrate any such sense of agreed-upon aims and realities. Some remarks of Terry Eagleton help to make this difference clear. 'It is not surprising', he writes, 'that classical models of truth and cognition are increasingly out of favour in a society where what matters is whether you deliver the commercial or rhetorical goods. Whether among discourse theorists or the Institute of Directors [or, one might add, Pentagon strategists] the goal is no longer truth but performativity, not reason but power' (Eagleton 1986, p. 134). And again (from the same essay): 'postmodernism persuades us to relinquish our epistemological paranoia and embrace the brute objectivity of random subjectivity; modernism [on the other hand] is torn by the contradictions . . . and the pressures of a quite different rationality which, still newly emergent, is not even able to name itself' (p. 144). This comparison could apply, at least in broad outline, to the two contrasting instances of American and Soviet nuclear discourse.

Reagan's speech was in fact an advertisement for his new SDI or 'Star Wars' project, marking a decisive turn away from the doctrine of deterrence (or 'mutually assured destruction'). And so it came about that the received nuclear wisdom of three decades was abandoned, more or less overnight, in favour of a wholly incompatible series of hypotheses, wagers and assumptions. All the experts now lined up to convince us that deterrence had always been a dangerous illusion and had never provided the kind of security claimed by its erstwhile champions (most often the very same people). In effect, these experts let the whole argument for deterrence go by default, but only in order to replace it with a new, more wildly extravagant scenario. Nothing could more aptly exemplify the postmodernist retreat from consequential thinking into a realm of substitute fantasy projections. The sheer *impracticability* of Star Wars — its reliance on as yet merely dreamed-of technology and the likelihood that in any case it just wouldn't work — is matched only by the rhetorical overkill of Reagan's presentation. Indeed, it is precisely this maximal distance between rhetoric and reality that marks out the speech as a signal instance of postmodern discourse. And yet — as Derrida reminds us — such language possesses a performative power, an influence on the course of US–Soviet rivalry, whose effects 'have at least as much importance as a given set of technological mutations that would, on both sides, be of such a nature as to displace the strategic bases of an eventual armed confrontation' (p. 26). Even the slightest shift of rhetorical stance may produce far-reaching and wholly unforeseeable consequences.

As one instance, Derrida cites the idea that the US might conceivably *prevail* in nuclear war, a notion let drop (unsuspectingly, it seems) by Caspar Weinberger in a 1982 policy document. Such talk clearly implied a move away from the so-called 'logic' of deterrence and a readiness to contemplate fighting — and at some stage winning — a limited or 'theatre' nuclear war. However absurd in realist terms, this innovation in the rhetoric of US–Soviet exchange was perceived on both sides as a change of strategic heart, one whose potential destabilising effect would henceforth need to be reckoned with by the experts. But — and this is Derrida's point — no reckoning could possibly cope with a chain of performative acts and responses whose 'logic' so far outruns any rational calculation. 'Among all the acts of observing, revealing, knowing, promising, acting, simulating giving orders, and so on, the limits have never been so precarious, so undecidable' (1984, p. 23). Such is indeed the 'postmodern condition' of which Lyotard provides (up to a point) the most acute diagnosis. But to let the analysis go at that without conserving some ground for rational critique is an attitude complicit with the wildest forms of nuclear-strategic doublethink.

The US Navy and the Ministry of Defence currently sponsor all kinds of research in the humanistic disciplines that would scarcely seem to have much practical military use. These disciplines include not only translation-theory, speech-act analysis, generative grammar and other such broadly systematic approaches — where there might be some conceivable pay-off in terms of information technology — but also poetics, literary theory, hermeneutics and even (Derrida is willing to believe) advanced work in the rhetoric of deconstruction. For the nuclear predicament is now so impossibly complex, so far beyond the grasp of any straightforward decision-making power, that strategies (to repeat) 'cannot do without a sophistry of belief and the rhetorical simulation of a text' (Derrida, p. 24). All the more reason that responsible workers in this field should address themselves urgently to countering the effects of this misapplied rhetorical expertise.

To move beyond this nuclear proliferation of missives and missiles, in order to re-appropriate the grounds for a rational critique of this nuclear neurosis, a clear understanding of the discursive tactics employed by Soviet and US texts is essential. At this point, then, our narrative focus will shift from general theoretics to an in-depth analysis of the way specific Soviet and US texts seek to secure assent for their individual positions. Since the Soviet strategy remains both uniform and immediately accessible, only one text — Yuri Andropov's 1983 Nuclear Address — will be analysed. This text is a pardigm of all the Soviet texts issued, even the most recent. The US rhetorical strategy, on the other hand, reveals its structural grammar only with prolonged exposure to a number of different texts. This has necessitated the inclusion within our analysis of various State of the Union addresses, along with one inaugural address. The reason for choosing these particular American texts is that in their totality they give at least a potentially expansive view of the strategy employed, while the individual instances of US nuclear policy, drawing as they do from a cultural image bank, give a decidedly fragmented picture of the 'logic' which structures their discursive formations. That logic does, however, come into sharp relief when juxtaposed with the overtly classical modes which surface in the corresponding Soviet text.

Starting with the Soviet rhetorical strategy, then, Andropov's text[2] is constructed in a discursive style which places it squarely within the tradition of the European Enlightenment. Indeed, it shares with the Enlightenment its humanist values, its basic faith in reason, as well as its empirical view of language. This particular view, the empirical, treats language as a transparent medium, a vehicle to convey information, a window through which the process of thought becomes invisible. Inherent in this view of language is the belief that there is a one-to-one correspondence between the signifier (in the instance of the Andropov text, the 'word') and the referent (once again, in the Andropov text, the 'deed'). Inherent also is the belief in a 'real world', a world independent of language and its speaking subject(s), but one which language, if it is proper, pure, and perspicuous, will represent in order that the individual, the subject, through the auspices of reason, or common sense, is able to construct a model of that world outside of him or herself. For the empirical thinker, then, language's main function is to convey fact, information, and report about the 'real world'. Underlying this view of language is the tendency, touched on briefly in our introduction, to assume that if a word exists then so must its real-world referent, the 'object' or 'concept' to which it stands in the relation of a signifier. In tone, presuppositions and style, Andropov's address perfectly reflects both the empirical view of language and the larger concerns of the European Enlightenment. Thus, in describing the Soviet response to American allegations of an 'unprecedented build up of nuclear armament', we read:

> Of course, malicious attacks on the Soviet Union produce a natural feeling of indignation here, but our nerves are strong, and our policy is not based on emotions. It rests on common sense, realism and a profound sense of responsibility for the future of the world.

Common-sense, realism, a profound sense of responsibility for one's fellow man, an enlightened critique based on reason — these were, and still are, characteristics of the European Enlightenment discourse. Within this discourse the individual, his experiences, and the power of his rational faculties are given priority; indeed, reason not emotion, common sense not desire, provide a boundary in which the thinking being is able to frame his actions (the 'her' was conspicuous by its absence in the Enlightenment discourse and has yet to surface in its Soviet nuclear expression). They provide a guideline by which the rational subject is able to find his way to a hard-headed vision of the way things are. Andropov's text clearly displays this discursive history, and in doing so reflects an accompanying rhetorical concern for its audience. The text is manifestly context-sensitive in that the audience it seeks to address is America's Western European allies, all of which share as part of their respective discursive histories the common experience of the European Enlightenment. It is also interesting to note that the text was translated and released by the Novosti Press, the official Western Soviet agency, simultaneously in German, English, French, and Spanish — all languages of countries which at the time were considering giving, or had already given, the Pentagon sites for their Pershing 2 and Cruise missiles.

The text itself, employing as it does the mode of logos, reason, quite naturally argues a case for the total 'unreasonableness', and by extension 'unreality' of the American position. Its argument, staying within the perimeters of the rational mode of persuasion, first presents American thinking on the nuclear arms issue as open to serious scrutiny:

> It goes so far for the sake of its imperial ambitions that one begins to doubt whether Washington has any brakes at all to prevent it from going beyond the point at which any thinking being must stop.

It then proceeds to amplify further the advanced irrationality of American nuclear ambitions by describing 'Washington's' continual effort to gain a superior strategic position as 'an unbridled militarist psychosis'. The dislocation of 'Washington' from 'America' allows the metaphor of the body politic to take shape, and as for its rhetorical intention — one need not be a psychiatrist to understand the inferred lack of reason exhibited by the mind of that practising body, the American administration.

Throughout the text, America's foreign policy is constantly portrayed as a species of last-ditch unreason. And those 'blinded by anti-communism' are themselves portrayed as minds unable to 'ponder' the consequences of American policy. To be reasonable, the Andropov text argues, is to see the nonsense of American strategic thinking, the unreality of its aims, and the heavy responsibility it alone bears for an 'insane' nuclear arms-race. The concluding page of the Soviet text underlines its main rhetorical mode by this urgent appeal: 'Mankind has not lost, nor can it lose its reason'.

Reason, however, is not the only mode of persuasion the Soviet text utilises. Ethos, ethics, is another of the three principal modes outlined by Aristotle in his *Rhetoric*, for gaining assent to one's arguments. Interestingly enough, the ethical appeal made by the Andropov text derives from what the Soviets take to be a disjunction between signifier and referent, or 'word' and 'deed', in American foreign policy. This part of the argument is first framed in terms of actions and their accompanying speeches:

> Peoples judge the policy of a government primarily by its actions. That is why when the US President bombastically declares from the United Nations rostrum his commitment to the cause of peace and to the self-determination and sovereignty of peoples, these declarations, made for effect, can convince no one.

The distance between what is said and what actually occurs, the dislocation of the signifier with respect to its referent, becomes the subject for ethical consideration in this next powerful rhetorical thrust:

> One must say bluntly that it is an unattractive sight when, intent upon smearing the Soviet people, the leaders of such countries as the United States resort to what amounts almost to obscenities alternating with hypocritical preaching about morality and humaneness. The world is well aware of such moralising. In Vietnam, morality as understood by the leaders in Washington was brought home with napalm and toxic agents, in Lebanon it is being hammered in by naval gun salvoes, in El Salvador this morality is being imposed by genocide. The list of crimes can be continued.

Here the rhetorical gesture is as unambiguous as its message: we have the power but we are holding it in check. This reserve, this capacity to 'learn the lessons of history', this ability to distinguish between fact and fiction — all these orbiting potentialities find their nucleus in the faculty of reason. A straightforward correspondence between signifier and referent permits a reasonable, clear-headed interpretation of the way the world currently turns. The Andropov text advances the case for its own ethics of correspondence — and therefore of truth, reason, and realism — while simultaneously arguing the lack of such qualities in American policy statements. Before turning to the American sample, one more aspect of the Soviet text needs to be explored.

As Aristotle astutely observed over two thousand years ago, when men exercise in rhetoric — that faculty of determining the available means of persuasion in any given context — the purpose is usually to gather assent, to enlist an audience, to recruit, as it were, willing subjects for a cause. The Andropov text is no exception to this rule; rather, it solicits agreement with Aristotle's case by offering exemplary evidence. The audience the Soviet text wishes to enlist is America's Western allies, and the cause is the suspension of the 'unreasonable' deployment of Cruise and Pershing 2 missiles throughout Western Europe. What is not so clearly evident, however, is how rhetorically appropriate Andropov's text actually is. We have already touched briefly on the fact that this text's intended audience shared with the Soviet peoples an experience of European Enlightenment values, thus establishing a common denominator, a shared dialect as it were, in their respective discursive histories. The fact that the text so aptly appropriates this Enlightenment discourse is neither an accident nor simply a 'natural' turn of events.

This attempt to establish commonality is further extended by the stated fact that part of the USSR is European. Thus we have a geographical (or geo-political) as well as an intellectual link. What is even more striking in the Soviet instance is the total absence, in contradistinction to the American texts, of any cultural references. The cultural non-specificity of the text and the geo-political link work in unison with a prose style — one sparse in metaphor and structured by the universal principle of reason — to create a text which, in effect, licences itself to voice distinctly 'European' concerns. This inferred commonality of geographical, intellectual, and ethical roots is further amplified by the shared enlightened concern for all peoples:

> We, for our part, do not seek such a trial of strength. The very thought of it is foreign to us. The well-being of our people, the security of the Soviet state we do not separate from, nor, more so, do we set them against, the well-being and security of other peoples, of other countries.

Europe and how it is to be defined, the European audience and how it is to be enlisted — these are central concerns of the Andropov text, a text both built on the assumptions of rational critique, and subject to appraisal on the same terms. What needs to be stressed here, however, is that although the Soviet text presents itself as a rational, almost objective, narrative of the way things are, it is a piece of classically structured rhetoric, a text skilfully constructed to secure the assent of its audience. To see the text as merely a piece of rational discourse is to fall under its suasive powers, and in doing so, to miss entirely the nature of the rhetorical strategy that the text employs in seeking assent for its own position. In the final analysis, it is not a matter of delineating a narrative exchange between Soviet reason and American rhetoric; rather, it is detailing the difference in rhetorical strategies both employ while prolonging the arms-race. The small print in this nuclear debate clearly spells out the fact that both countries are involved in using missives, language formations, in an attempt to gain a foothold for their individual nuclear strategies.

President Reagan's addresses, then, also seek to enlist an audience, to define a boundary. But to understand the workings of his texts involves a great shift of cultural perspectives, language-games, rhetorical context and discursive formation between Europe and America, along with the totally dissimilar rhetorical strategies they each employ. To ignore one or the other of these differences is to read Reagan's speeches, as the Soviet text does, as the mindless babble of a pyschotic. While the Andropov text makes out a strong case for precisely this reading, to dismiss Reagan's speeches out of hand is also to ignore the fact that this 'pyschobabble' does, in a very real sense, enlist or interpellate its audience. As evidence one need only remark that Ronald Reagan, often cast as a refugee from the celluloid world of B-rated movies, is presently enjoying his second term as President of the United States. It also obscures the fact that this same rhetorical strategy has gained for Reagan and his Republican administration not only an enthralled audience but also the largest budget ever expended on the military of any nation in the history of our race — and this from a Democratic Congress. If for no other reason than its manifest persuasive power, the text bears closer scrutiny.

All of Reagan's texts cited here locate themselves in a narration of American history. This mythic history — here understood not as mere illusion but as history *constructed by* myth — is peopled by such larger than life characters as George Washington, Abraham Lincoln, Daniel Boone, Walt Whitman and John Wayne — all living legends eternally present in the same celluloid world from which Reagan emerged. To say that this mythic history runs deep in the American pysche is to understate the case by several degrees. In its many and varied expressions, this cultural myth encapsulates everything it means to be 'American'; it is the mirror to which every American President from Washington to Reagan has turned when America, whether through internal strife or external pressures, was suffering those crises of identity and conscience which accompany such self-appointed positions as 'freedom's friend', along with the resultant Koreas and Vietnams. The notion of identity, the right of territorial expansion, the absolute conviction of a divine mandate licencing that expansion, the ineluctable will of the individual empowered by that divine mandate — these are the remarkable durable stuff of which the myth is made. To confront American nuclear rhetoric is to confront that mythic pysche in all its religious fervour.

The view of language indigenous to the American texts has already been referred to, in the context of this chapter, as 'postmodern'. To see this view as new or unprecedented is, however, to misunderstand its genealogy. In point of fact, the postmodern view of language is decidedly *pre*-modern. It may, in its current expression, be grounded in a post-structural separtion of the signifier and the signified, it may even be aligned with Lyotard's post-rational critique of our cultural condition, but these instances find their antecedents in speculative philosophers and DeCopian texts prior to the Enlightenment. In its most basic form, the postmodern uses language not as a transparent medium through which a real world can be seen, but as the site of a performance, the locale in which a discursive reality, a *reading*, is constructed. Thus its main concern is with enactment, ritual, performance. Language in this context is empowered to do things, to inaugurate changes in the world. Here we need only think of such speech-acts as directives or declaratives whose very utterance may bring into being a whole new state of affairs.

Prayers, mantras, the matrimonial promise 'I do' are all seen, in their respective contexts, as being invested with this same power to effect changes in the world. In its wider application this view holds that language is both an instrument and an environment in which the human animal actualises its social potential. In point of contrast, whereas the rational-empiricist view of language focused on *fact*, *information*, and *report*, the postmodern view concerns itself with *impact*, *inspiration*, and *transport*. Whereas the empiricist conceptualised language as a means of conveying information about a real world outside, the postmodern conceptualises language as a surface, a film, upon which to inscribe the imaginings of the tribal collective. The postmodern turns the empiricist transparent window into a door, an entrance that offers access to a 'language-game' or cultural 'form of life', to borrow Wittgenstein's terms. In the specific instance of the Reagan texts, language is used in a ritualistic celebration of the game of being 'American'; it provides membership, citizenship, in a collectively imagined world of 'unlimited horizons', a 'land of freedom', a 'land of unbounded potential'. To speak this language is to be in this world; to be in this world is to know without thinking what is right, good, and just — in short, it is to know intuitively what it means to be 'American'.

A sampling of the texts will give some idea of the general character of Reagan's rhetoric:

> How can we not believe in the goodness and greatness of America? How can we not do what is right and needed to preserve this last, best hope of men on earth?
>
> After all our struggles to restore America, to revive confidence in our country and hope for the future ... we cannot, must not and will not turn back, we will finish our job. How could we do less; we are Americans ... America was founded by people who believed that God was their rock of safety. He is ours ... (1984)

> My fellow citizens, this nation is poised for greatness. The time has come to proceed toward a great new challenge — a Second American Revolution of hope and opportunity: a revolution carrying us to new heights of progress by pushing back the frontiers of knowledge and space; a revolution of spirit that taps the soul of America, enabling us to summon greater strength than we have ever known; and a

> revolution that carries beyond our shores the golden promise of human freedom in a world at peace ... In Europe, they call it the American Miracle. Day by day, we are shattering accepted notions of what is possible ... (1985)
>
> Tonight I have spoken of great plans and great dreams. They are dreams we can make come true. Two hundred years of American history should have taught us that nothing is impossible. History is asking us, once again, to be a force for good in the world. (1986)
>
> We are entering our third century now, but it is wrong to judge our nation by its years. The calendar can't measure America because we were meant to be an endless experiment in freedom — with no limits to our reaches, no boundaries to what we can do, no end point to our hopes. (1987)[3].

The postmodern use of language has been described, by way of post-structuralism, as a 'celebration of the signifier', and here, clearly, the signifier being celebrated is 'America'. But notice that the 'America' of Reagan's speeches has no real-world referent. There is no one-to-one correspondence linking up word with world, as the Andropov text was at pains to point out with reference to Libya, El Salvador, and Vietnam. This is not to say that there is no such place as America. It is simply to say that the 'America' of which Reagan speaks is a mythic construction, the stuff, as Prospero would say, of dreams. And yet, with all the fervour of the newly converted, the text articulates what it means to be 'American', that is, to be one who lives in this 'land of freedom', this land where 'men and women are free to follow their dreams'.

Most British readers will shake their heads in wonder when they first confront the exorbitant nature of this rhetoric. Who, they ask, could possibly be taken in by such posturing nonsense? But the way in which this fantasy has been naturalised is similar to the way a nation so 'space-age' in its thinking as to endorse the American militarisation of space is still made to live on the imaginary frontiers of kings, queens and princes. The basic mode of persuasion in both cases is *pathos*, emotion, whether that emotion is called 'patriotism', 'loyalty', 'duty', 'honour', or 'the logic of deterrence' (i.e. escalating hatred and fear). Whatever the differences of overt theme, the effect is just the same: the naturalisation of an attitude, a way of life, a mode of imagining which evades the requirements of rational, enlightened discourse. And yet this perfectly 'natural' way of conducting one's affairs is so intricately bound up with a mythic national identity that any inquiry into the logic or nature of its premises is taken as a well-nigh treacherous affront to both one's person and one's sense of communal belonging.

It is here that we may (with certain reservations) call upon Foucault's notion of discourse as the ensemble of organised modes of perception which articulate the dominant values and meanings of a given socio-political order. In the instances under discussion, the prevailing discourses are a set of statements which circumscribe, define, legitimise or prohibit what can and cannot be said in the name of 'America' or 'Britain' respectively. Notice also that in both cases there is a clearly marked set of prescriptive codes bearing on individual *actions* and deriving from those same imperative discourses. In the United States, there is even a branch of government which deals expressly with 'un-American activities'.

This might seem little more than a local digression from the task of analysing American nuclear discourse. But the two phenomena are closely bound up, as we hope to make clear in what follows. In point of practice, no discourse exists in isolation, but rather in a network of sometimes competing, often contradictory, always very different discourses. American nuclear rhetoric is a complex synthesis of many such plural instances: the discourse of American history, the discourse of the Pilgrim Fathers, the discourse of the pioneers and the untamed frontier, the discourse of the daring, courageous, Romantic individual, to name just a few. The result of synthesising these various discourses is a typically postmodern collage, a collage both of images and narrative lines. What should not be overlooked, however, is the specific function each image or narrative serves. Taking only one discourse, that of mythic history — a history made eternally present by a medium called television and a one-time animator named Walt Disney — we see how this myth functions to bind various divergent social groups together (Moss 1985). Furthermore, in binding these groups together, it provides social consensus, a consensus about what is good and not good for the mythic national body. This consensus in turn empowers the

Pentagon to carry out their various programmes in the name of this mythic body, or in the name of 'peace' or of 'freedom'.

To illustrate further this tie between the rhetorical strategy and a mythologised history, one need only review the nomenclature of the American weapons system. On the nuclear parade-ground, 'Hawkeye', 'Honest John', 'Minuteman' and 'Pershing' — all heroes of one or another American campaign — mix easily with godlike heroes such as 'Atlas', 'Hercules' and 'Thor'.[4] With so many gods and heroes superintending American policies and concerns, what is surprising is that the administration still feels the need for an executive branch such as the CIA. Of course, the CIA itself has performed, with missionary zeal, Herculean tasks in the name of 'peace' and 'freedom' in such godforsaken places as Chile, El Salvador, Nicaragua, and, most recently, Libya. In exemplary postmodern fashion, the American nuclear script no longer reflects reality; rather, reality begins to read more and more like a badly directed movie. The President of the United States, himself an actor, addresses the world community with lines from a B-rated movie: 'They can run,' he says, lifting a line from *The River of No Return*, 'but they can't hide'.

The connection between film, television and American rhetorical strategy goes much deeper than simply pastiching occasional cryptic but resonant lines. The whole structural logic of the addresses is that of a commercial. Like an advertisement, it never presents a rational, sequentially ordered argument; rather, it presents its position as a product associated with desirable things or attitudes. And like an advertisement, its main intention is not to sell a product — something Marshal McLuhan and Edward Carpenter tried to massage into our waking consciousness a few decades ago — but to increase the pleasure in its consumption. By constantly staging performances which link the product with what is desirable, the subject soon associates the two as inseparable. Furthermore, if we recall that the postmodern uses language as a point of access, of induction into a private, members-only game, then we begin to understand more precisely the way in which this game operates. The promise of pleasure, the euphoria of imagined importance, membership in a divinely inspired social order — such is the fabric of those rhetorical wings which support ideas like Manifest Destiny, or The Home of the Brave, or again, The Defenders of Freedom. The performance, the advertisement, the private language-game all come supplied with an appropriate set of rules. To enter into the game is to enact its rules, to live by the prohibitions set by the game, whether that game be Trivial Pursuit, Monopoly, or Saving the World from the Red Horde. It is these rules, these discursive guidelines, which determine the production of meaning in the postmodern grammar of nuclear debate. To see how this strategy manifests itself as a text — as a piece of sustained ideological discourse — our chapter will now turn to the foreign policy section of the 1985 inaugural address.[5]

> There are those in the world who scorn our vision of human dignity and freedom. One nation, the Soviet Union, has conducted the greatest military build-up in the history of man, building arsenals of awesome, offensive weapons ... We strive for peace and security heartened by the changes all around us. Since the turn of the century, the number of democracies in the world has grown fourfold. Human freedom is on the march, and nowhere more so that in our own hemisphere. Freedom is one of the deepest and noblest aspirations of the human spirit. People worldwide hunger for the right of self-determination, for those inalienable rights that make for human dignity and progress.
>
> America must remain freedom's staunchest friend, for freedom is our best ally, and it is the world's only hope to conquer poverty and preserve peace ...
>
> So we go forward today, a nation mighty in its youth and powerful in its purpose. With our alliances strengthened, with our economy leading the world to a new age of economic expansion, we look to a future rich in possibilities. And all of this because we worked and acted together, not as members of political parties, but as Americans.
>
> ... So much is changing and will change, but so much endures and transcends time ... we hear again the echoes of our past.
>
> A general falls to his knees in the hard snow of Valley Forge; a lonely President paces the darkened halls, and ponders his struggle to preserve the Union; the men of the Alamo call out encouragement to each other; a settler pushes west and sings a song, and the song echoes out forever and fills the unknowing air.
>
> It is the American sound; it is hopeful, big-hearted, idealistic, daring, decent, and fair. That's our heritage, that our song. We sing it still. For all our problems, our differ-

> ences, we are together as of old. We raise our voices to the God who is the author of this most tender music. And may He continue to hold us close as we fill the world with our sound ... God bless you and may God bless America. (1985)

Here, in marked contrast with the Soviet appeal to reason, we find an almost exclusive appeal to emotion and communal sentiment. The whole strategy is to create an emotional environment in which the proposition of the 'noble struggle' can transform itself into the surface structures of the various ethnic groups which constitute the American populace. Here the common ground which the Soviet text tried to establish through a shared intellectual heritage is established through the creation of a mythical unified body. The first person plural, *we* (its object-case, *us*, and the possessive *our*) is used no less than 38 times in the short (eleven-paragraph) section of the President's address. Obviously, the repeated use of the pronoun is designed to create a sense of community, a community built upon shared interests, struggles, concerns and obligations. Nor is the appearance of religious themes, the gesturing toward a divine providence, simply for the sake of mouthing pious platitudes. The fact that America was founded by people seeking religious freedom, the continued presence of a deep-rooted belief in the convenant with God, the religious undercurrents of all the ethnic communities are here brought resoundingly together in the name of a unified America. The fact that this religious nerve is central to the cultural reflex should not be overlooked; for those who write the text of American nuclear strategy are constantly massaging that nerve.

And so, to recapitulate what has been said so far: the American discourse functions *not* as a transparent window onto a real world, but as the communal point of entry into a world that is created discursively by means of various rhetorical devices. This world, once again, is not the confused, contradictory but perhaps at last *intelligible* place that confronts the project of enlightened critique. On the contrary, it is another world, one (as Reagan says) 'lit by lightning', a world in which 'freedom is on the march'. In short, it is a world wholly projected through the power of language to conjure up alternative realities, alternative myths of freedom, destiny and self-authorising truth. By collaging scenes from the world of Walt Disney, by staging a cacophony of intertextual echoes and allusions, the Reagan speech very forcefully enacts the grammar of assent. Indeed, the performative nature of this text is such as to gain emotional assent at a level of unconscious identification where reason has no part to play. Like an advertisement that operates entirely by subliminal suggestion, the Reagan text circumvents every kind of rational argument, every obstacle that might yet be placed in its way by those who think to doubt the wisdom of this folk-hero President. Offering what appears to be unlimited scope for personal freedom, promising untold happiness for the free individual, it none the less carefully seals the sale of 'America' with a binding 'no escape' clause. For, as we have seen with Milton's call for citizenly freedom, an internal policing operation is here set in train. To be 'American' is to be true, that is loyal without thought, to the values of Reagan's 'America'. Furthermore, to question the rationale of US nuclear policy is to be 'un-American'; it is to 'weaken the American position' and thereby, implicitly, to align oneself with the forces of evil. Any rational critique is effectively marginalised, placed beyond the bounds of decency and truth by the very rules of the American nuclear discourse.

The 'logic of deterrence' perfectly exemplifies this stage of terminal unreason. The more afraid *they* are, so its argument goes, the more secure must we be in possession of these weapons. To question the reasonable basis of that logic is to lessen their fears, and thereby to weaken our strategic position. The logic of deterrence thus becomes yet another Catch-22, the no-escape clause so tellingly depicted in Joseph Heller's famous parable for our times. There seems no way out of the chronic double-bind which imposes its terms on the very discourse of 'reasonable', self-respecting thought. And yet to ignore the summons of reason, to enlist in the army of 'freedom', to bear (if only by yielding to such rhetoric) the 'weapons of peace' is to become just one more subject through whom the discourse of militant *un*reason speaks. For the logic of 'deterrence', as Derrida says, is performative through and through, given over to 'rhetorical-strategic escalation' and possessing 'neither reason nor measure'. To grasp the nature of this postmodern nuclear discourse is at least to make a start in the process of resisting its suasive powers.

Notes

1. This work grew partly out of collective research into nuclear poli-

tics and the rhetoric of deterrence, carried out by members of the Cardiff Critical Theory seminar. The authors would like to acknowledge the stimulus of many exchanges with (among others) Catherine Belsey, Fakhradin Berrada, Fred Botting, Terence Hawkes, Kathleen Kerr, Jane Moore, Jamal Samir and Chris Weedon.

2. The Andropov address was a communiqué issued by the Novosti Press Agency Publishing House, 1983, published in English, German, French and Spanish.

3. The quotations from the State of the Union address are from, in order, *Keesing's Archive* cf. no. 5, vols XXX (p. 32731), XXXI (p. 33454), XXXII (p. 34163), and XXXIII (p. 34938).

4. Moss (1985) provides a revealing analysis of both the function of myth and its underlying connection to the nomenclature of the US weapons system.

5. President Reagan's Inaugural Address was taken verbatim from *Keesing's Archive*, vol. XXXI (February 1985), pp. 33387-90.

References

Adorno, T.W. and Horkheimer, M. (1972) *Dialectic of enlightenment.* London: New Left Books

Barker, Francis (1984) *The tremulous private body: essays on subjection.* London: Methuen

Blake, N. and Pole, K. (1983) *Dangers of deterrence: philosophers on nuclear strategy.* London: Routledge and Kegan Paul

—— (1984) *Objections to nuclear defence: philosophers on deterrence.* London: Routledge and Kegan Paul

Chilton, P. (ed.) (1985) *Language and the nuclear arms debate: nukespeak today.* London: Francis Pinter

Derrida, J. (1984) 'No apocalypse, not now (full speed ahead, seven missiles, seven missives)'. *Diacritics*, XX, pp. 20-31

Eagleton, T. (1986) *Against the grain: selected essays.* London: New Left Books/Verso

Foucault, M. (1978) *The history of sexuality, volume one: introduction.* New York: Pantheon

—— (1980) *Power/Knowledge: selected interviews and other writings.* Brighton: Harvester Press

—— (1985) *The Foucault reader.* Ed. P. Rabinow. New York: Pantheon

Habermas, Jürgen (1972) *Knowledge and human interests.* Trans. Jeremy J. Shapiro. London: Heinemann

Lyotard, J.-F. (1984) *The postmodern condition: a report on knowledge.* Manchester: Manchester University Press

Milton, J. (1931) *Areopagitica, vol. IV of the Selected Works.* Ed. F.A. Patterson. New York: Columbia

Moss, P. (1985) 'Rhetoric of defence in the United States: language, myth and ideology'. In P. Chilton (ed.) *Language and the nuclear arms debate: nukespeak today.* London: Francis Pinter

Norris, C. (1986a) 'On Derrida's "apocalyptic tone": textual politics and the principle of reason'. *Southern Review* (Adelaide), XIX, pp. 13-30

—— (1986b) 'Whose game is it anyway? or the politics of post-modernism'. (Review of Lyotard.) *Southern Review*, XIX, pp. 334-43

—— (1987) 'Derrida, Kant and nuclear politics'. *Paragraph*, IV, pp. 47-73

Walzer, M. (1986) 'The politics of Michel Foucault'. In D. Hoy (ed.) *Foucault: a critical reader*. Oxford: Blackwell, pp. 51-68